# READING MILL: STUDIES IN POLITICAL THEORY

# Reading Mill: Studies in Political Theory

Ian Cook
*Lecturer in Political Theory*
*Murdoch University*
*Murdoch*
*Australia*

First published in Great Britain 1998 by
**MACMILLAN PRESS LTD**
Houndmills, Basingstoke, Hampshire RG21 6XS and London
Companies and representatives throughout the world

A catalogue record for this book is available from the British Library.

ISBN 0–333–69609–3

First published in the United States of America 1998 by
**ST. MARTIN'S PRESS, INC.,**
Scholarly and Reference Division,
175 Fifth Avenue, New York, N.Y. 10010

ISBN 0–312–21204–6

Library of Congress Cataloging-in-Publication Data
Cook, Ian, 1960–
Reading Mill : studies in political theory / Ian Cook.
  p.   cm.
Includes bibliographical references and index.
ISBN 0–312–21204–6 (cloth)
1. Mill, John Stuart, 1806–1873—Contributions in political
science.   I. Title.
JC223.M66C66  1997
320'.092—dc21                                         97–41421
                                                            CIP

To Sally, Jack and Nicholas

# Contents

# Acknowledgements

Many people have played important roles during the various stages of this project. I cannot hope to name all of them or their particular contribution. In the face of the fact that someone will be overlooked, I extend particular thanks to:

My friend Debbie Kearns for her help in fine-tuning this manuscript. Don Fletcher for his contribution to this project and so much more. Graeme Duncan for his advice and encouragement. Sally Kirk for still being there. Hugh Collins, Garry Rodan, Ian Scott and Horst Ruthrof for their support. Barbara Sullivan, Diane Zetlin, Michael O'Regan, Rodney Smith, Peter Lightbody and Geoff Wood for their friendship. Beryl Cook, Jeanette Black, Robyn Cooper and Carolyn Cook for being my family. Brett, Desleigh and Megan Loretz for being like family. Sue Harris and Linda Buckham for combining happiness and competence. Robert Burrowes for his special way of seeing things. Richard Hall, Michael Salla, Ray Land, Ralph Summy, Andrew Crevald and Michael O'Toole for the tennis. Timothy O'Rourke, Richard Hall, Seamus Parker, Ray Pagliano and Jane Grigg for the dancing. The folks of Jack Cook Park for the exercise. The Toads for being the Toads – especially Damien Ledwich, Andrew Fraser and Steve Stockwell. Mark Bracken, Shane Woolmer, Joe Crawford and David Baillie for the distractions in Brisbane. Gary Wickham, Michael Sturma, Anthony Sayers for the distractions in Perth. Janet Turley, Jack Turley, Edward Turley and Hugh Lions for my memories of them.

I also thank The University of Toronto Press Inc. for permission to use material from *The Collected Works of John Stuart Mill* and *The Australian Journal of Political Science* for permission to use material in Chapter 1 which had been previously published in an article contributed to that journal (Cook, I. 'Political Theorising: Four Conceptions of the Nature of Theory', *The Australian Journal of Political Science*, Vol. 26, No. 3, pp. 510–25). Finally, I would like to thank staff at Macmillan for their assistance and an anonymous reviewer who provided invaluable assistance in preparing this manuscript for publication.

# A Note on the Citation of Mill's Works

Unless otherwise indicated, all citations of Mill's works refer to the *Collected Works of John Stuart Mill*, edited by John M. Robson (Toronto: University of Toronto Press, 1963 and following years). Material from the *Collected Works of John Stuart Mill* has been reproduced with permission of The University of Toronto Press, Inc.

Citations will include an abbreviation of the title of the work, the volume of the *Collected Works* in which that work is located and the page number of the volume of the *Collected Works*. A reference to *On Liberty*, for example, will appear as (OL 18: page number)

*A System of Logic Ratiocinative and Inductive*: SOL
*August Comte and Positivism*: ACP
*Autobiography*: A (Note: The Toronto edition of the *Collected Works* has, for the most part, the final version of the *Autobiography* on every second page)
'Bentham': B
'Chapters on Socialism': COS
'Civilisation': Cn
'Coleridge': C
*Considerations on Representative Government*: CRG
*Essays on Some Unsettled Questions of Political Economy*: UQPE
John Stuart Mill – Harriet Taylor Mill Correspondence: JSM–HTMC
Letter to Thomas Carlyle: LTC
'Miss Martineau's Summary of Political Economy': MM
'On Genius': OG
*On Liberty*: OL
'On Marriage': OM
*Principles of Political Economy*: PPE
'Rationale of Representation': RR
'Reform in Education': RIE
'Remarks on Bentham's Philosophy': ROB
'Spirit of the Age': SOA (Mill wrote more than one article with this title; the particular article is indicated by an additional number that precedes the volume number)

'The Claims of Labour': COL
'The Gorgias': TG
'The Negro Question': NQ
*The Subjection of Women*: SOW
'The Use and Abuse of Political Terms': UAPT
'Thornton on Labour and Its Claims': TLC
*Three Essays on Religion*: TER

# Introduction

Many people have read Mill and one hopes that many more will. Political theorists are regular Mill readers. That they belong to a specific category of readers might lead to the conclusion that political theorists will read Mill in largely the same way. I once thought this. But I was wrong. Political theorists do not read Mill in the same way. This is one result of the co-existence of systematically different conceptions of political theory (and, as a result, what it is to be a political theorist). Some political theorists rarely, if ever, read Mill or others like him because of their conception of political theory. This book is an exploration of different ways of reading Mill that reflect different conceptions of what it is to be a political theorist.

Edmund Husserl's works provided me with a starting-point for a sophisticated sense of the ways in which reading can be understood to be oriented. Husserl introduced me to the idea of 'intentionality'. Intentionality involved the idea that minds were always directed in some way to what they addressed. There was no simple thing called 'looking', or if there was it was only a name for a lot of different ways of looking. Looking could be interrogating, deciding, evaluating in terms of some purpose, or interpreting. It could also be many other activities.

Husserl's works encouraged a consideration of the implications of intentionality for being a person. Or, alternatively, they encouraged the project of bringing the idea of intentionality to the question of being a person. Husserl's phenomenology incorporates the idea of constitution, which is the mental process of making sense of things (fitting them into some order that we can use to know things about the world). That the process of constitution had as its primary object the self was a conclusion that was fairly easy to draw in developing and elaborating upon the idea of constitution. In short, people are primarily oriented toward making sense of themselves.

But we never encounter ourselves just being. We encounter ourselves in action. We are making sense of ourselves in doing what we do. For those of us in universities, who often find ourselves pursuing something called knowledge, our attempts at making sense of the world have to involve attempts at making sense of ourselves pursuing knowledge.

1

That some of us do this in the context of being or trying to become a political theorist is important to this story.

Other factors also shaped this project. Central to these was an assumption that being a political theorist meant reading the works of political theorists, especially the ones found in those types of textbooks that covered the history of political theory. The consequence of this assumption was the view that to be a political theorist was to read someone whose works belonged in these sorts of texts. Many of these thinkers wrote in languages other than English. This was a problem for someone who can only read English and knew that reading translations could count against me. This was one factor behind the decision to study the works of John Stuart Mill.

Another, more important, factor was a sense that the sort of liberalism that Mill's works had stimulated and shaped was in decline. In intellectual circles his liberalism is called modern, revisionist, or social liberalism. In politics and journalism it tends to be known as 'wet' liberalism. These sorts of liberals rejected the liberalism of *laissez-faire* or a minimal state. Liberals like Mill believed that government had an important role in ensuring people had access to the means by which they could improve their lives. That, among other things, government had a responsibility to pursue social justice. This liberalism produced the welfare state and allowed government ownership of important resources and state-provided education.

This form of liberalism came under attack from intellectuals of the left and right. Sceptical liberals, like Hayek and Nozick, rejected government as incapable of knowing much about and responding to what people wanted. Socialists rejected individuality and treated this form of liberalism as a means by which liberal-capitalist hegemony was maintained and workers effectively 'bought off'. In politics this form of liberalism was under attack from those who rejected the idea that government could be relied on to do anything much that was good. These thinkers also rejected the idea that some wealth should be redistributed not simply to alleviate absolute poverty but to create a social or public environment conducive to the general well-being of all members of society (though, for various reasons, it would tend to be used by only a sub-section of them). This form of liberalism was under attack from the 'greed is good' philosophy that involved the rejection of care for others and advocacy of care of the self. These attacks stirred my interest in an author who had been indoctrinated into classical liberalism but had rejected many aspects of classical liberal doctrine. And he wrote in English.

At least one decision had been made. The other decision to be made, returning to Husserl, was how to read Mill. This might have begun with the question: 'how have others read Mill?' But it didn't. Instead, it started with the question: 'how do political theorists read?' That this was the starting-point for this project explains a great deal about this book.

Or, at least, it does when I tell you that my reading about how political theorists read took me to books and articles that dealt with the question: 'what is political theory?' Reading this literature resulted in the fairly rapid conclusion that the political theorists who wrote them tended to fall into four different types.[1] There were some variations but mainly their writings followed four main themes. So I decided to write about those themes and to use them to read Mill's work. My aim was to demonstrate that Mill could be read in different ways by different political theorists.

The four ways of reading Mill and being a political theorist have been labelled traditionalist,[2] historicist, linguistic and behaviouralist.[3] In the first chapter, each of these conceptions of political theory is outlined (and a decision not to read Mill through the behaviouralist conception explained). In the following three chapters Mill's works are read through orientations taken as typical of the traditionalist, historicist and linguistic conception of political theory. These chapters were written to demonstrate as much as could be demonstrated about how different political theorists read Mill differently.

In retrospect, which is always a safe place to look at things, I now realise that somehow the question 'what do political theorists read?' had been bypassed, or elided. How this happened is now clearer to me. Being taught, and therefore trained, through one of the conceptions of political theory that was available meant that I already 'knew' what political theorists read. They read the works of people like Mill and they read the works of people who wrote about people like Mill. They wrote books that had chapters that dealt with Plato, Aristotle, Aquinas, Hobbes, Locke, Mill and Marx. They wrote articles in which they examined specific aspects of the works of Plato, Aristotle, Aquinas, Hobbes, Locke, Mill or Marx. Or they wrote books and articles in which they examined these thinkers in combinations. Or they wrote books that looked at the same questions that had been studied by people like Plato, Aristotle, Aquinas, Hobbes, Locke, Mill and Marx.

Some readers will have already deduced that my first exposure to political theory had been provided by a traditionalist and I had assumed the traditional canon as defining the sorts of things that political theorists read, wrote about and used to organise their courses. A sense of the character of an historicist conception came later. This resulted both from an increase in the numbers of historicist political theorists, especially Marxist scholars, and my exposure to new teachers. I knew something of the behaviouralist revolution. As a good traditionalist, however, I was hostile to it and its methods. I knew little of linguistic philosophy and so was unsullied by its implications for the texts of political theory. So I was left with the traditional list of political theorists and chose Mill.

I knew what to read, but was uncertain as to how to read Mill's works. Thinkers like Husserl had disturbed my thinking sufficiently to prevent me from simply reading Mill without thinking about what it is to read as a political theorist. That I was also trying to *be* a political theorist may also have influenced me and I took this to involve learning how to do what they did. Reading Foucault's works had made me more sensitive to the processes and forms of disciplinarity. This may have been one reason for focusing on the ways in which the sub-discipline of political was produced and reproduced. Althusser's works had also increased a sense of the ways in which forms of study constructed, or produced, their objects.

All this led to the writing of this book. It has been organised into five chapters. The first four have already been mentioned. The first deals with the question: 'what is political theory?' as a way of getting to the different conceptions and practices of political theory on the part of political theorists. The second is a traditionalist reading of Mill's works. The third an historicist reading. The fourth a linguistic reading. (I take up the question of why I have not included a behaviouralist reading of Mill's works at the end of Chapter 1. In short, I argue that most, if not all, behaviouralists wouldn't read Mill as part of their being political theorists.) The fifth is a reconsideration of the four conceptions of political theory. After I had dealt with this question and tried to exemplify different ways of reading Mill, I thought it would be useful to return to the question by way of a consideration of possibilities with respect to unifying political theory around a single conception. This single conception might be produced either by eliminating some of the conceptions of political theory available or by combining some or all of them into a single definition of political theory.

My position is that there is little point in trying to unify these approaches and that neither of these ways of generating a single conception and practice of political theory makes any sense or serves any purpose. I enjoy the fact that political theorists do different things.

I think that the different things they do are all valuable and important. I also believe that the academic sub-discipline of political theory would be better served if political theorists recognised, tolerated and encouraged difference. This is the reason that I make preliminary suggestions toward a sensitivity to difference on the part of political theorists.

While this book was inspired more by Husserl's work, Richard Rorty's work provides a more accessible and familiar statement of one of its basic ideas. This is the view that, even if it was desirable, no means exists through which some final statement can be made about political theory apart from the statement that it denotes a set of possible practices. Any final statement requires an epistemological foundation. That is to say, anyone who says that political theory is a particular practice derived from a particular conception of its nature will always be asked how they know that political theory is as they say it is.

Rorty's anti-epistemological position is one explanation of my resistance to the idea that there is a way of finally answering questions like these, apart from discussing what political theorists do when they are being political theorists. According to Rorty, that form of philosophy organised around the question 'how do you know?' was misleading. Rorty referred to this position as 'the metaphysics of presence'. This position, according to Rorty, 'was designed precisely to facilitate argument, to make questions like "How do you know?" seem natural, and to make a search for first principles and natural resting-places seem obligatory. It assumes that all of us can tell such a resting-place when we see it and that at least some of our thoughts are already there.' (1985: 462–3) In Rorty's view, the problem with the question 'how do you know?' was that 'it assumes that we know what knowledge is like and can tell when we have got it. But this notion of knowledge as an introspectable state is just one more Platonic myth.' (1985: 463) Political theorists are only likely to understand themselves and others if they free themselves from this Platonic myth.

If the conceptions of political theory that govern the behaviour of political theorists are different and lead them to read differently works that, for whatever reason, are taken to be works of political theory, then all that is possible for political theorists is to recognise that such differences are part of the way different political theorists practise political theory. Without some final position from which conceptions of political theory can be judged, political theorists must reconcile themselves to diversity. This book is intended as a contribution toward this process of reconciliation.

# 1 Answers to the Question: What is Political Theory?

## INTRODUCTION

The only legitimate answer that can be given to the question 'what is political theory?' is that no definitive answer can be given to this question. This has been the case for some time. In 1968 McDonald noted that 'political theorists are not agreed among themselves about what political theory is or what its uses should be.' (1968: 2) In 1976 Miller observed that 'political theorists, are notorious for their disagreement about the proper object of their study.' (1976: 1) In 1981 Gunnell wrote that 'it has been difficult, since at least the mid-1970s, to specify the content of political theory as a sub-field of political science ... and to distinguish a definite set of issues'. (1981: 440) Nothing has occurred since 1981 to suggest that political theorists have come any closer to being able to provide a single definitive answer to the question 'what is political theory?'

One potential source of the confusion is that political theory coexists with a number of related concepts and practices. Gould and Thursby summed up this aspect of the problem of defining political theory when they wrote:

> The multiple current meanings of political theory range from a synonym for political philosophy to the designation of 'if ... then' propositions and formal model construction. It must be admitted, therefore, that political science, political theory, political thought, and political philosophy have not been used consistently in the same sense by all scholars of the subject field; uses in different senses can be cited for each of them. Sometimes the three latter terms are used as synonyms; sometimes they are distinguished. One is reminded of the exchange between Alice and Humpty-Dumpty in Through the Looking Glass:
>
> > 'The question is,' said Alice, 'whether you can make words mean so many different things.'
> > 'The question is,' said Humpty-Dumpty, 'which is to be master – that's all.'

Such mastery within a scholarly discipline entails either inefficiency or failure in communication. Short of consensus in usage, each writer must specify the meaning he intends for each of these terms or impose upon his reader the additional burden of ascertaining the intended meaning.

(Gould and Thursby 1969: 1–2)

While this quotation makes it clear that the relationship between political thought, political philosophy and political theory cannot be clearly specified, some discussions of political thought and political philosophy have been treated as useful for the elaboration of the different conceptions of political theory.

Gould and Thursby's concern that the confusion 'entails either inefficiency or failure in communication' is important in that it is an implicit recognition of the consequences of the problem for political theory as an academic discipline. My reading suggests that the confusion is not and was not random and that there are patterns in the literature that denote different conceptions and practices of political theory. These patterns resulted in the derivation of four conceptions of political theory (and, as a result, four different ways of answering the question 'what is political theory?'). These four conceptions of political theory will be dealt with in separate sections of this chapter. These sections focus attention on the different ontological and epistemological principles that underpin each conception and the ways in which those who adopt this conception read works of political theory.

The conceptions of political theory discussed in this chapter and book are self-conceptions, ways of understanding, and practices that can be identified from literature on the nature of political theory and from interpretations of works of political theory. While they come close to describing the practices of living and dead political theorists, their relationship with these political theorists cannot be fully clarified. They may be understood as ideal types. These are, as Abercrombie, Hill and Turner suggest, 'hypothetical constructions, formed from real phenomena, which have an explanatory value. "Ideal" signifies "pure" or "abstract" rather than normatively desirable.' As these authors went on to point out, 'the precise relationship between ideal types and the reality to which they refer remains obscure'. (1988: 117) That these four conceptions are ideal types means that they are not intended to be understood as exact matches or reproductions of any work produced by political theorists who adhere to a particular conception. They have been abstracted from the works of a number of political theorists who have reflected on the question 'what is political theory?'

## TRADITIONALIST ANSWERS

For those who adopt a traditionalist conception, political theory is a dialogue between significant thinkers in which basic or essential truths of politics are uncovered. 'Whatever else they have done,' McDonald wrote in 1968, 'political theorists in the Western tradition have been conducting a dialogue with each other.' (1968: 4) This perspective has remained current and, over twenty years later, Zerilli wrote: 'Political theory, it is often said, is a conversation – a transhistorical dialogue that links voices of the present with those of the past in a discourse concerning the meaning of public life.' (1991: 252)

The 'great conversation' (Germino 1975: 230) of the tradition is often taken to have originated with the ancient Greeks. Political theory 'was invented at a particular place, namely among the Hellenes in what we now call Greece, and at a more or less specific time, during the fifth century before Christ'. (Sabine 1973: 3-4) J. Peter Euben's article, 'The Battle of Salamis and the Origin of Political Theory', was 'an essay about the origins of politics and political theory in classical Athens'. (1986: 359) As a result, Germino wrote, contemporary political theorists do not have 'to invent political theory; that was invented long ago'; their role, in his view, is to continue a tradition that, 'with its endless possibility for growth and development, has continued into our own time'. (1972: 147)

### Being and Knowing (Traditionalist)

Traditionalists conceive of 'great' thinkers, whose works form the traditional canon, as rising above mundane levels of human existence and achieving a state of mind from which universal propositions are derived. A great political theorist is one who 'manages to achieve a broader perspective and to provide generalisations which transcend the immediate conditions of his time'. (Hacker 1961: 5-6) Great political theorists 'develop an understanding of life and politics that allows them to contribute to the resolution of problems that are fundamental to all forms of political organisation.... These theories are products of their age but they are also ageless....' (Plamenatz 1963: xxi)

For Strauss, political theory is like all forms of philosophy which, 'as quest for wisdom, is quest for universal knowledge, for knowledge of the whole'. (1957: 368) This is the reason that many traditionalists believe that the tradition contains 'perennially valid principles' (Germino 1967: 102) or 'truths and insights which are of permanent relevance for anyone who thinks philosophically about man and society'. (Barry 1982: 3–4) That political theorists belong to specific communities with specific problems is no constraint on their capacity to produce truths about politics. 'For every political situation contains elements which are essential to all political systems....' (Strauss 1959: 64)

The main difference between greats of political theory and others is that the former pursue knowledge further, often in unorthodox ways. 'Many of the most famous political theorists are specifically concerned with dispelling the mists of error which, in their view, becloud men's minds and corrupt their actions.' As a result, Spragens continued, these theorists 'see themselves battling the forces of sophistry and illusion which enchain men politically ... [and] attack those political attitudes and institutions which they see as based on false consciousness'. (1976: 19–20)

The capacity which most clearly distinguishes great political theorists from others is their capacity for insight or intuition. 'Feeling necessarily has a great part in searching for the truth.... A great idea is one that symbolises and unifies not only facts and beliefs that are clearly present to consciousness but also intuitions and impulses that have not been focused upon and given form.' (Tinder 1974: 7) According to Hacker, 'it is in these metaphorical or poetic moments that the "timelessness" of the "Great Books" comes to the fore'. (1969: 115) The possession of insight or intuition, as a supra-logical and synthetic perception, is one of the distinguishing characteristics of great political theorists. 'Like all great political theorists,' Jacobson wrote, 'Hobbes conjures up by an act of imagination, then deploys by an act of poetry, what trembles just beneath the consciousness of us all.' (1978: 59)

These ideas readily lead to a form of idealism. This reflects the traditionalist's sense of the significance for society of ideas generated by the great thinkers. Great ideas induce change by altering people's sense of reality and possibility. 'An idea is a kind of light; many of the great political ideas have the power of illuminating not only what is but what ought to be.' (Tinder 1974: 12)

These 'great ideas' are infrequent and emerge unpredictably. The list of great political theorists is short. 'Of course,' Tinder wrote, 'only a few great thinkers create the ideas that illuminate reality and thus guide action and research.' (1974: 13–14) Traditional political theory is highly individual. Probably as a result of the sort of intellectual attitude it requires, political theory 'appears to be a form of understanding akin to art in that individuality is an important part of it.' For, de Crespigny and Minogue continued, a great political theorist finds 'a problem where none was found before, and usually goes on to suggest a certain type of solution. These types of solution are irreducibly individual.' (1975: xiv)

The ways in which great political theorists look at themselves and their society places them somewhat outside the communities to which they belong. A great political theorist is not a person 'who panders to mass movements; in tension with his environment, he is much more frequently a loner or outsider than a team man'. (de Crespigny and Minogue 1975: xv) Thus, in Plamenatz's view, when compared with lesser thinkers a 'really great thinker' is 'idiosyncratic ... [and] more liable than they are to be misunderstood because he has more to say that is unfamiliar'. (1963: x)

That the 'great conversation' of political theory is timeless means that political theorists derive their inspiration, more often than not, from other thinkers far removed in time and culture. As Condren put it, they 'treat all past philosophers as their contemporaries; or as Hegel argued, philosophical events generate themselves in a way different from other events; they are somehow outside time'. (1979: 55) In a commentary on Plamenatz's *Man and Society*, Miller wrote: 'Successive chapters of that book reveal Plamenatz holding a conversation with the leading political minds since the Renaissance, a conversation in which he subjects their assumptions and definitions to a rigorous and subtle analysis.' (1983: 3)

**Reading Political Theory (Traditionalist)**

The ontological and epistemological underpinnings of the traditionalist conception of political theory lead to specific ways of reading works of political theory. These underpinnings determine both the works that are studied and the ways in which they are studied. Political theory derives from an individual and transcendental attitude by which essences are intuited and ideas provided through which reality may be more adequately perceived. Works of political theory have to be read in a way that reflects this.

The canon of great works of political theory is the central focus for those who wish to become political theorists and possibly make their own contribution to the tradition. 'Those of us who study or teach political theory take its importance almost for granted. We know that the classic works of political theory embody the searching reflections of some very great minds on profound issues that confront every man and woman.' (Spragens 1973: v) Reading is not some slavish pursuit of the ability to 'parrot' the greats of the tradition. Political theorists have 'to come to terms with these thinkers of the past', Plamenatz wrote, 'to make up our minds about them, if we are to learn to think more clearly than they did'. (1963: xiii) Reading 'is never simply a question of learning and borrowing from past masters, but also one of seeing them as exemplars of the interdependence of philosophy, theory, and explanation, such that we might understand the powers and limits of different possibilities, and gain a critical awareness of our own'. (Warren 1989: 612)

The purpose of reading the great works of political theory is to develop the capacity, where this is possible, to make one's own contribution. Thus, according to Germino, 'the role of tomorrow's political theorist will be essentially the same as that of ... today and yesterday'. This theorist 'will strive to exhibit ... those qualities of openness, love of wisdom, concern with the perennial problems of human existence, realism, critical detachment, and intellectual integrity which were found to be the hallmarks of political theory in every age'. (1967: 216) This means, in Hacker's view, that 'we should cease and desist from proving the "Great Books" wrong'. For 'if we are to allow the "Great Books" admittance because they can explain political behaviour in a valid way, then we should do it with good grace'. (1969: 115)

Traditionalists read works of political theory as responses to the fundamental problems of human existence. For the traditionalist, people in all places and at all times have faced, are facing or will be faced with the same basic problems. The works of great thinkers offer important insights to all people and can be read in ways that allow for an understanding of, if not a solution for, current issues in political life. 'The great political theorists continue to be read today virtually as if they were contemporaries because they were centrally concerned with the problems ... [of] societal existence.' (Germino 1967: 41) For, as Spragens pointed out, the '"perennial questions" reappear with a persistence which clearly marks them as central to the concern of political theory.' (1976: 8) The great works contain 'ways of looking at man and society which are of perennial interest.... Man and his social condition do change from age to age but they also remain the same...'. (Plamenatz 1963: xvii)

The question of what people are like, or the question of human nature, is one of the more frequently asked, and one of the most important, of the 'perennial issues' of political theory. From this perspective, political theorists are understood to base their theories on their 'understanding of man's essential human nature'. (Germino 1967: 102) For this reason, Nagel argued that political theory is 'hostage to human nature' (1989: 911), while Duncan simply acknowledged that 'any prescriptive political theory ... makes assumptions, which may be tacit, about human nature'. (Duncan 1983: 11)

Closely related to the question of human nature is the question of the proper or virtuous way of life. 'The good life is the existential realisation (or actualisation) of the known truth in the lives of single persons and in political societies.' (Sandoz 1972: 298) Thus, for Parekh, 'a political argument tends eventually to escalate into one about an ideally good life'. (Parekh 1968: 196) The works of the great thinkers of traditional political theory 'are more than attempts to explain society and government, and more also than apologies for or attacks upon the established order. They are philosophies of life....' (Plamenatz 1963: xiv)

If some trajectory can be identified that leads from the question of human nature to that of the good life, this trajectory may be said to continue to the question of the good society. 'In effect, the political philosopher-theorist asks the question: "What would society resemble if it brought out the best of which men are capable and if it were organised around the norms and priorities of the most fully developed human types?"' (Germino 1975: 244) Or, as Plamenatz put it, 'there is always a close connection between a philosopher's conception of what man is ... and his doctrines about how man should behave, what he should strive for, and how society should be constituted'. (1963: xvi) As a result, 'political theory ... presents an ideal of collective life, and it tries to show people one by one that they should want to live under it'. (Nagel 1989: 903) The question of the best form of social organisation is a central, in some views the ultimate, concern of political theorists. 'In short,' Spragens wrote, 'the theorist must confront the question that is often taken in abbreviated accounts as the question of political theory: What is the good society?' (Spragens 1976: 77)

To read a work of political theory is to interrogate that work with respect to the views implicitly or explicitly presented with respect to human nature, the good life and the good society. That these are the defining questions of political theory means that traditionalists read all great thinkers in order to develop their understanding of these fundamental concerns of human being. In Plamenatz's view, the great works of political theory 'contain most of the important ideas and assumptions still used or made, whether by students of society and politics or by persons engaged in political controversies'. (Plamenatz 1963: x) While no particular work can be understood to contain all that can be said on these questions and to contain some final answer to them, each contributes important insights and allows a political theorist to develop and offer their own answers.


## HISTORICIST ANSWERS

For the historicist, political theories are situated responses to problems that arise within a political theorist's particular situation or context. Political theories are produced by historically located individuals seeking to resolve problems encountered in their personal and/or social lives. Political theories refer directly to and are only meaningful in the light of the conditions within which they were articulated. Political theorists are situated beings, within this conception, whose works must be understood in terms of the situation of their writing. To properly understand them, then, 'past ideas should be studied in their historical contexts, which means going beyond the texts themselves to an exam-ination of the circumstances in which they were written'. (Lockyer 1979: 201) For 'historical situations determine at least in part the kind of visions that political thinkers can formulate'. (Berki 1977: 32)[4] Political theories do not refer to eternal problems or perennial issues, they refer to the situation in which they were written. So 'however universalist may be the terms in which a theory is couched, it is in fact coloured and probably called into being by the problems which confront the generation which devises it'. (Greaves 1966: 1)

### Being and Knowing (Historicist)

That historicists treat political theories as determined by the historical location of their authors means that the problems and solutions presented in works of political theory are only meaningful for and rele-vant to that particular situation. 'It would', Berki argued, '... have made no sense to argue in favour of free trade, *à la* Adam Smith, before the modern expansion of commerce and production, or to depict an ideal of individuality, as John Stuart Mill does, before the rise of modern democracy.' (1977: 32) Works of political theory are useful and important as historical artefacts which, under certain conditions, might throw some light on aspects of a current situation; but only if they are not read as if they were timeless.

The major writers of political theory were not addressing the same questions; at most, they addressed what may appear to be similar questions in very different contexts. Universality was an illusion with respect to both questions and answers. In rejecting anything but a fairly empty notion of 'perennial questions', Skinner argued that 'what *counts* as an answer will usually look, in a different culture or period, so different in itself that it can hardly be in the least useful even to go on thinking of the relevant question as being "the same" in the required sense at all'. (1988a: 66)

If being is situated then being's interrogation of itself is specific to the site within which it finds itself. 'To discover ... that there are in fact no such timeless concepts, but only the various different concepts which have gone with various different societies, is to discover a general truth not merely about the past but about ourselves as well.' (Skinner 1988a: 67) Political theorists who took themselves to be confronting and answering questions of human being *per se* were mistaken. All that they were doing was posing and answering questions produced by the situation within which they found themselves.

A relationship of constraint or determination of a theorist's ideas by 'reality' or 'social reality' is fundamental to this conception of political theory. Political theories are produced within and for particular historical circumstances and depend on these circumstances for their meaning and force. Political theories may take shape in the minds of political theorists, but those minds are stimulated and constrained by historical circumstances. 'Political theories are secreted ... in the interstices of political and social crisis. They are produced, not indeed by the crisis as such, but by its reaction on minds that have the sensitivity and the intellectual penetration to be aware of the crisis.' (Sabine 1973: 3)

Crises and lesser forms of social tension not only force theorists to consider certain issues as pressing but also cause them to come to particular conclusions on those issues. C. B. Macpherson's discussion of the revision of classical liberalism is a strong version of this style of argument. According to Macpherson

> What made a change in the classical [liberal] political theory possible and necessary was not simply that the development of society had made the old assumptions invalid, but that the same development had produced a working class with some class-consciousness, some organisation, and some theories of alternatives to capitalist relations (Chartism, Owenism, etc.). Working-class consciousness, we may say, both made the old theory invalid and made it obvious that it was invalid. (1973: 200)

Knights offered a more limited version of this approach in his treatment of Locke's *Second Treatise of Government*. In this study Knights 'tried to show that Locke's interest in Filmer coincided with his participation in the petitioning campaign of 1679–80, and that much of chapters 13 and 14 of the *Second Treatise* appear to have been influenced by the politics of the time'. (1993: 110)

## Reading Political Theory (Historicist)

Two factors must be taken into account when reading a work of political theory. The first is the nature of the situation within which it was generated. The second is the individual political theorist who responds with a political theory to that situation. Understanding a political theory requires examining the interaction between a political theorist, whose works are under consideration, and the situation in which that theorist wrote. Individual and context must be brought together if a theorist's works are to be properly understood. 'It would seem vital in reading a text to know the circumstances of its composition, something about the author's purposes in writing as best as we can ascertain them, something about his intellectual and political friends and foes, and the nature of the immediate audience he is addressing.' (Wood and Wood 1978: 11)

Interpreters must work hard to avoid imposing a meaning that derives from their own time on to a work written in another time. A political theory studied 'with little or no attention given to its social origins ... is studied as if it were written in our own times. We approach it from our own historical vantage-point, bring to it our own time-bound values and assumptions, our own conceits....' (Wood and Wood 1978: 12) Paying careful attention to a theorist's 'history' is an important corrective to misinterpretation.

The agenda of the historicist is quite clear when it comes to the interpretation of a political theory. Attention is not simply devoted to the words committed to paper by a political theorist. Given that a theorist's 'history' is taken to play a significant role in determining a theorist's meaning, a study of that 'history' is also required and the works themselves become only one of the means by which a theorist can be understood. Skinner could accept the traditional 'classics' as foci for study, but 'the degree of primacy which this assigns to the classic texts is simply that they become one obvious focus around which it might seem appropriate to organize some of our historical researches'. (1988c: 101) Choosing to begin with the 'classic texts' is not essential. Skinner was careful to make clear that the classic texts 'do not ...

represent the sole or even the most interesting focus we might choose'. (1988c: 101). They simply provided 'one potential answer to the inescapable question of where our historical researches ought to begin'. (1988c: 101)[5]

While the choice of historical context for reading may not be the last choice, that it is one of the first is significant. Analysis of a political theory involves as much history as it does theory, because the full appreciation of a political theory requires an understanding of the context that stimulated and delimited it. 'There is in every political theory a reference to a pretty specific situation, which needs to be grasped in order to understand what the philosopher is thinking about.' (Sabine 1939: 3) As a result, 'to reconstruct, as nearly as one can, the time, the place, and the circumstances in which it was produced is always an important factor in understanding a political theory'. (Sabine 1939: 3–4)[6]

That all historicists pay attention to history in their reading does not mean that all historicists understand history in the same way. Identifying the type of material that bears upon the meaning of a work of political theory is crucial for historicist modes of interpretation. For their interpretation of political theories to begin, historicist analyses must provide principles for 'closing the context' (Dunn 1968: 98).[7] This is an ontological and epistemological issue that quickly becomes a question of method. If the context within which theorists find themselves determines what they meant when they wrote, then specifying the nature of this context for the purposes of reading a work of political theory is a central issue of method.

At least three different types of context have been used by those who adopt a historicist method for the interpretation of works of political theory. All three are suggested in this quotation from Berki: 'The largest context is the historical development of Western society and the state. The second is the intellectual background of the writer, with special reference to the availability of linguistic forms and scientific or literary ideas with which he could express himself or communicate his intentions. The third context is the writer's personality.' (1977: 32)

These different ways of 'closing the context' of a political theory result in significant differences with respect to the type of material treated as relevant for the analysis of the works of a political theorist and the claims that can be made on the basis of this material. All three may be brought together, but the intellectual dexterity necessary to enable an analyst to combine the material that bears upon each context seems more readily available in theory than in practice. With few exceptions, historicist analysts tend to rely upon one or other of the three contexts referred to above.

The first, and broadest, context within which a work or corpus of works of political theory is read is the general social context. 'What sets the agenda for political theory, accordingly, is what is going on in society.' (Dunn 1985: 1) Neal Wood provided his sense of the research project fundamental to social-historicist analysis in the following quotation:

> If we are to discover in any precise way how the individual theorist and his theory can be related to the socio-political turmoil of his age, it is necessary to examine in some detail the situation of conflict and to elucidate the issues, the alignment of social forces and their nature. This requires a careful assessment of the polity and the economic aspects of the society in which the theorist is living and writing. Then we must determine the nature of the existing social structures, of class divisions, of the prevailing system of status, the connection between class and status, and their relationship to the state. (1978: 348)

The amount of information necessary for such an analysis may be extensive, but 'this social knowledge, far from being mere "background material" or "window dressing", is absolutely essential to any basic understanding of a political theory'. (Wood 1978: 348)

That political theorists are intellectuals means that they can also be understood to be influenced by works produced by other intellectuals. As a result, their theories can be read as responses to their intellectual situation or elaborations on and responses to the works by which they have been influenced. The context for interpretation in this case is a theorist's intellectual context and or inheritance. 'It is hard to imagine serious reflection which begins de novo, which is not sublimated to a higher level by a richly developed literary-philosophic tradition, transmitted in the form of writings.' (Bloom 1980: 115–16)

For some commentators, the tradition of political theory provides a theorist with a sense of the basic issues to be addressed and of the basic forms of the solutions available with respect to these issues. According to Lockyer, 'there exists a rational connection between a particular author's views and his problem situation – crucially including his intellectual inheritance'. (1979: 215) Skinner, on the other hand, exhorts historians of ideas to 'focus not just on the text to be interpreted but on the prevailing conventions governing the treatment of the issues or themes with which the text is concerned'. (Skinner 1988b: 77)

The final context that may be used to read a work of political theory is the personality of its author. Biography and psycho-biography become essential tools for a proper reading of a work of political theory. This approach is somewhat more controversial because it involves the introduction of material sometimes considered to be inappropriate to academic study. This form of historicism delves into the private; an uncomfortable thing for those who would maintain a separation between the public and private. For example, Hirschmann used what she called a feminist approach to uncover significant psychological dynamics behind liberal political theory. Her analysis demonstrated 'how the gender-related experiences that object relations theory articulates can be used to gain a deeper understanding of the epistemological grounding of obligation and of the structural gender bias that voluntarist theories embody'. (1989: 1243)

However the context is closed, the primary interpretive objective of the traditionalist is to use that context as something against which a work, or set of works, of political theory is read. If theorists are writing in and about their situations then to understand what they mean requires understanding those situations.

## LINGUISTIC ANSWERS

The linguistic conception reflects a reaction among some political theorists to the 'linguistic turn' in philosophy and, more specifically, the later works of Ludwig Wittgenstein. The effect of these works was to lead to a reorientation of philosophy and change in the conception of the role of the philosopher. This led some political theorists to reconsider their role and to adopt very different research agendas. No longer were theorists concerned with reflecting upon, and sometimes resolving, the perennial issues of political theory. They simply offered observations and sometimes advice with respect to the language used in discussions about politics.

### Being and Knowing (Linguistic)

Central to the linguistic turn was Wittgenstein's repudiation of the view that 'that the essential function of language is to depict or to describe the world'. (Fann 1969: 5) Whereas people had believed that languages 'could perform their function only if they consisted of models or copies

of reality, ... this belief has been shown to be mistaken'. (1953: 41–2)
Instead, words could only be understood in terms of the activities in
which they were used. 'Wittgenstein ... tries to show that there is not
something which stands behind the words. He therefore urges us to
seek understanding not by looking behind language, but at the language
games themselves in which words are used.' (Danford 1978: 196)
Word use 'cannot be understood merely by looking at the word, it can
only be understood in contexts – both linguistic and social'. (Fann
1969: 68) A concern with linguistic and social aspects of word use is
reflected in a concern with language-games. For by language-games
Wittgenstein 'means not only language as a system of linguistic signs,
but also all the activities belonging to the use of this sign-system'.
(Specht 1986: 137)

The use of the word 'games' indicates that there is a plethora of
activities in which words are used. The image also alludes to the fact
that while the same word might occur in a number of games, its
meaning will change in accordance with each game in which it is used.
A tennis ball may be used in tennis or a game of catch. It does not mean
the same thing in both instances. As Heap put it, 'concepts, such as
chopping, sawing, eating, aiming, fishing, flying, fighting, justifying,
and insulting do not necessarily or even usually have a single set of
properties that are evidenced by every action that can be called "chopping," "sawing" ... "justifying" or "insulting"'. (1977: 179)

From this perspective, the language available to any speaker or
writer 'can be seen as an ancient city: a maze of little streets and
squares, of old and new houses, and of houses with additions from
various periods; and this surrounded by a multitude of new boroughs
with straight regular streets and uniform houses'. (Wittgenstein 1963:
8) Learning to speak a language involves acquiring a variety of technical and non-technical language-games. Thus, when a person 'learns
what one might call special technical languages, e.g., the use of charts
and diagrams, descriptive geometry, chemical symbolism, etc., he
learns more language games'. (Wittgenstein as quoted in Zabeeh 1971:
335) The image of the language of a mature person that this created for
Wittgenstein was 'of a nebulous mass of language, his mother tongue,
surrounded by discrete and more or less clear-cut language games, the
technical languages'. (Wittgenstein as quoted in Zabeeh 1971: 335)

The use of 'game' is important in that it also indicates that language
is rule-governed. Rules, not reality, allow words to be used meaningfully. 'Knowing a language consists of knowing the conventions that
govern its units, and making sense in it consists of using it according

to the conventions.' (Flathman 1973: 12) Thus, 'there are rules that govern describing something as a tree, a telephone, an obelisque, and so on'. (Flathman 1973: 16) The notion of rule should not be taken too seriously, however. 'What, then,' Hund asks, '*did* Wittgenstein mean by "rule"? What emerges is that he made no distinction at all between rules and habits, or custom, and that he defined rules in terms of habits.' (1991: 73) Thus, according to Hund, 'both Austin and Wittgenstein identified rules ... with what people do "as a rule"'. (1991: 74)

Rules, or conventions, of use determine the ways in which words or phrases may be meaningfully employed. 'Languages are public in the sense that the uses of units of which they consist are governed by conventions or rules known, accepted, and usually followed by those who speak them. Knowing a language consists of knowing the conventions that govern its units, and making sense in it consists of using it according to the conventions.' (Flathman 1973: 12) To understand a speaker or writer is to recognise the conventions of their languages and to interpret the words and phrases they use in terms of those conventions.

One consequence of this is that the same word may be bound up with a variety of activities and governed by a variety of conventions. Its meaning differs as a result of these alternative uses. As a result, 'the search for the true or correct meaning or use of words and sentences is a wild goose chase'. (Weldon 1953: 28) Weldon criticised those political theorists who inquire into the essential meanings of words such as 'justice', 'freedom' and 'authority' because 'words do not have meanings in the required sense at all; they simply have uses'. (1953: 19) To pursue the 'true meaning' of such words is to misunderstand the possibilities available to political theorists. 'They are not the names of Ideas or archetypes ... for they are not the names of anything. To know their meaning is to know how to use them correctly, that is, in such a way as to be generally intelligible, in ordinary and technical discourse....' (Weldon 1953: 19)

## Reading Political Theory (Linguistic)

The conventional use of words is a necessary starting-point for the analysis of the use of words by political theorists. If political theorists are to articulate meaningful theories those theories must rely upon, even when they challenge, the conventions that govern the meaningful use of words. 'The languages are the primary focus of attention; individual authors are of importance because they use and modify them. A language of discourse is never the intentional or unintentional creation of any particular thinker, yet it may incorporate the entire vocabulary and range of argumentation used by a writer on any occasion. The language is prior to the speaker.' (Boucher 1985: 151) As Pocock wrote: 'Each of us speaks with many voices, like a tribal shaman in whom the ancestor ghosts are all talking at once; when we speak, we are not sure who is talking or what is being said....' (1984: 29)

Questions of the intentions of particular speakers are not significant. Factors that might have shaped such an intention are ignored. For Pocock,

> language consists of a number of already formed and institutionalised structures. These embody and perform speech-acts, but they perform the intentions of the user only through words formed by sedimentation and institutionalization of the utterances performed by others whose identities and intentions may no longer be precisely known. There is a double sense, then, in which the words that perform my acts are not my own: in the first place, they are words used by others and only borrowed by me, and in the second place, they have been institutionalized to the point where they cannot finally be reduced to the speech-acts of known individuals.
>
> (Pocock 1984: 30–1)

This parallels Ricoeur's argument that 'with written discourse, the author's intention and the meaning of the text cease to coincide'. (1971: 534)

The relationship between use and activity indicates another important feature of Wittgenstein's approach to language. This is his concern with understanding languages as reflecting 'forms of life'. Forms of life include that set of social relations of which language-games are part. 'Following a rule, making a promise, giving an order, and so on, are customs, uses, practices, or institutions.... They presuppose a society, a form of life.' (Fann 1969: 74)

While all political theorists might be said to focus on words, the orientation of the linguistic political theorist differs from other political theorists. All might agree with Miller that 'careful attention to the use of language is an essential part of political theorising'. (1976: 6) Significantly fewer would accept Pocock's argument:

> There are still striking discoveries to be made by scholars prepared to look empirically at the language, rather than immediately at the theory, or philosophy; even of thinkers whose works have been the

subject of centuries of discussion. To know a language is to know the things which may be done with it, so that to study a thinker is to see what he attempted to do within it.... (1971: 28)

The method to be used in reading political theory is not as straightforward, however, as might be inferred from the above quotation from Pocock. Greenleaf clearly understated the methodological problems for those who adopt a linguistic conception of political theory when he wrote that 'in purpose it is simply analysis of the language and concepts employed in political and moral discussion'. (1972: 472)

At least three linguistic approaches appear to have resulted from the ontological and epistemological principles that underpin the linguistic conception of political theory. Some linguistic analysts seek to develop a taxonomy of uses for particular words. Others take the language of those who study politics to be a specific language game and seek to clarify the meanings of words to facilitate the study of politics. A final, and less common approach, is to adopt a 'therapeutic' mode of analysis in which alternative uses of particular words are used to reflect upon problems in the forms of life of the community of users that adopt these alternative uses.

The taxonomic approach strongly reflects the descriptive character of linguistic analysis. While she has generally gone beyond the taxonomic Pitkin has indicated the descriptive character of this form of linguistic analysis:

Philosophy has the capacity for making us aware of our own method of representation, our conceptual system - both that it is a conventional, conceptual system, and how it represents, how it is to be 'read'. To do so, philosophy need only make fully clear for us the assumptions and conventions we already have. That is why Wittgenstein so often stresses the purely descriptive, nonreformational character of philosophy; it 'may in no way interfere with the actual use of language; it can in the end only describe it'. Philosophy 'leaves everything as it is'.

(Pitkin 1972: 298)

One of the more consistent practitioners of this form of linguistic analysis is Richard Flathman. (1973, 1987) According to Flathman, the role of philosophy is not 'to teach us something we did not previously know; it is merely to "assemble reminders" of what we already know, of what we know by virtue of the fact that we are speakers of a language'. (1973: 5)

Taxonomists observe the limits to philosophy that resulted from the linguistic turn by simply attempting to describe word use. In a discussion of 'law' Weldon offered a number of alternative uses and suggested that: 'It is important to distinguish these different uses of "law", since endless argument and confusion have arisen because ... they have been recklessly mixed up together.' (Weldon 1953: 65) Berlin's 'positive' and 'negative' liberty may be understood as a type of taxonomic analysis. (Berlin 1969) Harding began an article on 'the state' with the following statement: 'This article aims to trace the development of the concept of the state through the use of the word by politicians and lawyers as well as by theorists, without prejudice as to what "state" ought to mean.' (1994: 57) In his article 'Rights: An Essay in Informal Political Theory', Tushnet dealt 'with questions about how political actors, including judges, actually used words like rights rather than with questions about how such words can best be defined in relation to other words'. (1989: 404)

Other political theorists who adopt the linguistic conception do more than provide taxonomies of uses. They treat discussions about politics on the part of political scientists as technical uses which require careful attention to ensuring clarity of meaning. A concern with technical use usually results in attempts to stipulate, or reconstruct, the meaning of words when these meanings have been confused by multiple uses in both technical and non-technical activities. Political theory facilitates the study of politics by contributing to the precision that may be achieved in that study.

> One important characteristic of a body of knowledge is that it is conveyed through a rather specialised language, by which we mean that words are used in certain special senses and that certain concepts and categories are treated as fundamental to an understanding of the subject. To a large extent, any specialised language represents an artificial creation because it is self-consciously constructed to express meanings and definitions as precisely as possible.
>
> (Wolin 1960: 11–12)

Those who practise stipulation or reconstruction often take political theory to be the means by which words that are part of the specialist activity of studying politics are given the precise meanings required by specialist users.

Stipulation is often justified as necessary for the resolution of some 'technical' problem or to serve some heuristic purpose. Weldon noted that 'like most other words in ordinary use, "justice" has no single nuclear meaning. There is no precise criterion for its correct employment.... We can, if we find it convenient to do so, give it a precise or fairly precise meaning, and then it ceases to be vague or ambiguous and becomes a technical or semi-technical word.' (Weldon 1953: 22–3) Sometimes the purpose of stipulation is to 'clear away' the confusions that surround the meanings of words. Weldon accepted that the word 'law' had a variety of uses, but thought that it also had 'a lot of religious and semi-mystical ingredients ... [which] need to be taken out and discarded if we are to talk at all clearly about "law" and its relation to other political words'. (1953: 61–2)

A champion of this style of linguistic analysis is Felix Oppenheim, who argued that 'to make political concepts suitable for political inquiry, it seems to me necessary to reconstruct them, i.e., provide them with explicative definitions; these must in certain cases deviate from ordinary language to avoid ambiguities and valuational overtones'. (1981: 1) Oppenheim rejected 'ordinary language' as 'too blunt a tool to be of use for scientific investigation'. (1981: 177) His intention was to 'sharpen the tools' of those engaged in the scientific investigation of politics.

Pitkin's *Wittgenstein and Justice* (1972) was the first, and remains the most fully developed, attempt to apply the therapeutic approach to political theory. This 'therapeutic' approach picks up on Wittgenstein's attempt to cure philosophers of their tendency to disconnect words from their uses. This disconnection led philosophers to believe that by resolving divergences in the use of words they did away with the tensions that surrounded these alternative uses.

Wittgenstein's position does not require abandoning works that address 'those characteristic interminable controversies familiar in the history of political theory, which persist over generations, are taken up by one able theorist after another, and yet are never resolved'. (Pitkin 1972: 314) Indeed, Pitkin recognised 'the paradoxical quality of conceptual "insights", the way they simultaneously conflict with and depend on ordinary usage'. (1972: 287)

Wittgenstein's later philosophy, however, required a different approach to these controversies:

If we approach such controversies from a Wittgensteinian perspective, we see that each side seems to have a point, that either one taken separately can persuade us. We are tempted to reject one side only because the other seems convincingly right, and we assume that they cannot both be right. But perhaps they can both be (partially) right, each extrapolated from a valid insight or example; or perhaps only the extrapolations are in conflict. Then a simultaneous contemplation of what is right in each view might produce a new synthesis, or at least a perspicuous overview of why we are torn between the two positions.

(Pitkin 1972: 314–15)

This is not a call for some 'mindless acceptance of any and all views'. (Pitkin 1972: 315) But it is a call for an awareness of the extent to which the dilemmas of political theory may be intractable. 'Sometimes a philosopher questions conventions shaped by language games that are truly forms of life, truly natural to human beings in all times and places, and which literally cannot be changed.' (Pitkin 1972: 293)

Pitkin's therapeutic approach was aimed at removing the 'disease' caused by conceptual puzzlement through an awareness that it cannot be overcome and must simply be accepted. Thus 'the sign of a successful treatment is that the illness disappears. Philosophical problems are not so much solved but dissolved; given a perspicuous view of our grammar, we cease to be puzzled.' (Pitkin 1972: 288) Philosophical puzzlement does not disappear because its source disappears. It disappears because the desire to resolve the tension created by the feature of word use that was its source is removed. This is the most important contribution of 'therapy'.

These variations on a theme may constitute different linguistic approaches to the reading of works of political theory, but all reflect careful reflection upon the use of words. The significance of the linguistic turn for political theory was that the meaning of words and confusion over meanings derived from the language-games and forms of life of which they were part. Taxonomic approaches identify the rules or conventions that govern different uses of the same word. Stipulation, or reconstruction, introduces clear rules or conventions that technical users can rely on to ensure clarity in communication. Therapeutic approaches treat the conceptual confusions and disagreements on the part of users of a word by inducing recognition of the way that their uses are governed by different rules or conventions which cannot be reconciled.

## BEHAVIOURALIST ANSWERS

Those who adopt the behaviouralist conception of political theory see their project as bound up with the development of a science of politics.

They treat political theory as one element of the activity of investigating, and in some cases predicting, political behaviour. Theorising functions in two ways: in the development of hypotheses that are to be tested via the observation of human behaviour; and in the assimilation of the results of testing into a body of knowledge constituted through the scientific investigation of political aspects of human behaviour.

## Being and Knowing (Behaviouralist)

Observation is central to the study of politics for the behaviouralist. This explains Bentley's argument that actions are the true subject matter of the political scientist:

> We know nothing of ideas and feelings except through the medium of actions. This ... will be misunderstood if it is taken to mean that the ideas and feelings are there and that the action is merely a "medium".... In fact, the action is what we have given us. It is our raw material. The ideas and feelings, as such, are not given facts; they are not fixed points from which we can start to argue. They are ways of talking about the facts ... (1956: 14–15)

All inquiry into the nature of politics must be based upon observation and must be capable of being linked to further observation. One of the central tasks of the behaviouralist is to employ techniques that allow for the interrelation of observations. Two of the more important of these techniques are the survey and inferential statistics – particularly computer-supported techniques. 'The essence of the survey was the actual observation of forces in operation, with an effort to measure these forces and to standardise some system of measurement.' (Merriam 1970: 127)

Once observations have been made they can be used to develop generalisations about political behaviour. Ultimately, behaviouralists desire to formulate generalisations that explain political behaviour. This is where the political theorists plays a key role. 'Political theory is concerned, ideally, with the search for parsimonious explanations of political behaviour, processes, and systems.' (Eulau and March 1969: 51) Parsimonious explanations, however, are more of an ultimate, perhaps ever elusive, goal. 'Although the goal of scientific work is nothing less than the achievement of universal validity for its propositions, I doubt that a theory of politics as such is, at least for the present and immediate future, a feasible research strategy.' (Eulau 1969: 15) Merriam, on the other hand, remained optimistic: 'Possibly the door of human nature is closed by some decree of nature against the scientist, but it is possible that we have not found the key that will unlock it.' (1970: 219)

One feature of the explanations the behaviouralists seek is that they must be acceptable and evident to all, that is, are verifiable. 'Empirical theorists attempt to determine ... facts which help to explain man's activities on this earth. They do this with the following criterion as a guide: that any explanation which is given may be verified in principle through the use of man's sense apparatus (the five senses of seeing, smelling, hearing, touching, and tasting), without relying on a sixth sense.' (Froman 1962: 17) The goal of political scientists is 'knowledge that can be tested, verified, and shared among different investigators, regardless of their personalities and preferences'. People, Deutsch continued, are 'part of nature', and, as a result, a considerable amount about their 'behaviour can be known, much as facts about other parts of nature can be known'. (Deutsch 1971: 16)

The following quotation from Froman is probably an over-statement of the sentiments of behaviouralists, but traces of this persist.

> Truths (true statements) are said to be established in empirical theory when there is a high degree of correspondence between statements made about the world and the results of experiments and research which are designed to verify the statements. The ability to predict behaviour in the future ... is central to the demonstration of true statements. If one can predict future behaviour, this is strong support that the concepts one employs in explanation have a high degree of utility and that statements using these concepts are true. (1962: 17–18)

The link between the utility of concepts and prediction indicates the extent to which theory results from and is dependent upon the techniques available for testing propositions.

Few behaviouralists refuse to pay lip-service to the significance of discussions of the normative issues of politics. Most take the propositions generated in these discussions to be untestable, however, and consider normative inquiry to be the province of philosophy and not political science and the political theory that services it. 'On the question of whether behavioral science can arrive at judgments of what is "good" and what is "bad", the answer is that it cannot – that such judgments are, indeed, the task of ethics as a separate enterprise.' (Eulau 1969: 12) Indeed, for the behaviouralist 'the exclusion of value consideration in the form of biases that distort scientific inquiry is desirable'. (Deutsch 1971: 16) The goal in political scientific work is knowledge about facts.

The systematic accumulation of facts is only possible when study is guided by techniques or procedures that allow a community of scholars to cooperate to achieve an increase in the predictive power of generalisations. The accumulation of observations and the development of empirical methods that can be taken up by all students of political science is essential. 'Codification as a theoretical enterprise is necessarily a collective endeavour. As empirical research areas become more numerous and specialised, authoritative appraisal of research findings and their cumulation into a body of systematic knowledge will require the collaboration of specialists. Theorising in the past has largely been highly individualistic.' (Eulau and March 1969: 55) Political science requires a community of scholars working with similar methods on similar phenomena oriented by theorists who facilitate collaboration and the development of more robust generalisations.

The results that derive from empirical investigation and the generalisations made from them must be capable of providing the basis from which further empirical work and generalisations may be made by others in the scientific community (either contemporaries or future generations). Apter noted

> a revamping of the traditional curricula of post-graduate work to ... present a broader training, first in the canons and criteria of scientific work generally, and secondly in the general principles of social behaviour and organisation. The first emphasises the setting up of a researchable problem and the legitimate ways of handling that problem in order that fruitful and reliable conclusions can be obtained. The latter stresses the generalisable potentialities of the problem and its conclusions so that the area in which the student does intensive and detailed work can be related to other problems and issues in the field. (1957: 747–8)

Previous approaches to the study of politics were rejected as fundamentally inadequate. Behaviouralists were troubled by 'the extreme eclecticism and individualism of effort in political science. The field seemed to them to lack all the characteristics of a discipline, especially the constant accumulation of tested theories, a high degree of meaningful communication among its practitioners, and a high degree of cooperative research activity.' (Eckstein 1969: 360) The explanation for this state of affairs was that political scientists 'have no common language, no common problems, no significant methodological agreement in the field as a whole ... because we do not have a comprehensive and shared model (or conceptual scheme) of the political process which could guide our researches and give them a collectively coherent structure'. (Eckstein 1969: 360)

Behaviouralists placed much of the blame for the lack of such a 'comprehensive and shared model' at the feet of political theorists, especially traditionalists. 'The classic tradition, of course, is less concerned with describing and explaining political behaviour and processes than with speculating about the goals of political action and prescribing relevant modes of political conduct.' (Eulau and March 1969: 52)

Behaviouralist political theory, on the other hand, facilitated research and reflected the increase in knowledge achieved through empirical studies and reflection upon these studies. Deutsch put it bluntly:

> There is only one way to know whether our knowledge in fact has grown. No matter how different our theories may look on the surface, by how much has their truth content increased? How many new existential statements do they imply, in addition to the old ones included in their predecessors? How many new facts, relations and possibilities have we discovered, how many earlier conjectures confirmed or even modified, or else refuted? What new predictions can we make and test, what new political, social or legal actions, what new laws or institutions, now seem possible and perhaps worth trying? (1971: 19)

The problem was that while other parts of the political science community engaged in recording their observations, they were not used by political theorists, who continued to pursue idiosyncratic paths.

This individualism prevented political theory from adequately fulfilling one of its functions, which is to unite the political scientific community. 'Where other branches of political science may concentrate their attention on partial forecasts or partial descriptions of the political process, or of particular political phenomena, it remains the task of political theory to persist in the search for an orderly picture of the entire political system....' (Deutsch and Rieselbach 1965: 139) An effective political theorist had to work within the scientific community to facilitate the research carried out by other members of that community and to identify further avenues for that research.

## Reading Political Theory (Behaviouralist)

The behaviouralist conception orients the theorist and interpreter to a different set of questions from those that arise within other conceptions of political theory. As Wolin has suggested, 'the advocates of science have set themselves the objective of developing a theory which will serve as a guide for empirical inquiry'. (1968: 125-6) Some of the questions generated concern the adequacy of methods for observing and predicting behaviour. One measure of adequacy is a theory's utility in generating, synthesising, or otherwise providing valid generalisations from the data available. Political theory functions 'as a source of conceptual frameworks, operational concepts, and logical relationships for the use of the political scientist'. (Glaser 1969: 82) The burden placed upon theorists is to make their theories useful for those members of the community who engage in the observation of political behaviour. For only those theories that provide testable hypotheses can be treated as appropriate for political science.

The 'classic' texts of political theory are unlikely to be of great interest to the behaviouralist. They were too often associated with approaches to the study of politics explicitly rejected by behaviouralists. Behaviouralists sought to revolutionise the study of politics through their use of new techniques for the accumulation and processing of data. Theory functioned only in close association with these techniques. Other forms of theory had no place in the behaviouralist project. As Held observed, behaviouralists 'sought to displace the theoretical frameworks of normative political theorists by the development of empirical theory; and ... decisively rejected the history of political theory as the primary source of interpretation, and the basic meaning of theory, in political science'. (Held 1991: 12)

Behaviouralist political theorists are self-consciously different from the other types of political theorist discussed in this chapter. Indeed, many political theorists who adopt other conceptions deny that behaviouralists are political theorists. Different sorts of claims are made that derive from this different function of political theory. A different training for political theorists is required. This is largely a training in the use of techniques for survey and statistical analysis. Those claims that cannot be expressed in a form that can be taken up for these methods are useless to the behaviouralist.

## Not Reading Mill (Behaviouralist)

The constraints that derive from the behaviouralist conception frustrate those who hold to other conceptions of political theory, for these constraints render uninteresting many works often taken to be classics of political theory. The traditionalist McDonald was clearly irritated by behaviouralist attitudes to political theory: 'To ask theorists dead a thousand years to abide by our restricted, formal definitions of theory is futile. To justify the reading of political theory by asking how we may use it is not only premature but philistine.' (1968: 3) Ultimately, many texts that have been taken as objects for intensive study by other political theorists are ignored or considered minor contributions.

> The method most commonly employed in politics has been that of observation, development of shrewd hypothesis, and attempts at verification by observation, but without any special effort in the direction of numerical or statistical analysis. This is the way by which Aristotle, Machiavelli, Bodin, Montesquieu, Bagehot, Bryce, and others endeavoured to arrive at political conclusions. Very often they reached results that are attributable to the insight of a skilled observer. They might also be called political psychiatrists.
>
> (Merriam 1970: 186)

Political psychiatrists are not political scientists or political theorists who contribute significantly to the development of political science. Their works may be interesting but, from this perspective, they are not particularly useful.

Despite his interest in rigour and science Mill's works are not works of a behaviouralist political theorist. McCloskey observed

> The claim that truth, knowledge, rational and vital belief, progress, etc., are promoted by liberty is clearly an empirical claim. It cannot be tested experimentally, but empirical research into a range of societies in which liberty has or has not been enjoyed, is clearly relevant to such a claim. And, whilst the evidence may be too indefinite to establish or conclusively to refute this contention, it will nonetheless be of value and of much greater value than these speculations of Mill. (1964: 55)

In short, Mill's claims cannot be tested.

I do not believe that Mill's works can feasibly or credibly be reconstituted 'as if' they were written by a behaviouralist. First because it would require too much in the way of reconstitution. Such a reconstitution would not reflect Mill's orientation or that of behaviouralist political theorists. The second reason for not attempting a behaviouralist reading of Mill's works is to maintain a sense of the primacy of technique in the behaviouralist approach to theorising. If theorising is bound up with the techniques for data accumulation and processing that are available, theory must be written for these techniques. The priority of the technical cannot be underestimated. To write behaviouralist political theory requires a sense of the nature of available techniques and limitations that derive from them.

While primitive statistical techniques were available in Mill's time his familiarity with them was limited and his use of them even more so. He was not self-consciously and explicitly committed to this conception of theory and, as a result, did not make claims of the type to be expected from this type of theorist. He did not adopt an intellectual practice that came about almost a century later.

> Mill's theory of democracy cannot be neatly divided into empirical and normative parts. Even though some of the key propositions Mill puts forward can be regarded as mainly normative or mainly empirical, the theories of government and development, as well as of his major arguments, employ not only both kinds of propositions but also various hybrids of them. In this respect Mill follows the example of the leading political theorists of the past and departs from the practice of twentieth-century social scientists and theorists who turn a logically acceptable distinction between normative and empirical statements into a dichotomy between kinds of theories.
>
> (Thompson 1976: 184)

None of this diminishes the worth of behaviouralist political theory. It merely registers the sense of difference felt by those who adopt the behaviouralist conception of political theory. That Mill's works cannot be read through a behaviouralist conception indicates the specificity of this conception. Behaviouralist political theory cannot be written unselfconsciously. To treat a behaviouralist conception with the respect that it deserves requires not applying such a conception to Mill's works.

## CONCLUSION

Each of the conceptions of political theory outlined reflect different self-conceptions on the part of political theorists. This, however, does not mean that adherents of each conception necessarily recognise a difference between themselves and adherents of other conceptions. The behaviouralists are those most self-consciously different from the other practitioners of political theory. Those who may be designated traditionalist, historicist and linguistic political theorists may sometimes be mistaken for each other. There are three reasons for this. The first relates to apparent similarities in their behaviour; the second to similarities in their training; the third stems from their desire to deny limitation in their practice of political theory.

Both the traditionalist and the historicist believe in the significance of the intellectual and of intellectual questions. They both perceive their roles to be practical and engaged. They also treat intellectualising as an appropriate initial method for dealing with issues with which they are faced – that is, they both accept the validity and necessity of theory. Both treat the 'great works' of political theory as worthy of attention. On many occasions traditionalists and historicists may seem to be doing the same thing and may believe that they are doing the same thing. The less they articulate the deeper purposes behind what they are doing and the less they are generally self-conscious and express this self-consciousness the less they will be open to differentiation.

Linguistic political theorists may also be confused with traditionalists and the historicists. Both the linguistic theorist and the traditionalist can write about words and both may treat the meaning of words as significant. They can both quite happily read the 'great works' of political theory in terms of what some thinkers meant by certain words. Indeed, a common traditionalist approach to reading political theory, which derives from a traditionalist ontology and epistemology, is to read works as answers to questions like 'what is the essential meaning of "justice", "liberty" or "equality"?'. That this might appear like a linguistic approach obscures the fact that an inquiry into the use of 'justice' means very different things for a traditionalist and a linguistic political theorist. The orientation toward 'essences' basic to a traditionalist approach is fundamentally different from the orientation toward 'use' basic to a linguistic approach. Similarly the linguistic theorist and the historicist may want to investigate the meaning of certain words. Both will be interested in claims made by commentators and spokespeople. But both are driven by divergent ontologies and epistemologies that make the two enquiries into meaning vastly different enterprises.

The training of political theorists also contributes to their capacity to be confused for each other. Most courses in political theory are constructed around either a body of works or a set of key concepts. The objects, as it were, of political theory are constituted prior to the methods that will be brought to bear in reading these texts or discussing these concepts. That the training of a political theorist is often less oriented to methods and more to objects means that their training makes it difficult for them to recognise differences among themselves. Given that the differences between political theorists relate to methods and not objects, most political theorists will have little awareness of their differences.

Yet another reason that political theorists who practise different types of political theory often seem to be doing the same thing relates to their refusal to accept those limitations that derive from their conception of political theory. The ontological and epistemological principles that underlie each of the conceptions of political theory construct certain possibilities for being and for being a political theorist. These possibilities are limited because these epistemological principles derive from particular ontological principles which construct certain possibilities for human being. A self-conscious commitment to a particular conception of political theory requires the acceptance of the limitations that derive from that conception. Few theorists are comfortable with such limits. Most resist systematic and self-conscious limitation. Most political theorists want to do more than can be done within any one of the conceptions of political theory outlined in this chapter. Most engage in activities that reflect more than one of the conceptions discussed.

These observations are not intended as criticisms. I do not and cannot imagine that political theorists have or had explicit commitments to the conceptions of political theory outlined in this book. Most of the work done in generating the conceptions was done on the basis of inferences rather than explicit statements of intention. Relatively few political theorists have spent much of their time developing and articulating coherent conceptions of political theory.

The only significant exceptions are the behaviouralists. Their conception is much more bound up with a particular process of disciplining than the others. The behaviouralist political theorist is required to self-consciously adopt the ontological and epistemological principles of behaviouralist approaches to political science. This reflects, in part, the hostility from those who adopt other approaches toward this approach to the study of politics and political theory.

Each of the three remaining conceptions of political theory is applied in a reading of Mill's works in the chapters that follow. These applications are intended to reinforce a sense of the alternative natures of the three remaining conceptions of political theory (the preceding discussion of the behaviouralist conception and the discussion of the conception in Chapter 5 provide the only grounds for accepting that this is an alternative conception). These are not definitive versions of traditionalist, historicist or linguistic readings of Mill's works. Definitive versions of ideal types do not exist. Their purpose is simply to augment the discussion of the three conceptions of political theory of this chapter with a representation of them in practice to achieve a more complete understanding of the conceptions. Once this theoretical discussion has been augmented by a demonstration of the conceptions in practice some discussion of the value, problems and possibilities for unification of the conceptions can be undertaken in Chapter 5.

# 2 Reading Mill within a Traditionalist Framework

### Introducing Traditionalist Reading

The traditionalist conception is the most familiar of the three approaches to reading Mill exemplified in this book – even if it is considered objectionable by some political theorists. Much of the literature written about Mill can be understood to sit comfortably within this analytical framework. Certainly there may be the odd reference to Mill's historical location (understood usually as an intellectual location or a social location) in some works and to his use of words in others. Most of these, however, can either be read down or are so deeply situated within the framework of the pursuit of essential questions that they pose no real problem for using these works within a typical traditionalist reading. Historical references are sometimes contained in a preamble to a typical traditionalist reading of Mill's works and rarely interrupt that reading. Reference to word use is usually within a standard theme of traditionalist approaches: as the pursuit of the essential meaning of justice, freedom and the like to which Mill's works are taken as a contribution. The following reading eschews reference to Mill's times or to his use of words and is oriented exclusively to his investigation of the key questions of human being: human nature, the good life and the good society. These questions are taken to be eternal problems of human being, the answers to which great thinkers like Mill have directly contributed.

### INTRODUCTION

To read Mill's works as a traditionalist is to encounter a mind confronted by and wrestling with fundamental existential questions. The first of these questions is the primary question of human being: 'what am I?' The second is the question 'how should I live?' and the third: 'how should we live?' A search for answers to these questions is central to traditionalist political theory and they are otherwise understood as the questions of human nature, the good life and the good

37

society. Like all great political theorists, Mill provides insights into and opens up the possibility of answering these basic existential questions.

Mill's works help us to develop our own answers to these traditional questions. The subtlety of Mill's responses to the fundamental questions of political thought makes his works a rich source of inspiration for contemporary political theorists. To read Mill's works is to engage with a mind of great insight and sophistication.

This chapter is divided into three sections that cover Mill's view on human nature, the good life and the good society. These views have been discerned from Mill's positions with respect to other related issues. Mill did not organise his works around answers to the problems of human nature, the good life and the good society. But as with all great thinkers of the tradition of political theory, his works are addressed implicitly to these questions.

## HUMAN NATURE

Mill's political theory can only be understood if an analysis begins with his conception of human nature. As Mill himself suggests: 'The first question in regard to any man of speculation is, what is his theory of human life?' (B 10: 94) This is the first question because it provides the basis from which a political theory develops. To resolve those issues that go to the proper ordering of a person's life and of a society requires starting with human nature.[8]

Mill's position with respect to three issues will be discussed for the purposes of determining his 'theory of human life'. These are: the human psychology; necessity versus free will; and the nature of women. Basically, Mill takes the view that human nature is significantly malleable with few inherent or natural characteristics and that character, as a result, is a product of both volition and environment. In developing his conception of human nature, then, Mill emphasises both external and self-determination.

### Psychology

Mill's understanding of human psychology represents a modification to associationism. While he accepts basic associationist principles, he rejects the view that the mind is wholly a product of external stimuli and believes that individuals have inherent character traits or dispositions that cannot be fully overridden.

Associationists believe that the human mind is a simple recording device. At its inception the mind is without content. Content is acquired as experiences are recorded in the mind. These experiences have positive or negative 'value' according to the sensations present during the experience. Experiences are connected, or associated, with other experiences through an experiential connection. An experiential connection is completed when two or more experiences are experienced together on a sufficient number of occasions to develop a permanent link.

Packe describes the associationist version of the development of the mind thus:

> All minds started as much alike as all stomachs or hands or any other physical organs. They were all blank sheets forced to record every experience which the senses introduced to them: and, in the event of a repeated sequence of experiences, to recall the order in which they came about, so that the last events in the sequence could be predicted from the first with such certainty that they could be said to have been caused by them. Thus, minds differed only so far as they recorded different chains of experiences, and from them formed different habits of association. (1954: 14–15)

This view of mental processes means that minds are open to being trained and a particular character produced. All that is required in order for particular responses to be 'programmed' into an individual's mind is the repetition of patterns of experiences.

For associationists, all forms of mental events can be understood through 'laws' of association. 'A desire, an emotion, an idea of the higher order of abstraction, even our judgments and volitions when they have become habitual, are called up by association, according to precisely the same laws as our simple ideas.' (SOL 8: 856) Individuals differ in their behaviour as a result of their acquiring different associations. There is no such thing as 'one universal character, but there exist universal laws of the Formation of Character.' (SOL 8: 864)

Mill modified his associationism by accepting the operation of 'natural tendencies of the mind'. (UQPE 4: 315) The modification Mill is making to the doctrine of association is intended as a refinement and not a refutation. Mill identified 'natural differences which really exist in the mental predispositions or susceptibilities of different persons'. As a result, Mill continued, 'the idea of some particular pleasure may excite in different persons, *even independently of habit or education*, very different strengths of desire, and this may be the effect of their different degrees or kinds of nervous susceptibility'. The effect of these differences does not mean that some people feel pleasure when others do not; they merely 'render the pleasurable sensation itself more intense in one of these persons than in the other'. (SOL 8: 857 emphasis added) Mill does not retreat from his associationism but accepts that different minds have different propensities to form particular associations and that all minds have some natural tendencies.

Mill asserts a 'natural indolence' (PPE 3: 795) on the part of people. This was probably one example of 'the bad propensities of human nature [which] are only kept within bounds when they are allowed no scope for their indulgence'. (SOW 21: 289) Negative dispositions are not the only ones Mill identified as he also drew attention to 'the social feelings of mankind; the desire to be in unity with our fellow creatures ... [as] already a powerful principle in human nature...'. (U 10: 231)

Mill believes that, in most instances, these negative tendencies or predispositions could be overridden. For him, all individuals had a duty with respect to their 'own nature as in respect to the nature of all other things, namely not to follow but to amend it'. (TER 10: 397) These tendencies can be overridden if society is structured to override these undesirable natural tendencies and create desirable artificial ones. The English, in Mill's view, are

> farther from a state of nature than any other modern people. They are, more than any other people, a product of civilization and discipline. England is the country in which social discipline has most succeeded, not so much in conquering, as in suppressing, whatever is liable to conflict with it. The English, more than any other people, not only act but feel according to rule. In other countries, the taught opinion, or the requirement of society, may be the stronger power, but the promptings of the individual nature are always visible under it, and often resisting it: rule may be stronger than nature, but nature is still there. In England, rule has to a great degree substituted itself for nature. The greater part of life is carried on, not by following inclination under the control of rule, but by having no inclination but that of following a rule. (SOW 21: 313)

Mill's basic commitment to associationist principles is evident in his view that natural tendencies could be displaced. 'For Mill asserted, not only that human nature changed significantly, and that consequently one could not build universal theories on the basis of its form in any particular historical society, but that it could be shaped deliberately.' (Duncan 1973: 251) The effect of natural differences of mind could not be discounted but they were not decisive in character formation. For

Mill, 'differences in education and in outward circumstances are capable of affording an adequate explanation of by far the greatest portion of character; and ... the remainder may be in great part accounted for by physical differences in the sensations produced in different individuals by the same external or internal cause'. (SOW 21: 859) Mill accepted some natural differences between minds, and dispositions in all minds, that affected their capacities to form associations, but he did not reject the basic principles of associationism.

## Necessity and Free Will

Mill's conception of character-formation almost immediately introduces the question of the extent to which individuals actually control their actions. Mill believes that the choice of answers to this question is usually taken to be a choice between treating human actions either as determined or as the result of the exercise of free will. In his view, however, the choice between determinism, or necessity, and free will is a false choice. According to Mill, the choice is usually presented as being between the view that holds 'human volitions and actions to be necessary and inevitable' and the view 'that the will is not determined ... but determines itself; that our volitions are not, properly speaking, the effects of causes, or at least have no causes which they uniformly and implicitly obey'. (SOL 8: 836) Mill rejects both of these positions.

Properly understood, Mill believes, the doctrine of Necessity was just the position 'that, given the motives which are present to an individual's mind, and ... the character and disposition of the individual, the manner in which he will act might be unerringly inferred: that if we knew the person thoroughly ... we could foretell his conduct with as much certainty as we can predict any physical event.' (SOL 8: 836–7)

Prediction is possible only if the conditions that determined a person's behaviour persist. If these conditions change, new behaviour will result. That, in Mill's view, people have the ability to change their own circumstances means that their behaviour is not beyond their control. For Mill, predictions represent 'hypothetical rather than ... categorical statements. Instead of stating impossibilities or inevitabilities they merely set down what will or will not happen, if intervening causes do not apply'. This makes possible 'the crucial possibility of human control'. (Smith 1980: 239) Will asserts or reasserts itself as the capacity to introduce new conditions which result in changes to behaviour.

Mill is a determinist, not a fatalist:

A necessitarian, believing that our actions follow from our characters, and that our characters follow from our organization, our
education, and our circumstances, is apt to be ... a fatalist as to his
own actions, and to believe that his nature is such, or that his education and circumstances have so moulded his character, that nothing
can now prevent him from feeling and acting in a particular way, or
at least that no effort of his own can hinder it. (SOL 8: 840)

Mill rejects this position as 'a grand error' and asserts that a person
possesses the 'power to alter his character. Its being, in the ultimate
resort, formed for him, is not inconsistent with its being, in part,
formed by him as one of the intermediate agents'. (SOL 8: 840)

In short, individuals can change themselves by changing their associations. 'Thus we do have the power to intervene, to inject into
circumstances new factors which will modify our characters and so
change the direction of will and desire.' (Garforth 1979: 40) That character is formed primarily through external causes means that new
causes will result in changed behaviour. 'A man's character is not a
straitjacket which restricts his behaviour no matter how he struggles. A
man can alter his character if he wants to do so; thus he can alter his
actions, too.' (Ryan 1974: 86)

To this extent, and only to this extent, is Mill sympathetic to the free-
will doctrine. This doctrine keeps 'in view precisely the portion of the
truth which the word Necessity puts out of sight, namely the power of
the mind to co-operate in the formation of its own character, and has
given to its adherents a practical feeling much nearer to the truth than
has generally ... existed in the minds of the necessitarians'. (SOL 8:
841–2) Those who believe in necessity or free will are both wrong and
right. The former err when they neglect the possibility of overcoming
past causes by introducing countervailing causes. The latter err when
they fail to recognise the power of prior determinants of behaviour.

## Women

A central part of any political theory is the way in which differences
between men and women are presented. Mill's views on association and
necessity and free will mean that he treats observable differences
between the 'natures' of men and women as, for the most part, the
result of different conditions under which their characters are formed.
He considers the inequality in the social positions of men and women
to be socially induced. 'Women are as capable as men', he wrote, 'of

appreciating and managing their own concerns, and the only hindrance to their doing so arises from the injustice of their present social position.' (PPE 3: 953)

In short, women in Mill's society have been trained to fill a subservient position and were made submissive toward and dependent upon men:

> All women are brought up from the very earliest years in the belief that their ideal of character is the very opposite to that of men; not self-will, and government by self-control, but submission, and yielding to the control of others. All moralities tell them that it is the duty of women, and all the current sentimentalities that it is their nature, to live for others; to make complete abnegation of themselves, and to have no life but in their affections. (SOW 21: 271–2)

Mill denies some essential or necessary inequality between men and women. 'There is no natural inequality between the sexes; except perhaps in bodily strength; even *that* admits of doubt....' (OM 21: 42) He does not deny the possibility of natural differences, but leaves the resolution of this question to the future. 'No one can safely pronounce that if women's nature were left to choose its direction as freely as men's,' Mill wrote, '... there would be any material difference, or perhaps difference at all, in the character and capacities which would unfold themselves. (SOW 21: 305)[9]

Though Mill does allude to unequally distributed differences between the sexes, he argues that there is 'a certain proportion of persons, in both sexes, in whom an unusual degree of nervous sensibility is constitutional...'. Mill believes this sensibility to be 'hereditary, and ... transmitted to sons as well as daughters; but it is possible, and probable, that the nervous temperament (as it is called) is inherited by a greater number of women than of men'. (SOW 21: 308) Thus it would be a mistake to assume with respect to the sexes that the 'differences of feeling and inclination only exist because women are brought up differently from men, and that there would not be differences of taste under any imaginable circumstances'. (SOW 21:334)[10]

Mill believes that a great majority of the differences that exist between the sexes are the product of differences in upbringing and general socialisation. He accepts that some of the differences may derive from differences in the natural tendencies of women and men. He concludes that a woman's character does not begin in exactly the same state as a man's and that some of the basic building-blocks of character differ between the sexes.

**Human Nature**

Mill treats by far the greatest proportion of human character as due to the environment within which it is formed. He refers to

> the vulgar error of imputing every difference which [one] finds among human beings to an original difference of nature. As well might be said, that of two trees, sprung from the same stock, one cannot be taller than another but from greater vigour in the original seedling. Is nothing to be attributed to soil, nothing to climate, nothing to difference of exposure – has no storm swept over the one and not the other, no lightning scathed it, no beast browsed on it, no insect preyed upon it, no passing stranger stript off its leaves or its bark? If the trees grew near together, may not one which by whatever accident, grew up first, have retarded the other's development by its shade? Human beings are subject to an infinitely greater variety of accidents and external influences than trees, and have infinitely more operation in impairing the growth of one another; since those who begin by being strongest, have almost always hitherto used their strength to keep the others weak. (NQ 21: 93)

Mill clearly sides with those who emphasise nurture over nature, when it comes to the essential political issue of human nature. 'He broke with the pseudo-scientific model ... of a determined human nature, endowed at all times with the same unaltering needs, emotions, motives, responding differently only to differences of situation and stimulus, or evolving according to some unaltering pattern.' (Duncan 1973: 34) To understand human beings is not to identify their fixed characteristics (e.g. aggression, competitiveness, sociability, or empathy) but to recognise their malleability. Mill projects an openness with respect to human existence that allows individuals to choose their character and destiny. 'Mill's entire view of human nature turns out to rest ... on his perception of human lives as subject to perpetual incompleteness, self-transformation and novelty....' (Berlin 1959: 18)

THE GOOD LIFE

Mill's views on psychology, necessity, education and women provide the foundations for his conception of the morally correct, or good, life. A fuller understanding of his conception of the good life requires consideration of his views on individuality, pleasure, and traditions or customs. Mill's image of the good life begins with his view that individuals should take responsibility for their behaviour and pursue ends that reflect their particular inclinations. This does not mean that he advocates mere self-assertion. Mill is concerned that individuals choose to pursue higher ends and carefully consider the possibilities expressed in traditions or customs.

## Individuality

Individuality, as individual self-motivation and self-direction, is crucial for Mill. His view that human beings are significantly mutable in character leads Mill to charge each of them with the responsibility for their development. The highest form of character is only possible if individuals consciously and freely take control of their character and actions. Though his modified associationism leads Mill to acknowledge that an individual's character can be influenced, even formed, by external factors, he rejects such manipulation, at least when it comes to adults: 'Nobody denies that people should be taught and trained in youth, as to know and benefit by the ascertained results of human experience. But it is the privilege and proper condition of a human being at the maturity of his faculties, to use and interpret experience in his own way.' (OL 18: 262)

A good education is only effective if it is reinforced by the individual engaging in self-directed activity. 'Instruction is only one of the desiderata of mental improvement; another almost as indispensable, is a vigorous exercise of the active energies....' (PPE 3: 943) Excessive outside interference undermines strong character and prevents an individual's development. Mill prizes 'a character which is self-reliant, rational in its assessment of the world, tolerant, wide-ranging in its interest, and spontaneous in its sympathies.... coercion is logically at odds with the creation of such a character.' (Ryan 1970: 254–5)

People must determine their own ends if they are to develop their individuality. Choosing and individuality are inextricably linked for Mill. A human differs 'from animals primarily neither as the possessor of reason, nor as an inventor of tools and methods, but as a being capable of choice, one who is most himself in choosing and not being chosen for'. (Berlin 1959: 8) To refuse to choose is to deny one's humanity. 'Those who are unable or who refuse to exercise their human capacity for choice ... have lost or surrendered that which is distinctively human, that which marks them out from the rest of nature and from the artefacts of human creation....' (Ten 1980: 68–9)

Unless individuals are given and take up the opportunity to choose they will not develop. Human beings have to determine and pursue their own destinies to grow and remain strong. 'Human nature is not a machine to be built after a model, and set to do exactly the work prescribed for it, but a tree, which requires to grow and develope [*sic*] itself on all sides, according to the tendency of the inward forces which make it a living thing.' (OL 18: 263)

Moral actions also require individuality. To act morally is to choose to act morally. A moral person does not merely follow others. 'Morality consists of two parts. One of these is self-education; the training by the human being himself, of his affections and will.... The other and coequal part, the regulation of his outward actions, must be altogether halting and imperfect without the first....' (B 10: 98) The highest natures are self-produced. Their exemplary character is not merely evidenced by the paths chosen but also by their being freely chosen. 'Individuality for Mill, therefore, consists in part in the readiness to make deliberate and considered choices between alternative beliefs and patterns of life, and in part in the direction and content of such choices.' (Ten 1980: 69)

**Pleasure**

One aspect of the direction and content of proper choices is that they are toward the higher rather than the lower pleasures. This position begins with Mill's view that pleasures are 'intrinsically different: there are higher and lower among them'. (Davidson 1957: 123) For Mill, to pursue higher pleasures is to express and expand one's humanity. He distinguishes between pleasures that can be enjoyed by all animate beings and pleasures that are peculiarly the province of mature human beings.

> Few human creatures would consent to be changed into any of the lower animals, for a promise of the fullest allowance of a beast's pleasures; no intelligent human being would consent to be a fool, no instructed person would be an ignoramus, no person of feeling and conscience would be selfish and base, even though they should be persuaded that the fool, the dunce, or the rascal is better satisfied with his lot than they are with theirs. They would not resign what they possess more than he, for the most complete satisfaction of all the desires which they have in common with him. (U 10: 211)

The distinction between animal pleasures and human pleasures is not a matter of quantity and is based upon the quality of the pleasure. Quality is determined by 'the preference felt by those who, in their opportunities of experience, to which must be added their habits of self-consciousness and self-observation, are best furnished with the means of comparison'. (U 10: 214) Thus, 'when Mill uses *happiness*, he means the happiness that *rational* reflection would approve, not *any* pleasure a man *happens* to pursue.' (Cowling 1963: 32) Only those with higher natures can identify these superior pleasures. 'Mill's "pleasures" are not ... phenomena which can be exactly identified and measured; and the propositions he makes about them cannot be shown to rest upon any process of induction. What he has to rely upon is experience – the discriminating experience of educated minds.' (Britton 1953: 75-6)

Those with higher natures are not immune from the siren call of the lower pleasures. The ability to appreciate higher pleasures requires continuous cultivation. 'Capacity for the nobler feelings is in most natures a very tender plant,' Mill writes, 'easily killed, not only by hostile influences, but by mere want of sustenance....' People 'lose their high aspirations ... because they have not time or opportunity for indulging them; and they addict themselves to inferior pleasures, not because they deliberately prefer them, but because they are either the only ones to which they have access, or the only ones which they are any longer capable of enjoying'. (U 10: 212-13) Maintaining the ability to appreciate higher pleasures requires effort and diligence. Refined sensibilities may become dulled and a sense of the superiority of the higher pleasures can be lost if no effort is made in this direction.

One of these higher pleasures is the enjoyment of the intellect. In this Mill agrees with the Epicureans and 'there is no known Epicurean theory of life which does not assign to the pleasures of the intellect, of the feelings and imagination ... a much higher value as pleasures than those of mere sensation'. (U 10: 211) Intellect is both a means for appreciating the higher pleasures and a higher pleasure in itself.

Another of Mill's higher pleasures derives from a concern for others. To pursue personal happiness directly is not, he thinks, the path to that end: 'Those only are happy ... who have their minds fixed on some object other than their own happiness; on the happiness of others, on the improvement of mankind....' (A 1: 145) Selflessness provides a higher form of pleasure than selfishness. Indeed, the latter leads away from pleasure of superior quality. A person's 'highest pleasure comes when he does not directly seek it; his own happiness is found in doing good to his fellows or to other sentient creatures'. (Davidson 1957: 124-5)

The pursuit of pleasures other than those of the intellect and self-lessness meant an impoverished and unfulfilled life. 'Next to selfishness,' Mill wrote, 'the principal cause which makes life unsatis-factory, is want of mental cultivation.' (U 10: 215) Mill 'claims that the quality or kind of happiness is important in assessing its value; moreover, the most valuable kinds of happiness are those that engage humans in developing and exercising certain capacities.... To be more specific, the most valuable forms of happiness are those of engagement in the use of intellectual, affective and moral or caring capacities.' (Donner 1993: 156) Mill's good and happy life requires the pursuit of these virtues. To pursue other ends is to pursue lower pleasures and no amount of these will fill the lacuna left by the absence of the higher.

## Tradition and Custom

That individuals must choose for themselves does not mean that they should pay no heed to the views of others and ignore competing perspectives.

> The steady habit of correcting and completing his own opinion by collating it with those of others, so far from causing doubt and hesi-tation in carrying it into practice, is the only stable foundation for a just reliance on it ... knowing that he has sought for objections and difficulties, instead of avoiding them, and has shut out no light which can be thrown upon the subject from any quarter – he has a right to think his judgment better than that of any person, or any multitude, who have not gone through a similar process. (OL 18: 232)

Correct opinions concerning proper behaviour come only through extensive consideration of the positions held by others.

The views and practices of contemporaries are not the only ones an individual needs to take into account. Traditions and customs that embody the views of preceding generations must be taken into account and, when persuasive, should be adopted. Mill's understanding of the role and function of traditions, or customs, is complex. He is wary of a reliance upon tradition or custom but he does not dismiss them as valueless.

Mill considers the 'despotism of custom' a major obstacle to human improvement, since it prevents people from pursuing improvements in their social arrangements. (OL 18: 272) Mill cites the situation in 'the East' as a case of the debilitating effects of unchallengeable customs. 'The greater part of the world has, properly speaking, no history, because the despotism of custom is complete. This is the case over the whole East. Custom is there, in all things, the final appeal; justice and right mean conformity to custom; the argument of custom no one ... thinks of resisting.' (OL 18: 272)

Despotism of custom is not the problem facing Europe, however. In this case, the problem is unreflective obedience to unceasing changes in fashion. In this case, despotism of custom 'is not precisely stationariness. It proscribes singularity, but it does not preclude change, provided all change together.' (OL 18: 273)

Change for the sake of change is as much a despotism of custom as a resistance to all change. When it comes to politics, then, the 'fact that a certain set of political institutions already exist, have long existed, and have become associated with all the historical recollections of a people, is in itself ... a property which adapts them to that people, and gives them a great advantage over any new institutions in obtaining that ready and willing resignation to what has once been decided by lawful authority...'. (ROB 10: 17) One sign of a durable political community is that there are core values that are commonly respected, and which it is 'lawful to contest in theory, but which no one could either fear or hope to see shaken in practice...'. (C 10: 134)

Mill criticises radical French philosophers of the eighteenth century for 'unsettling everything which was still considered settled, making men doubtful of the few things of which they still felt certain; and in uprooting what little remained in people's minds of reverence for anything above them...'. (C 10: 137) Tradition and custom should not be done away with in one clean sweep because greater circumspection is required in achieving social change. Indeed, this is Mill's main contention with respect to traditions, or customs: if they are to be replaced, this should only occur after careful reflection with respect to gains and losses. Mill dismisses both unreflective rejection of traditions and blind allegiance to them.

The role of tradition or custom is a difficult one for Mill. His solution is to accept both the importance of obedience to tradition or custom *and* the need to continually draw all beliefs and practices into question. Mill recognises 'a tendency in the best beliefs and practices to degenerate into the mechanical ... unless there were a succession of persons whose ever-recurring originality prevents the grounds of those beliefs and practices from becoming merely traditional...'. (OL 18: 267) Even those beliefs and practices most conducive to social well-being would become impediments to social well-being without continual reconsideration. Reconsideration is not automatic repudiation. Thoughtless rejection of custom or tradition is as dangerous as unquestioning acceptance. 'Mill is not opposed to tradition and custom as such. Either to reject or accept customary practices, without considering their claims as opposed to alternative patterns of behaviour, is equally to refuse to exercise choice.' (Ten 1980: 70)

## The Good Life

Mill does not prescribe a complete code of behaviour and instead provides only a general indication of the character of the good life. 'Mill's conception of an ideal human character did not run in terms of a narrowly prescribed pattern of conduct or a particular pattern of tastes which society was justified in forcing on the individual. Mill was rather concerned to stress certain broad features of a desirable kind of life....' (McPherson 1982: 269–70) This is not an omission on his part, but derives from his emphasis upon individuality. Mill believes that 'different kinds of excellence of character are possible, and they are also desirable, both because this permits an experimental way of living, and because variety is itself a thing to be enjoyed'. (Britton 1953: 73–4)

Mill also rejects detailed prescription on the ground that moral codes are excessively abstract and often impractical. Besides, to develop a moral code is also to encourage others to develop competing moral codes.

> Those who cherish any one of the numerous *a priori* systems of moral duty, may learn ... how plausible a case may be made for other *a priori* systems repugnant to their own; and the adepts of each may discover, that while the maxims or axioms from which they severally set out are all of them good, each in its proper place, yet what that proper place is, can only be decided, not by mental intuition, but through the practical consideration of consequences.... (TLC 5: 650)

Mill's reluctance to develop an *a priori* moral system doesn't mean that he has no sense of the general features of the good life. The good life is freely chosen. It involves the pursuit of higher pleasures. It incorporates a recognition of the need to take traditions into account for the making of informed choices and for the maintenance of social cohesion. It is not selfish.

Mill's good life is a mixture of individual self-creation and social responsibility that manifests itself in a desire to live the good life in order to benefit others. This is not achieved by prescription or coercion, but by example. 'The love of virtue, and every other noble feeling, is not communicated by reasoning but caught by inspiration or sympathy from those who already have it. . . .' (TG 11: 150) When a good person looks to others s/he 'considers their welfare, not by telling them how to live, but by considering in what way how *he* and *she* lives affects them'. (Struhl 1976: 160)

## THE GOOD SOCIETY

Just as the general features of the good life follow from human nature, so too do the general features of the good society follow from those of the good life. An understanding of Mill's conception of the good society, however, can be enhanced through a consideration of his views with respect to history, the stationary state, socialism, the proper role for government, education and 'self-regarding' actions.

### History

For Mill, history is a record of constant change in humanity and society. This record is, for the most part, positive. 'He believes in progress in the usual sense. That is, he believes that the general tendency of history, with minor exceptions, is toward what he calls a better and happier state.' (Gildin 1964: 295–6) This explains Annas's suspicion that Mill 'is dominated by a linear picture of Progress'. (1977: 187)

Change occurs in fairly discrete stages which represent distinct types of improvement. 'Mill sees a continuous line of development from slavery to self-government, with each stage prepared by the learning of a specific lesson, that is, by the acquiring of a new character trait on the part of the population as a whole.' (Magid 1963: 687) One of the tasks of those who study society is to understand the laws 'which regulate the succession between one state of society and another ... to find the laws according to which any state of society produces the state which succeeds it and takes its place.' (SOL 8: 912) Such a project, Mill believes, 'opens the great and vexed question of the progressiveness of man and society; an idea involved in every just conception of social phenomena as the subject of a science.' (SOL 8: 912)

That society follows a trajectory and history is not a random meander does not mean that this development is smooth. Mill does not treat forward movement as necessary, even if he tends to expect it. Mill's optimism is guarded. He believes that although there is a tendency toward improvement there is also a tendency toward stagnation, if not regression. In Mill's view, 'there is an incessant and ever-flowing current of human affairs towards the worse, consisting of all the follies, all the vices, all the negligences, indolences, and supineness of mankind...'. (CRG 19: 388) This current 'is only controlled, and kept from sweeping all before it, by the exertions which some persons constantly, and others by fits, put forth in the direction of good and worthy objects'. (CRG 19: 388) Historical progress continues only through the efforts of those who pursue the good life. Mill is not, as Cranston alleges, 'taken in by the myth of inevitable progress...'. (1958: 22)

Nor does Mill consider all change to be improvement. In his view 'the laws of human nature might determine, and even necessitate, a certain series of changes in man and society, which might not in every case, or which might not on the whole, be improvements' (SOL 8: 913), though he remained committed to the view 'that the general tendency is, and will continue to be, saving occasional and temporary exceptions, one of improvement; a tendency towards a better and happier state'. (SOL 8: 914) This makes sense of Ryan's conclusion that Mill 'makes it quite clear that he believes that change is inevitable but that improvement is not. In other words, his view of history was progressive in the sense of presupposing cumulative change, but not optimistic in the sense of supposing that change would always be for the better'. (Ryan 1974: 47)

## The Stationary State

One aspect of society that will not always improve is its economy. What economists of Mill's time called the stationary state was inevitable, but not lamentable. Mill believes that development will cease in the economic sphere, but not in the intellectual and cultural spheres – indeed, he suggests that the cessation of economic progression will allow for progression in these other spheres.

Mill assumes that economic development is finite. He accepts 'that the increase of wealth is not boundless: that at the end of what [political economists] term the progressive state lies the stationary state...'. (PPE 3: 752) For these political economists 'the impossibility of ultimately avoiding the stationary state ... must have been ... an unpleasing and discouraging prospect; for the tone and tendency of their speculations goes completely to identify all that is economically desirable with the progressive state...'. (PPE 3: 752) Mill, on the other hand, embraces the inevitability of the stationary state. For him, economic torpidity does not imply cultural or intellectual torpidity.

Mill acknowledges that economic development is a stimulus to the human intellect, but thinks it a base form of stimulation. A decline, or even cessation, of economic stimulation will allow other stimuli to operate. 'That the energies of mankind should be kept in employment by the struggle for riches ... until the better minds succeed in educating the others into better things,' Mill writes, 'is undoubtedly more desirable than that they should rust and stagnate. While the minds are coarse they require coarse stimuli....' (PPE 3: 754)

Once these coarse stimuli have done their work, they become impediments to, not sources of, social development. Freed from the oppression of economic necessity people will develop in ways not possible while burdened by that yoke. 'The best state for human nature is that in which, while no one is poor, no one desires to be richer, nor has any reason to fear being thrust back, by the efforts of others to push themselves forward.' (PPE 3: 754) In Mill's view, society was moving to the stage at which material needs will be satisfied and people will be 'left free to give themselves with undivided energies to political, moral and intellectual development, to the enjoyment of nature, and to the influences of solitude, "the cradle of thoughts and inspirations"'. (MacCunn 1964: 39) In short, Mill's 'stationary state looked comfortable, without bustle, and fit for the life of a philosopher'. (Zweig 1979: 11)

## Socialism

It is becoming clear that Mill is no unqualified supporter of capitalism. The stationary state to which he looks forward bears little resemblance to market-regulated possessive individualism. Indeed, Mill advocates a form of socialism as the desirable successor to capitalism. He is not dismissive of capitalism, since he treats historical development as necessarily proceeding through definite stages, but concludes that it is not the end-state of human history.

Capitalism is necessary, but it is only one stage in social development. A system of private property is merely one of the alternatives available to humanity. For Mill,

The idea of property is ... variable like all other creations of the human mind; at any given time it is a brief expression denoting the rights over things conferred by law or custom of some given society at that time; but neither on this point nor on any other has the law and custom of a given time and place a claim to be stereotyped for ever. (COS 5: 753)

Replacing capitalism with another form of economic organisation would merely reflect the adoption of new laws and customs. Such a change may represent progress in that it will more adequately reflect the stage that humanity and society has reached in the historical process. Capitalism is part, not the end, of human history. 'To the ... advocate of a private property economy ... Mill could respond that communism is at least as feasible as existing private property economies, and thus, at least as capable of improvement.' (Panichas 1983: 258)

That systems of exchange are pervasive is no ground for claims of their inviolability. Mill accepts that the processes of material production are largely invariable. Methods for the distribution, on the other hand, can be altered. Thus, in Mill's view, 'the conditions and laws of Production would be the same as they are, if the arrangements of society did not depend on Exchange, or did not admit of it'. However, 'exchange is not the fundamental law of the distribution of the produce, no more than roads and carriages are the essential laws of motion, but merely a part of the machinery for effecting it.' (PPE 3: 455)

Systems of distribution will change according to the stage of development that society and humanity have attained.

Two issues are central to Mill's assessment of an economic system. The first is the fairness of the distributions generated within that system. The second is the extent to which people have an incentive to labour. Mill perceives a real choice between capitalism and socialism, especially given defects in capitalism on the former count.

> If the institution of private property necessarily carried with it as a consequence, that the produce of labour should be apportioned as we now see it, almost in an inverse ratio to the labour – the largest portions to those who have never worked at all, the next largest to those whose work is almost nominal, and so on in a descending scale ... if this or Communism were the alternative, all the difficulties, great or small, of Communism would be as dust in the balance. (PPE 2: 207)

Mill believes capitalism to be open to improvement without recourse to dramatic change, but his position is not fixedly in favour of capitalism on the issue of fairness.

Mill also doubts the incentive to labour provided under capitalism: 'I am not undervaluing the strength of the incitement to labour when the whole or a large share of the benefit of extra exertion belongs to the labourer. But under the present system of industry this incitement, in the great majority of cases, does not exist.' (PPE 2: 204) From this Panichas concludes:

> The incentive argument assumes that persons work better, more productively, when workers directly receive and fully control the benefits or fruits of their own labour. But, as a matter of fact, in a modern private property economy (England) where wages are the predominant form of remuneration for labour, it is not the case that persons fully control and directly receive the benefits of their own work. Thus, insofar as feasibility is concerned, the incentive argument works at least as well (if not better) against a modern society with a private property economy as it does against communism. (1983: 257)

The system Mill accepts as most likely to lead to both a more just system of distribution and an increase in the level of incentive to labour is 'worker democracy'. 'The form of association ... which if mankind continue to improve, must be expected in the end to predominate,' he wrote, 'is ... the association of the labourers themselves on terms of equality, collectively owning the capital with which they carry on their operations, and working under managers elected and removable by themselves.' (PPE 3: 775) While Mill qualifies such comments, nonetheless, he tends to the view that ownership of the means of production will and should pass out of the hands of individuals and into those of collectives.

The equality of control of collectivised industries allows Mill to claim that this system is more just than capitalism. A key feature of the collective system is a sense of labour as a public service. In Mill's view, people are 'capable of a far greater amount of public spirit than the present age is accustomed to suppose possible, History bears witness to the success with which large bodies of human beings may be trained to feel the public interest their own. And no soil could be more favourable to the growth of such a feeling, than a Communist association....' (PPE 2: 205) If public-spiritedness failed, other mechanisms might fill the gap; as 'independently of the public motive, every member of the association would be amenable to the most universal, and one of the strongest, of personal motives, that of public opinion'. (PPE 2: 205)

Mill's collectivism does not ignore or discount the incentives provided by competition. He criticises many socialist schemes for failing to recognise the value of competition. Mill finds himself in agreement 'with the Socialist writers in their conception of the forms which industrial operations tend to assume in the advance of improvement...'. He also shares 'their opinion that the time is ripe for commencing this transformation, and that it should by all just and effectual means be aided and encouraged'. However, he repudiates completely 'the most conspicuous and vehement part of their teaching, their declamations against competition'. (PPE 3: 794)

Mill also rejects any form of collectivism that involves the centralisation of control over the economy. Ownership and control of the productive resources of a community should be taken out of the hands of individuals, he believes, but they should not be vested in the hands of a single authority.

> The very idea of conducting the whole industry of a country by direction from a single centre is so obviously chimerical, that nobody ventures to propose any mode in which it should be done; and it can hardly be doubted that if the revolutionary socialists attained their immediate object, and actually had the whole property of the country at their disposal, they would find no other practicable mode of exercising their power over it than that of dividing it into portions, each made over to the administration of a small Socialist community. (COS 5: 748)

Mill believes socialism to be desirable when the appropriate social conditions have developed, but rejects state socialism. 'He always distinguishes two sorts of socialism, "state socialism" and "cooperative socialism", and it is only the latter ... which he looks upon at all sympathetically.' (Collini 1977: 244)

Mill proposes a syndicalist form of socialism in which the productive resources of society are divided among small groups. He believes that efficiency and the proper administration of those resources would result from this form of organisation. In support of this, he argues that 'a mixed agricultural and manufacturing association of from two thousand to four thousand inhabitants under any tolerable circumstances of soil and climate would be easier to manage than many a joint stock company'. (COS 5: 738-9)

Syndicalism is superior because it allows for communal ownership, and the incentives that derive from it, while also providing for competition. Mill characterises this competition as 'a friendly rivalry in the pursuit of a good common to all' (PPE 3: 792). He insists 'that competition should not be done away with: it should continue to operate both between and within the co-operative units....' (Platteau 1985: 21) A further advantage of syndicalism is that people will be required to take responsibility and exercise choice with respect to the management of communal affairs. 'There is one final, and far from insignificant, structural feature of market cooperation that generates the spreading of public spirit and perhaps generous sentiments. This is the wide distribution of the managerial prerogative.' (Arneson 1981: 217)

## The Proper Role of Government

Mill's sense of historical progress means that he is reluctant to predetermine the proper functions of government. He is suspicious of government intervention, as he fears the loss of opportunities for the expression of individuality. On the other hand, he accepts that government must also positively intervene to promote well-being and development amongst citizens. 'Mill's stress on the malleability of character under the influence of education and social institutions ... led him away from ... evaluating social policies and institutions solely from the standpoint of their effectiveness in satisfying existing wants, and brought him to think about them also from the standpoint of their tendency to generate improved wants and forms of character.' (McPherson 1982: 252)

The basic test that Mill advocates in determining the proper role of government was that of convenience.

> There is a multitude of cases in which governments, with general approbation, assume powers and execute functions for which no reason can be assigned except the simple one, that they conduce to a general convenience. We may take as an example, the function ... of coining money.... Prescribing a set of standard weights and measures is another instance. Paving, lighting and cleansing the streets and thoroughfares, is another.... Making or improving harbours, building lighthouses, making surveys in order to have accurate maps and charts, raising dykes to keep the sea out, and embankments to keep rivers in, are cases in point. (PPE 3: 803)

The provision of basic social infrastructure is not the only role that Mill advocates, however.

Like all liberals, Mill believes government must play a role in controlling anti-social behaviour. During a consideration of the various 'ends or uses of government', Mill argues that 'the first and most fundamental of all ... is to enable mankind to live in society without oppressing and injuring one another'. (RR 18: 18) This is necessary to ensure that those who work feel assured that the benefits that they accrue from their labour will be protected. 'Insecurity of person and property', he wrote, 'is as much as to say, uncertainty of the connexion between all human exertions or sacrifice, and the attainment of the ends for the sake of which they are undergone.' (PPE 3: 880)

In Mill's view, government must also exercise surveillance and control over the use of natural resources. For him, natural resources 'are the inheritance of the human race, and there must be regulations for the common enjoyment of it. What rights, and under what conditions, a person shall be allowed to exercise over any portion of this common inheritance, cannot be left undecided. No function of government is less optional than the regulation of these things....' (PPE 3: 801)

Government must also take care of those incapable of either understanding or defending their own interests. Paul argues that in Mill's view 'the individual was not the best judge of his own interests in all cases'. As a result, she continues, Mill 'is ... willing to supplant the judgments of individuals in the marketplace when he feels that those judgments are misdirected'. (1978: 146)

A clear justification for protection is where a person is 'an infant, or a lunatic, or fallen into imbecility. The law surely must look after the interests of such persons.' (PPE 3: 803) Ryan argues that Mill also accepts government protection for working people. According to Ryan, Mill's consideration of the economic role of government 'is based on a clear understanding of the way the costs of social and technological change fell on an unprotected working population. It is, for instance, a proper task of government to see that the impact of innovation does not fall too heavily on a particular section of society.' (1974: 170)

Mill extends the category of those whose interests must be protected to include those in love and planning to marry, on the basis that this is another category of people capable of acting improvidently. 'There are other cases in which the prudence and forethought, which perhaps might be exercised by the people themselves, are exercised by the state for their benefit; marriage not being permitted until the contracting parties can show that they have the prospect of comfortable support.' (PPE 2: 158) In Mill's view, those 'laws which ... forbid marriage unless the parties can show that they have the means of supporting a family, do not exceed the legitimate powers of the state....' (OL 18: 304)

A further set of services that should be provided by government includes those services in which no individual has a specific interest or opportunity for recompense and yet from which all derive some benefit. 'Take for instance a voyage of geographical or scientific exploration. The information sought would be of great public value, yet no individual would derive any benefit from it which would repay the expense of fitting out the expedition....' (PPE 3: 968)

Another function for which government is responsible is to provide 'by means of endowments or salaries, for the maintenance of what has been called a learned class'. (PPE 3: 968) Mill recognises that the benefits of maintaining this class are neither direct nor tangible. He believes, however, that benefits stem from having such activities pursued, rather than from the direct satisfaction of some need on the part of the populace.

Above all else it is the responsibility of government to provide positive stimuli to its citizens. 'A government cannot have too much of the kind of activity which does not impede, but aids and stimulates, individual exertion and development.' (OL 18: 310) A crucial test of good government, in Mill's view, is the extent to which it provided for 'the improvement of the people themselves.' (CRG 19: 403) Thus, 'the most important point of excellence which any government can possess is to promote the virtue and intelligence of the people themselves'. (CRG 19: 390) A government should do what is necessary to support an individual's pursuit of self-improvement. 'As the end of life is self-development, the prime duty of government for him is to assist self-development.' (Anschutz 1963: 46)[11]

Improvement cannot result from coercion. 'The state should be sparing of direct command and interdiction; but by aid, encouragement and advice, the state ought to see to the education of its citizens.' (Ryan 1974: 57) Mill distinguishes 'authoritative interference of government' from a non-authoritative form in which 'a government, instead of issuing a command and enforcing it by penalties, adopts the course so seldom resorted to by governments, and of which such important use might be made, that of giving advice, and promulgating information...'. (PPE 3: 937)

Good government also encourages people to involve themselves in public services. 'The government which encourages active participation in its operations by all its citizens is better ... than one which is more orderly but encourages its citizens to be passively obedient to the commands of a ruling group, whatever the morality and justice of those commands.' (Magid 1963: 685) Mill notes 'the practical discipline which the character obtains, from the occasional demand made upon the citizens to exercise, for a time and in their turn, some social function'. (CRG 19: 411) The greater the individual's involvement in these functions the greater their development. 'If circumstances allow the amount of public duty assigned to him to be considerable, it makes him an educated man.' (CRG 19: 411)

## Education

Mill's views on education are closely tied to his views on the proper role of government. For him, education is one of the chief means through which government pursues the development of individuals. 'Government is a purposeful enterprise. Its objective, reduced to simplest terms, is to educate its citizens.' (Hacker 1961: 574)

That individuals receive a proper education is crucial, for a lack of proper education will impede social progress. 'Convinced that a great gulf separated men as they are from men as they might become ... it was to education that Mill turned to bridge this gulf....' (MacCunn 1964: 67) Mill 'saw education (rightly conceived, of course) as a creative force, an essential means to truth, to intellectual rigour, to strength of character, to the release of individual potential.' (Garforth 1979: 23) As Davis notes, Mill's 'strong advocacy of education [is] to promote a society of autonomously acting individuals...'. (1985: 353) Education was the primary means through which society would develop intellectually and culturally. Selfishness and its social costs could only be addressed properly through education. In Mill's view, the 'inferior efficacy of public and social feelings is not inevitable – [it] is the result of imperfect education'. (COS 5: 740)

Mill believes that all children must be educated. If necessary, this may require both placing pressure upon parents to send their children to school and making those schools available to all. 'It is therefore an allowable exercise of the powers of government, to impose on parents the legal obligation of giving elementary instruction to children. This, however, cannot be fairly done, without taking measures to insure that such instruction shall be always accessible to them, either gratuitously or at a trifling expense.' (PPE 3: 948–9)

That the main purpose of education is to promote individuality means that schools provided by government should not be the only ones available. Mill argues that 'the government must claim no monopoly for its education ... must exert neither authority nor influence to induce the people to resort to its teachers in preference to others, and must confer no peculiar advantages to those who have been instructed by them'. (PPE 3: 950) Mill is suspicious of an education system controlled by the ruling body within a society. He believes that 'a general state education is a mere contrivance for moulding people to be exactly like one another...'. As a result 'an education controlled by the State should only exist ... as one among many competing experiments, carried on for the purpose of example and stimulus, to keep the others up to a certain standard of excellence'. (OL 18: 302)

## Self-Regarding Actions

While Mill rejects *laissez-faire* approaches to government, he is careful to delineate as inviolable a certain type of individual actions. This type of actions is usually known as 'self-regarding'. The general rule Mill lays down is: 'The only part of the conduct of any one, for which he is amenable to society, is that which concerns others. In the part which merely concerns himself, his independence is, of right, absolute.' (OL 18: 224 )

Mill's concern with the protection of a sphere of independent individual action from government and society is a result of his desire to preserve and promote individuality. Protection is designed to enhance an individual's ability to act and choose freely. For Mill, 'in each person's own concerns, his individual spontaneity is entitled to free exercise'. (OL 18: 276) As Rees suggests, 'individuality and variety of character' can be achieved in a society 'if a principle were observed whereby every person was accorded an area of liberty in thought and action'. (Rees 1969: 358)

One justification for this protection is that the individual concerned is the only one directly affected by self-regarding actions. According to Mill, 'the interest which any other person, except in cases of strong personal attachment, can have in it, is trifling ... the interest which society has in him individually (except as to his conduct to others) is fractional...'. (OL 18: 276) He also suggests that 'the modern conviction ... is, that the things in which the individual is the person directly interested, never go right but as they are left to his own discretion; and that any regulation of them by authority, except to protect the rights of others, is sure to be mischievous'. (SOW 21: 273)

The limit point of individual freedom is a threat of harm to others. One of Mill's most famous dicta is that 'the sole end for which mankind are warranted, individually or collectively, in interfering with the liberty of action of any of their number, is self-protection.... the only purpose for which power can be rightfully exercised over any member of a civilized community, against his will, is to prevent harm to others'. (OL 18: 223)

This can only be understood in light of Mill's desire to have the notion of 'harm' construed narrowly. Mill qualifies his category of harm that justified interference in the individual's behaviour by introducing a further notion of illegitimacy in the act that causes harm. 'Acts, of whatever kind,' he writes, 'which, *without justifiable cause*, do harm to others, may be, and in the most important cases absolutely require to be, controlled....' (OL 18: 260 emphasis added). Mill denies that 'because damage, or probability of damage, to the interests of others, can alone justify the interference of society, ... therefore it always does justify such interference.' (OL 18: 292) An example of an act which may be perceived to cause harm, but which is not to be interfered with is where 'an individual, in pursuing a legitimate object, necessarily and therefore legitimately causes pain or loss to others, or intercepts a good which they had reasonable hope of obtaining'. (OL 18: 292)[12]

Mill is often misunderstood on this point. Many interpreters read into Mill's work a wide definition of harm. Ten offers an important correction to this reading: 'According to traditional interpretation, self-regarding conduct does not affect others at all except with their consent. But this interpretation is mistaken for Mill readily conceded that self-regarding conduct has certain adverse effects on others. His argument is that a principled defence of individual liberty will lead us to discount these effects on others.' (Ten 1980: 6) A healthy society, in Mill's view, is one in which its members construe harm narrowly and, as a result, maximise individual liberty.

**The Good Society**

Mill's good society is characterised by a complex interaction between individual sovereignty, social cooperation and government responsibility. It comes at the end of a process of historical movement that provided the necessary material and intellectual resources, especially access to education. The stationary state marked the end of social progress via the stimulation of material needs and the beginning of progress through the stimulation of intellect and culture. The production of material goods continues, but it is based upon collective and cooperative control of the means of production (but not centralised or uncompetitive control). This allows for fairness of distribution, equality of control and incentive to labour.

Schwartz identifies cooperative productive associations as central to Mill's good society.

> Co-operation fitted in perfectly with his whole doctrine of how to achieve the good society. From the moral point of view ... it strengthened the qualities of self-reliance and foresight of the individuals involved, the running of it taught them the virtues of self-government, and of freely accepted discipline and collaboration, together with the habit of continued and regular work. From the point of view of justice, each received, better than in any other system, the due reward for his abilities and exertions. From the economic angle, the advantages of large-scale enterprises were combined with the incentives of diffused poverty. From the social and political viewpoint, co-operation broke down the barriers between capitalists and workers, increased the intelligent participation of all in communal affairs, and transformed the citizenry so deeply that the ideals of democracy could be effectually realized.... (1972: 231)

Or as Mill himself puts it, 'we may, through the cooperative principle, see our way to a change in society, which would combine the freedom and independence of the individual, with the moral, intellectual, and economical advantages of aggregate production'. (PPE 3: 793)

Mill's good society directly reflects his views on human nature and the character of the good life.

> Education and opinion, which have so vast a power over human character, should so use that power as to establish in the mind of every individual an indissoluble association between his own happiness and the good of the whole ... so that not only may he be unable to conceive the possibility of happiness to himself, consistently with conduct opposed to the general good, but also that a direct impulse to promote the general good may be in every individual one of the habitual motives of action, and the sentiments connected therewith may fill a large and prominent place in every human being's sentient existence. (U 10: 218)

The malleability of human nature meant that those attitudes essential to the good life can be developed within the framework of the good society. This does not mean an attempt to generate uniformity of behaviour, but it does require the encouragement of an unselfish and cooperative approach toward social existence and self-development.

Mill 'sketches an inspiring picture of a society vigorous in thought, eager in discussion, strenuous in action, rich in varied modes of life, fertile even to eccentricity in "experiments in living", and peopled by citizens in whose energetic characters is reflected the many-coloured diversity of their many-coloured environment.' (MacCunn 1964: 72) His 'ideal or good society was to be characterised by equality, freedom of choice, diversity, tolerance, and individuality; by the absence of the negative effects of custom and social class; and by the presence of self-assertion and independence of its citizens'. (Hughes 1979: 524)


## CONCLUSION

Like all of the great political theorists, Mill's works offer insights which shed light on the fundamental questions of human existence and politics. His modifications to associationism combined with his views on free will and women deepen our understanding of human nature. His views on individuality, pleasure and traditions or customs are the basis upon which we can consider and develop our own sense of the character of the good life. Mill's views on history, the stationary state, socialism, the proper role for government, education and self-regarding actions help in developing an understanding of the possibilities of the good society.

While we may not be able to contribute directly to the tradition of political theory, to read and facilitate an understanding of Mill's works is an important contribution we can make to the preservation and continuation of that tradition. To keep these insights alive is to make no small contribution to social progress. While we may see no further than the giants upon whose shoulders we stand, we should not desist from standing on those shoulders. Great thinkers like Mill are rare. They are also precious. To preserve and make their insights available is no small service to humanity in its ongoing attempt to resolve the fundamental issues which shape individual lives and social organisation.

# 3 Reading Mill within an Historicist Framework

### Introducing Historicist Reading

The practice of traditionalist readings of the works of great political theorists has led to another way of reading Mill's works. The rejection of the traditionalist belief that certain human beings are capable of somehow 'rising above' their situation and reflecting on the transcendental problems of human existence resulted in a shift to understanding Mill in terms of a set of determinants on his thoughts and theories. In 1977 Collini argued that 'the historians employed in the Mill industry are now almost as numerous as its traditional operatives, the philosophers, and the task of situating Mill in the intellectual context of his time has begun'. (1977: 237) Once human being is understood to be situated, reading the works of political theorists becomes a process of situating those theorists within some 'historical' context that makes sense of what they were doing in writing and what they were saying in writing.

The following reading is, I hope, a simple and clear exemplification of historicist readings of Mill's works. It follows, clarifies and builds on the variety of historicist readings of Mill's works to be found in the secondary literature of an historicist form. This literature is driven by an historicist ontology and epistemology, that, as Collini suggested, is as common a reading of Mill as that driven by a traditionalist ontology and epistemology. This reading is focused on the same concepts that were dealt with in the traditionalist reading of Mill presented in Chapter 2.

## INTRODUCTION

Political theories are produced by people. People are not simple entities. They are a product of a complex interaction of the personal, the intellectual, and the social (or socio-political). At different points, and sometimes at the same point, an analysis of his works will reveal Mill the individual, Mill the intellectual and Mill the social commentator.

Each of these frameworks reveals important dimensions and the real meaning of Mill's political theory. Each allows an interpreter to get closer to an understanding of the historical figure John Stuart Mill. Each way of framing John Stuart Mill uses a particular set of contextual determinants. One historicist framework places those factors that were crucial to Mill's psychological development at the foreground of reading. From this perspective, a political theory is a form of biography, though an attenuated one.[13] Another framework gives a privileged position to those intellectual influences to which Mill was exposed. From this perspective, Mill's works are responses to works with which he was in 'contact' prior to or during writing. The third historicist framework places factors that refer to Mill's social conditions at the centre of reading. When understood through this set, Mill's political theory is a response to the social environment within which he wrote.

Though these frameworks may be combined, each will be applied separately to the interpretation of different elements of Mill's political theory. First, because this avoids the problems that the use of combined sets of contextual determinants seems to introduce to a reading; second, because most analyses of Mill's works use one or other of the sets of determinants in a reading of Mill's works.

This chapter is divided into three sections. Psychological determinants will be used first in a reading of Mill's views on association, necessity, individuality and women. Intellectual determinants will then be used in a reading of Mill's writings on pleasure, history and the stationary state. The final historicist reading of Mill's works will use aspects of his social conditions in a reading of his views on the proper role of government, self-regarding actions, socialism, traditions and customs and education.

## A PSYCHOLOGICAL-HISTORICIST READING

### Introduction

Many commentators on Mill's work have recognised that an understanding of the dynamics of his psyche is crucial to a proper appreciation of his political theory. Cranston recognised this when he wrote that Mill's 'personality holds more than the usual number of keys to the understanding of his work'. (1958: 5) Or, as Sawyier put it, 'Mill made conscious and/or unconscious use of his feelings about himself in working out the fundamental features of his moral philosophy.' (1985: 169) Mazlish has argued that most analyses of Mill's works shared the theme of 'the crucial role of his own personal development, his education, as both mirroring and inspiring the intellectual doctrines and positions that he espoused'. (Mazlish 1975: 149)

Two features of Mill's psychological development determined the shape of his political theory. The first was the nervous breakdown that resulted from the educational programme to which his father subjected him; the second, Mill's relationships with the key figures of his emotional development (his father, mother and Harriet Taylor). An appreciation of the role of the former in Mill's intellectual development is necessary for an understanding of his theories with respect to associationism, necessity and individuality. The second determined and explains his views on women.

## Psychological Crisis and Understanding Mill on Associationism, Necessity and Individuality

### *The Crisis*

Few interpreters of Mill's works have failed to refer to Mill's education. The amount and nature of the material to which the young John Stuart Mill was exposed made his a singular education. Mill himself referred to it as 'an education which was unusual and remarkable, and which, whatever else it may have done, has proved how much more than is commonly supposed may be taught, and well taught, in those early years...'. (A 1: 5)

James Mill's commitment to associationism justified the fervour with which he pursued his son's intellectual development. As an associationist, James Mill sought to control most aspects of the early stages of his son's development. This meant that John Stuart Mill was continually exposed to influences that were intended to develop his intellect and rationality and divert him from the pursuit of idle fancies. 'It was necessary on the intellectual side to prevent a child from cluttering its youthful brain with idle emotions, dreams or recreations.... anything which did not assist the main course of character and reason would only cloud the vision and dissipate clarity of mind.' (Packe 1954: 16)

In short, James Mill controlled almost every aspect of his son's intellectual development. James Mill 'dominated every moment of ... John's life. He supervised not only the boy's education (with fierce dedication and attention but also with chastisement and shaming), and arranged the child's life so that he (James) was sole companion in the only "play" the boy had – long educative walks.' (Sawyier 1985: 178)

James Mill even prevented John 'from having ordinary sibling contact, for he insisted that John be tutor (and responsible for the errors of) for his younger brothers and sisters.' (Sawyier 1985: 178)

Glassman has cautioned against the view that Mill was not loved, while emphasising the cost of that love. 'The *Autobiography* makes us understand that Mill was a deeply loved child. The work continually reminds us that few fathers have ever given more to a child than James Mill gave to John. We are also led to recognize, however, that few fathers ever have damaged a son so gravely and, it must be said, deliberately.' (Glassman 1985: 3)

Mill's own recollections of this time in his life suggest the sort of ambivalence to which Glassman alluded:

> The deficiencies in my education were principally in the things which boys learn from being turned out to shift for themselves, and from being brought together in large numbers.... It was not that play, or time for it, was refused me. Though no holidays were allowed, lest the habit of work should be broken, and a taste for idleness acquired, I had ample leisure in every day to amuse myself; but as I had no boy companions, and the animal needs of physical activity were satisfied by walking, my amusements, which were mostly solitary, were in general of a quiet, if not a bookish turn, and gave little stimulus to any other kind even of mental activity than that which was already called forth by my studies. (A 1: 39)

James's control continued well into John's adolescence and the effects of his upbringing would never dissipate completely.

His extensive and deliberate interference in his son's development gave James the impression of being Mill's creator. When Mill was 14 and leaving for France, his father took him aside.

> [He] told me that I should find ... that I had been taught many things which youths of my age did not commonly know; and that many persons would be disposed to talk to me of this, and to compliment me upon it. What other things he said on this topic I remember very imperfectly; but he wound up by saying, that whatever I knew more than others, could not be ascribed to any merit in me, but to the very unusual advantage which had fallen to my lot, of having a father who was able to teach me, and willing to give the necessary trouble and time; that it was no matter of praise to me, if I knew more than those who had not had a similar advantage, but the deepest disgrace if I did not. (A 1: 37)

Mill's clear recollection of this part of the conversation indicates the significance of his father's message for his psychological development. Mill wrote that he could recall 'the very place in Hyde Park' (A 1: 37) where the conversation took place. This suggests that his father's message was driven deep into his psyche.

The stresses to which Mill had been subjected resulted in a nervous breakdown when he was 21. This breakdown was to change not only Mill the individual but also Mill the theorist. Mazlish wrote that 'his mental crisis ... resulted in a kind of "new birth", of John Stuart Mill the person and of liberalism the doctrine'. (1975: 4) Mill's crisis brought him to question everything he had been trained to believe and desire.

> It was in the autumn of 1826 I was in a dull state of nerves, such as everybody is occasionally liable to; unsusceptible to enjoyment or pleasurable excitement; one of those moods when what is pleasure at other times, becomes insipid or indifferent.... In this frame it occurred to me to put the question directly to myself, 'suppose that all your objects in life were realized, that all the changes in institutions and opinions which you are looking forward to could be completely effected at this very instant: would this be a great joy and happiness to you?' And an irrepressible self-consciousness distinctly answered, 'No!' At this my heart sank within me: the whole foundation on which my life was constructed fell down. (A 1: 137-9)

Two aspects of Mill's 'crisis' are important. The first is his understanding of its cause; the second, the means through which he was released from his melancholic state. Both shaped key aspects of his political theory.

Mill attributed his crisis directly to his education. He came to believe 'that the description so often given of a Benthamite, as a mere reasoning machine ... was during two or three years not altogether untrue of me.' (A 1: 111) Mill determined that the source of his distress was the analytic mode of thought he had been taught to apply: 'Analytic habits may ... strengthen the associations between causes and effects, means and ends,' he wrote, 'but tend altogether to weaken those which are, to speak familiarly, a mere matter of feeling.' (A 1: 143) In short, the intellectual-rational had not been augmented with the emotional-spiritual. 'My education, I thought, had failed to create these feelings in sufficient strength to resist the dissolving influence of analysis....' (A 1: 143)

The resolution of Mill's 'crisis' occurred when Mill

> was reading, accidentally, Marmontel's Memoirs, and came to the
> passage which relates his father's death, the distressed position of the
> family, and the sudden inspiration by which he, then a mere boy, felt
> and made them feel that he would be everything to them – would
> supply the place of all that they had lost. A vivid conception of the
> scene and its feelings came over me, and I was moved to tears. From
> this moment my burthen grew lighter. (A 1: 145)

This event is significant for an understanding not just of Mill's psychological development but also the development of his political theory.
'The psychological implications of the Marmontel episode ... are
obvious enough, and, in view of the momentousness of the crisis, can
hardly be minimised. But more important in the present context are its
philosophical and political implications.' (Himmelfarb 1974: 6)

The 'Marmontel episode' can be interpreted in different ways.
Mazlish adopted a Freudian-style approach:

> What had occurred emotionally in the Marmontel episode that
> allowed Mill to move forward intellectually? The evidence indicates
> that by experiencing the death of his father imaginatively and by
> displacement to Marmontel's father, John was able to 'work through'
> his ambivalent and hitherto unexpressed feelings of love and hate for
> his father. On one side, we may conjecture that he could face the
> possibility of his father's death as the loss of the loved object on
> whom he most depended, by means of an imagined period of mourn-
> ing and melancholy. On the other side, we can see that he came to
> terms with his feelings of rivalry toward his father by vicariously
> killing him and then replacing him. (1975: 211)

In Mazlish's view, the source of the 'crisis' was an unresolved Oedipal
conflict and the termination of the 'crisis' indicated Mill's resolution of
that conflict.

This view is supported by the fact that Mill could not tell his father
about the effects of the education to which he had subjected him. Mill
had to suppress any desire to criticise any aspect of his education in
front of his father. 'My education, which was wholly his work, had
been conducted without any regard of the possibility of its ending in
this result: and I saw no use in giving him the pain of thinking that his
plan had failed....' (A 1:139)

Mazlish himself recognised that another understanding of the source
and resolution of Mill's crisis is available. 'Contemporary psychoanalysts

would tend to stress the reality factors and ego involvement rather more than in the classical libidinal picture we have just offered. The emphasis would be on depression stemming from the ego's awareness of its help-lessness, or at least difficulty, in achieving independence and an identity of its own.' (Mazlish 1975: 215)

An understanding of Mill's emotional development is the only way to develop a complete understanding of his views on associationism, necessity and individuality. It allows for an appreciation of Mill's modification to associationism, his re-interpretation of the doctrine of Necessity and the centrality and nature of individuality in his political theory. In each instance his views can be understood in light of the struggle in his political theory to resolve the crisis brought about by his education. 'Mill's life is an unceasing revolt against his father's outlook and ideals, the greater for being subterranean and unacknowledged.' (Berlin 1959: 11)

*Associationism*

Associationism was both one of the subjects of Mill's education and its philosophical justification. Mill believed that the application of associ-ationist principles had placed him in a vulnerable psychological position and ultimately led to his psychological breakdown.

> He had been taught Hartley's doctrine of the association of ideas and feelings; he well understood how, by planned education, a youth may be made to find his greatest happiness in working for the general good. And he also understood the fortuitous and unnatural character of the associations thus contrived. But he was in a peculiar position: he had himself undergone the educational process, and at the hands of a master. For a time it seemed that the education had succeeded: but suddenly, in 1826 the associations broke down. The idea of the general good was still there, but the pleasurable feeling was alto-gether absent. Why was this? Because in an emotional crisis of adolescence, it was all too easy for him to dissociate by intellectual analysis the feelings from their objects.
>
> (Britton 1953: 20)

Mill discovered in a direct and forceful manner that the system of asso-ciation was flawed, for it had led to his 'crisis'.

Two responses were available to Mill. He could reject the doctrine of association outright; or he could add to it in order to account for his experiences. The first is available because Mill had personally experienced the failure of the doctrine. Mill could not take this path. First, because it would require a repudiation of his own nature (since he had been formed under the principles of association); and second, because it would mean the rejection of his father.

Mill could not repudiate associationism because, Mazlish's 'contemporary psychoanalyst' might argue, this would require him to reject himself. Mill was a product of associationism and would not benefit from rejecting the doctrine. He was seeking to strengthen, not weaken, his psyche. Mill had to find a way to retain those aspects of the doctrine that were positive for his self-esteem while changing those aspects of the doctrine that he linked to his 'crisis'.

The second, more Freudian, reason Mill could not reject associationism was because this would have been counter to his Oedipal complex – strongly present in this case due to the all-pervasive influence of Mill's father. Part of that complex is a feeling of love toward the father. Mill was careful not to blame his father for his crisis and lack of contentment. He argued that James's rationalism was not due to the fact 'that he was himself cold-hearted or insensible; I believe it was rather from the contrary quality; he thought that feeling could take care of itself...'. (A 1: 113) At no stage did Mill reject his father as a role model. 'The result of James Mill's "intrusive" parentage is the lengthy story of John Stuart Mill's effort to free himself from his father, while at the same time retaining him inside himself.' (Mazlish 1975: 157)

Mill's solution, and resolution, was to modify associationism. His modification involved the introduction of natural tendencies of the mind that limited the efficacy of associationist training. The 'natural' attribute of feeling had to be incorporated into a theory that stressed the 'artificial' one of reason. Sociability and sympathy for others were examples of these natural feelings. They were also feelings that Mill could assert of his father. James's mistake had been to assume that everyone shared strength of feelings, 'that feeling could take care of itself'. John knew that it could not.

Mill required a new theory of associationism to find his way out of the 'crisis' he linked to his education; a theory that retained much that was central to the tenets of associationism, but introduced factors that could explain both the 'crisis' and its resolution. Mill's introduction of 'natural tendencies' of the mind allowed him to modify his father's influence without leading him to directly challenge his father. A direct challenge would have required a repudiation of himself as well as his father. A direct challenge could just as much weaken him as strengthen him.

*Necessity*

Associationism was not the only issue Mill had to address as a consequence of his 'crisis'. 'Necessity' was also important to his psyche and, as a result, took on enormous theoretical importance. Mill recognised his obsession with the 'problem' of necessity. He wrote that 'the doctrine of ... Philosophical Necessity weighed on my existence like an incubus. I felt as if I was scientifically proved to be the slave of antecedent circumstance; as if my character and that of all others had been formed for us by agencies beyond our control, and was wholly out of our own power.' (A 1: 175-7) Necessity weighed on Mill's mind and on his political theory.

Mill would be forever trapped in the straitjacket of the past, unless he could undermine the strict determinism of the Necessitarian's position. He 'desperately needed the assurance that real change and growth were possible! Deeply depressed by his circumstances in early manhood and bleak as to his future, one belief to which he had to cling was that there was some hope the future might be unlike the present.' (Sawyier 1985: 174) As a result, Mill 'wrestled with the philosophical issue of Liberty versus Necessity, struggling in highly abstract terms with the powerful emotions which were constricting his own most intimate life'. (Mazlish 1975: 227)

To lose the fight would be to relinquish hope for the future. 'The past had been structured by someone else ... and thus a belief in a real future entailed a belief that the die was not permanently cast, that John Stuart Mill could have some share in re-making himself.' (Sawyier 1985: 174) Mill's solution was to develop a theory in which human character was determined but which allowed individuals to introduce new determinants that changed their character.

> I pondered painfully on the subject, till gradually I saw light through it. I perceived the word Necessity, as a name for the doctrine of Cause and Effect applied to human action, carried with it a misleading association; and that this association was the operative force in the depressing and paralysing influence which I had experienced. I saw that though our character is formed by circumstances, our own desires can do much to shape those circumstances; and that what is really inspiriting and ennobling in the doctrine of free will, is the conviction that we have real power over the formation of our own character; that our will, by influencing some of our circumstances, can modify our future habits or capabilities of willing. (A 1: 177)

The 'pain' to which Mill referred is a clear indication of the psychological importance of the subject of Necessity.

Mill's response was to maintain something of the determinism of the Necessitarian position while affirming the capacity of individuals to bring about changes in their circumstances and character. Though he saw himself as a determined being, Mill needed to assert that this determination was not final. If it was, Mill would always be his father's creature and could never be his own. He could not assert himself, as a 'contemporary psychoanalyst' would argue he needed to do; or overcome and replace the father as a Freudian might believe was necessary for a resolution of his crisis.

## Individuality

Psychological factors are also central to an understanding of Mill's position on individuality. Mill's struggle to free himself from the dominating effects of his father provides a point from which his conception of and concern for individuality may be understood. Mazlish has relied on Mill's own testimony to support this approach to Mill's vigorous support for self-assertion:

> By engaging in a baffling and depressing Oedipal conflict with his father, he managed ... to fight his way clear of many of his former beliefs. As he wrote to Carlyle in 1832 'On the whole there are scarcely any left of the old narrow school of Utilitarians.' The old generation were gone. Of the new generation, John Stuart Mill says: 'None however of them all has become so unlike what he once was as I myself, who originally was the narrowest of them all, having been brought up more exclusively under the influence of a peculiar kind of impressions than any other person ever was. Fortunately however I was not crammed; my own thinking faculties were called into strong though partial play; and by their means I have been able to remake all my opinions.' (1975: 234)

Mill himself manifested the problem of a lack of individuality. This, in turn, stimulated his sense of the extent to which it was necessary for the healthy existence and development of human beings.

Sawyier was convinced that Mill's psychology provides an explanation for the strength of Mill's advocacy of individuality for all:

> We can surely understand that John Stuart Mill might be pushed by powerful feelings of self-hatred as well as by anger at his father for that gentleman's prolonged domination. I suggest that it was the combined force of these feelings which overwhelmed John Stuart

Mill and so, in effect, took over his pen as he began to write about the importance of individualism even for those who seemed least inclined towards it. (1985: 174)

Sawyier also argued that Mill's vehemence on this matter was a result of his struggle to assert his individuality. 'I am convinced ... that the actual source of Mill's passion for individualism came from some level of awareness within himself of how painful and difficult it really is to "individuate".' (1985: 177)[14] Individuality was central to Mill's political theory because it was central to his life. His personal project was to establish his individuality. The project he came to understand as central to human being was to establish individuality.

## Relationships with Key Individuals and Understanding Mill on Women

Mill's crisis is only one aspect of his psyche through which his political theory can be properly understood. His relationships with his parents and with Harriet Taylor also demand attention. Mill's views on women can only be understood in light of his relationships with the key individuals of his emotional life.

### Relationships with Key Individuals

James Mill's repeated interventions in his son's development have already been alluded to, but the nature of those interventions – or, at least, John Stuart Mill's perception of them – needs to be more directly addressed. One feature of James's character that his oldest son often commented upon was his temper. James Mill regularly engaged in what John considered to be surprising fits of temper. Mill repeatedly refers to his father's harsh treatment of him. Mill wrote that he 'was continually incurring his displeasure by my inability to solve difficult problems for which he did not see that I had not the necessary previous knowledge'. (A 1: 15) His father 'was often, and much beyond reason, provoked by my failures in cases where success could not have been expected...'. (A 1: 31) Mill wrote that 'both as a boy and as a youth I was incessantly smarting under his severe admonitions...'. (A 1: 39) Any attempt to question his father's views was unlikely to be met with respect. 'But my father was not one with whom calm and full explanations on fundamental points of doctrine could be expected, at least with one whom he might consider as, in some sort, a deserter from his standard.' (A 1: 189)

James Mill's baffling bursts of anger was not the only character trait with which John had to cope. James was also insensitive and subjected his son to vehement criticisms while depriving him of praise or support: 'From his own intercourse with me I could derive none but a very humble opinion of myself;' Mill wrote, 'and the standard of comparison he always held up to me, was not what other people did, but what a man could and ought to do.' (A 1: 35) As a result, Mill wrote that 'if I thought anything about myself, it was that I was rather backward in my studies, since I always found myself so, in comparison with what my father expected from me.' (A 1: 37)

James seemed to have manifested little concern or affection toward anyone. 'The element which was chiefly deficient in his moral relation to his children', Mill wrote, 'was that of tenderness' (A 1: 53), though Mill believed that his father 'resembled most Englishmen in being ashamed of the signs of feeling'. (A 1: 53)

One person for whom those feelings could have been reserved, but was not, was James's wife, Harriet. 'By the time John Stuart Mill was old enough to notice, his father ... was unable to conceal his contempt for his wife.' (Britton 1953: 10)[15] The contempt James felt and the psychological abuse that went with it were obvious to all. 'The disdain with which he now began to treat her shocked all his friends.' (Mazlish 1975: 153)

Mill's response to this, at least overtly, was to take his father's side. 'All too easily John Mill came to accept his father's estimate of his mother.' (Kamm 1977: 12) Mill's harsh and uncompromising attitude toward his mother was probably unfair and was definitely insensitive to his mother's situation. 'He is obviously seeing only through the eyes of his father.' (Mazlish 1975: 155) Mill considered his mother weak and even unloving. In an unpublished section of the Autobiography he wrote that 'a really warm hearted mother would ... have made my father a totally different being and ... would have made the children grow up loving and being loved'. Mill went on to suggest that Harriet Mill's children 'liked her because she was kind to them but to make herself loved, looked up to, or even obeyed, required qualities which she unfortunately did not possess'. (quoted in Hayek 1951: 31–2)

If Mill held his mother in low regard the woman he held in high regard was Harriet Taylor. According to McCloskey, Mill's 'strange relationship of adoration and subservience, even to an important degree concerning philosophical matters, to Mrs Harriet Taylor ... gave rise to important questions for Mill scholars, and has itself occasioned a rich literature'. (1969: 178)

Throughout his works, and especially the *Autobiography*, Mill referred to Harriet Taylor in terms for which the description 'glowing' would be an extreme understatement. As Davidson observed, Mill 'subsequently idealized [her] as the perfect embodiment of wisdom, intellect, and character'. (1957: 112) Mill called Harriet his 'precious guide, philosopher and friend' (as quoted in Hayek 1951: 165–6) and wrote that he did not judge Carlyle 'with any definiteness, until he was interpreted to me by one greatly the superior of us both – who was more of a poet than he, and more a thinker than I – whose own mind and nature included his, and infinitely more'. (A 1: 183) Harriet Taylor was even a match for his father: 'In the power of influencing by mere force of mind and character, the convictions and purposes of others, and in the strenuous exertion of the power to promote freedom and progress, he left, as far as my knowledge extends, no equal among men, and but one among women.' (A 1: 213)

Mill referred to his relationship with Harriet 'as the source of a great part of all that I have attempted to do, or hope to effect hereafter, for human improvement'. (A 1: 193) According to Mill, his 'only guide and oracle...'. (JSM–HTMC 3: 1029) was 'the inspirer, and in part the author, of all that is best in my writings'. (OL 18: 216) Mill's deferential attitude toward Harriet mirrored his attitude toward his father. He wrote in a letter to her: 'I want my angel to tell me what should be the next essay written. I have done all I can for the subject she last gave me.' (quoted in Hayek 1951: 205)

Harriet's position in Mill's life, as both intellectual and practical mentor, reveals an important dynamic within Mill's psychology. His domineering and aggressive father left Mill with an enduring need for external guidance. In an early draft of his *Autobiography*, Mill wrote: 'I was so much accustomed to be told what to do either in the form of direct command or of rebuke for not doing it that I acquired the habit of leaving my responsibility as a moral agent to rest on my father and my conscience never speaking to me except by his voice.' (quoted in Hayek 1951: 32) Mill transferred his dependence from his father to Harriet. 'For he was quite helpless without her, a fact which he attributed to the lack of practical training in his youth....' (Kamm 1977: 67) Mill's overriding need was to look up to someone. As a contemporary of Mill's wrote: 'It is safe to conclude that, if not Harriet or Helen [Harriet's daughter], someone else – man or woman – would have occupied the pedestal erected in Mill's soul during his impressionable childhood.' (quoted in Pappe 1960: 6)

*Women*

Mill's relationships with the key individuals in his life meant that he could readily identify with the injustice and debilitating effects of the dependent position of women. 'Together, his conscious and unconscious "mental" development pushed him into becoming the foremost champion of women's rights in the nineteenth century.' (Mazlish 1975: 330–1) Like him, women's characters had been formed by others and they were led to depend on others as a consequence. The vehement tones in which he defended women's rights to freedom was a response to his own dependence on others.

His resentment at his mother's failure to extract respect and obedience also resulted in a deep need on his part for women to have the strength of character necessary to stand up to the men in their lives. In part, Mill was expressing a wish about his own mother. He wished that she had been a stronger influence, both in protecting him from his father and bringing out greater affection in James. Thus 'his lack of sympathy toward his mother had something to do, paradoxically, with his strong view about sexual equality. His mother was visible, painful evidence of the "subjection" he found so distressing.' (Himmelfarb 1974: 192)

In part, Mill was expressing a wish about himself. According to Sawyier, the vitriol Mill directed toward those who did not pursue individuality, the disdain he expressed toward his mother and his excessive deference toward Harriet Taylor may be understood in terms of what she called Mill's 'self-rage'. 'Anger at a parent who has in some ways abused one is probably always accompanied by anger at oneself for having put up with it. This can be particularly applicable when the "putting up with it" involved not only passivity but also some feeling that one has unjustifiably abused other important persons because of this passivity.' (Sawyier 1985: 173–4) Mill would not be as dependent upon others as he was, if he had been able to resist his father's domination. If women were also spared such interference in their development they too would develop stronger characters and be more worthy of respect. Harriet Taylor was a rare example of a type of woman both possible and desirable.

The bitter memories of having had his character formed for him meant that he understood what this meant and was ready and willing to defend the rights of women. His own ability to achieve independence and self-determination meant that he was ready to support and encourage the same from women. His mother and Harriet Taylor reflect two sides of Mill's psyche. 'If Mrs Taylor represented for him the emancipated woman, his mother was the archetype of the enslaved woman. The titles of his essays – the "enfranchisement" and "subjection" of women – were, perhaps not by accident, the existential realities of his life.' (Himmelfarb 1974: 187)

## Conclusion

In his writings on associationism, necessity, individuality, and women Mill worked through his own psychological problems and dilemmas. His views on these subjects reveal a mind seeking release from those troubles he had carried with him for so long. These aspects of his political theory are central to and express his resolution of tensions caused by his upbringing. They can only be properly understood within this framework.

## AN INTELLECTUAL-HISTORICIST READING

### Introduction

Mill's psychology is not the only framework that allows for a proper and full understanding of his works. His absorption of complementary and divergent intellectual influences also provides a context for, and a motivation to write, political theory. A knowledge of the theories that were influential in Mill's life is vital for understanding his political theory. An appreciation of the works he read provides a key to unlocking the meaning of Mill's works.

A number of interpreters have noted the importance of Mill's intellectual influences for his political theory. According to Sabine, 'Mill's theory of political and ethical liberalism ... remained for the most part within the circle of subjects and of ideas native to his English tradition.' (1973: 647) For Anschutz, 'somewhere or other in his writings you can discern traces of every wind that blew in the early nineteenth century'. (1963: 5) While in Pappe's view 'Mill ... cannot be fully understood without realizing to what extent his mind was moulded by his immersion in Greek and medieval philosophy.... Britton does not mention Plato in his writings on Mill, and thus debars himself from access to an essential element in Mill's position.' (1960: 15–16)[16] According to Davis, Mill's was 'a life-long pursuit of "incessantly weaving ... anew" the fabric of his old ideas and education. It is this last quality that makes necessary an evolutionary approach to any study of Mill and his work. One must stay with him all the way or be found in dangerous waters of misconception and misrepresentation.' (1985: 345)

Mill saw himself very much as an intellectual intermediary. 'As the one man of his age who found himself in sympathy with conservatives and liberals, transcendentalists and empiricists Mill decided that he was ... duty bound to serve as a mediator between fiercely opposed schools of thought.' (Alexander 1965: 9) Mill wrote that he 'had always a humble opinion of my own powers as an original thinker, except in abstract science ... but thought myself much superior to most of my contemporaries in willingness and ability to learn from everybody...'. (A 1: 253-5) He commented with pride on his willingness 'to make room in my opinions for every new acquisition by adjusting the old and the new to one another'. (A 1: 259)

This resulted from Mill's sense that few systems of thought contained all that was to be discovered about the truth. For him, most of the 'rich veins of original and striking speculation have been opened up by systematic half-thinkers ... no whole truths are possible but by combining the points of view of all the fractional truths...'. (B 10: 94) In attempting to combine the 'half-truths' that he found in the intellectual influences to which he was exposed Mill produced a theory that drew from sometimes contradictory sources. His theory is marked by an openness and lack of dogmatism which allowed him to be influenced by theories with which he came into contact. Duncan wrote that Mill 'consciously chose "practical eclecticism" as a methodological principle, assuming that there was likely to be some truth in every doctrine...'. (Duncan 1973: 209)

Mill's political theory can be understood as being a response to his intellectual influences. In the following section, three aspects of his political theory will be analysed in these terms. These are: his conception of pleasure, his understanding of history, and his attitude to the stationary state. Mill's views on these issues can be understood in terms of an interaction between two philosophies with which he came in contact. His view on each of these issues was the product of the convergence of these intellectual influences.

## Bentham, Wordsworth and Understanding Mill on Pleasure

Two sources shaped Mill's views on pleasure. The first was the 'felicific calculus' of Jeremy Bentham. The second was the romantic poetry of William Wordsworth. In short, his position as to the nature of pleasure must be understood as an admixture of the positions of Bentham and Wordsworth. Mill's conception of pleasure started from a Benthamite orientation but was modified under Wordsworth's influence. Mill ceased to be a simple Benthamite. His contemporaries had to realise, Mill wrote, 'that Wordsworth, and all which that name implies, "belonged" to me'. (A 1: 163) Pleasures could not be treated as basically identical in Wordsworth's view. Some increased an individual's capacity to experience pleasure and even made possible other pleasurable sensations. Mill's approach to pleasure came to reflect both Bentham's orientation to the use of pleasure as a test for the efficacy of public policy, and Wordsworth's sense of the qualitative difference between various forms of pleasure and the edifying effect of some of these forms.

## Bentham

Bentham was a friend and mentor of James Mill and much of John's early training was derivative of Bentham's theories, both in form and content. 'If Bentham was the father of the Church [of Utilitarianism], James Mill was the first apostle and John Mill the chief novitiate. The oldest son and child prodigy, John had been reared for the express purpose of disseminating the true faith.' (Himmelfarb 1974: 4) Thus, according to Anschutz, 'it is of the first importance in trying to understand him that we should understand Bentham and James Mill, since it was within the framework provided by them that he tried to organize the new truths that he discovered for himself'. (Anschutz 1963: 6) Mill wrote that 'the Benthamic standard of "the greatest happiness" was that which I had always been taught to apply'. (A 1: 67) An understanding of his views on pleasure must begin with Benthamite utilitarianism.

The objective of Bentham's theory of utility explains much about his views on pleasure. Bentham sought to develop a calculus of felicity that could be used to assess public policies. Calculations require quantities. The quantities that were used for felicific calculus were pleasure and pain. According to Bentham, 'Nature has placed mankind under the governance of two sovereign masters, pain and pleasure.' (Bentham 1907: 2) Public policies could be assessed in terms of the extent of the quantities of pleasure and pain they produced.

The method, as Bentham outlined it, went as follows:

To take an exact account then of the general tendency of any act, by which the interests of the community are affected, proceed as follows. Begin with any one person of those whose interests seem most immediately affected by it: and take account:

1. Of the value of each distinguishable pleasure which appears to be produced by it in the first instance.
2. Of the value of each pain which appears to be produced in the first instance.
3. Of the value of each pleasure which appears to be produced by it after the first....
4. Of the value of each pain which appears to be produced by it after the first....
5. Sum up all the values of all the pleasures on the one side, and those of the pains on the other. The balance, if it be on the side of pleasure, will give the good tendency of the act upon the whole, with respect to the interests of that individual person; if on the side of pain, the bad tendency of it upon the whole.
6. Take an account of the number of the persons whose interests appear to be concerned; and repeat the above process with respect to each. Sum up the numbers extensive of the degrees of good tendency, which the act has, with respect to each individual, in regard to whom the tendency of it is good upon the whole: do this again with respect to each individual, in regard to whom the tendency of it is bad upon the whole. Take the balance; which, if on the side of pleasure, will give the general good tendency of the act, with respect to the total number or community of individuals concerned; if on the side of pain, the general evil tendency, with respect to the same community.

(Bentham 1907: 30–1)

The method that emerges was a mathematical determination of appropriate social policy, which Mill considered 'the most remarkable example afforded by our times of the geometrical method in politics'. (SOL 8: 889)

Mill was impressed by Bentham's system: 'He has ... it is not too much to say, for the first time introduced precision of thought into moral and political philosophy.' (B 10: 87) The means by which this precision was achieved was a quantitative conception of pleasure. Bentham dismissed the question of whether the experience of a particular pleasure was good for people. He was simply interested in the quantities of pleasure and pain that would result from actions and social policies.

*Wordsworth*
Wordsworth's approach to pleasure began with his Pantheism.

Wordsworth found the contemplation of nature to be a source of deep spiritual enlivenment. 'From nature doth emotion come', he wrote. (Wordsworth 1959: 456) According to Beer, Wordsworth's poetry suggested 'a direct influx of power from nature to the very roots of the primary being'. (Beer 1978: 89) Wordsworth's poetry is littered with references to the enlivening and uplifting effects of natural phenomena. The *Prelude* contains the following passage Wordsworth wrote: 'Ye motions of delight, that through the fields / Stir gently, breezes and soft airs that breathe / The breath of Paradise, and find your way / To the recesses of the soul...'. (1959: 430)

Wordsworth wanted to convey a sense of the uplifting character of certain experiences, especially those of nature: 'The passions and the heart flourish best where they are educated within their own element – that is, among the forms and energies of nature itself.' (Beer 1978: 85) Wordsworth differentiated between pleasures on the basis of their propensity to improve the person who experienced them. All pleasures were not the same; some were uplifting, others merely satisfying. Wordsworth wrote: 'The inferior Creatures, beast or bird, attun'd / My spirit to that gentleness of love, / Won from me those minute obei-sances / Of tenderness, which I may number now / With my first blessings...'. (*Prelude* 1959: 290) Wordsworth's appreciation of the tenderness he derived from these experiences made them more valuable to him.

Other experiences of nature initiated changes in Wordsworth that enhanced his appreciation of his world. Three days of roaming in the countryside induced him to write:

> That in life's every-day appearances
> I seem'd about this period to have sight
> Of a new world, a world, too, that was fit
> To be transmitted and made visible
> To other eyes, as having for its base
> That whence our dignity originates,
> That which both gives it being and maintains
> A balance, an ennobling interchange
> Of action from within and without,
> The excellence, pure spirit, and best power
> Both of the object seen and the eye that sees.
>                              (*Prelude* 1959: 476)

That a person could be changed in this way meant that such pleasures were more valuable than others that initiated no change.

An enhancement of the ability to find pleasure in nature was not the only benefit of these experiences. Another was an increase in the ability to derive pleasures from the imagination. This is illustrated by the following passage:

> 'Twas doubtless nothing more
> Than a black rock, which, wet with constant springs
> Glister'd far seen from out its lurking-place
> As soon as ever the declining sun
> Had smitten it. Beside our Cottage hearth,
> Sitting with open door, a hundred times
> Upon this lustre have I gaz'd, that seem'd
> To have some meaning which I could not find;
> And now it was a burnished shield, I fancied,
> Suspended over a Knight's Tomb, who lay
> Inglorious, buried in the dusk wood;
> An entrance now into some magic cave
> Or Palace for a Fairy of the rock;
>
> (*Prelude* 1959: 294)

Wordsworth delighted in the playful stimulation of imagination that natural objects brought.

This was in marked contrast to Bentham's appreciation of imagination; for although he accepted imagination as capable of affording pleasure, his approach was very different. For Bentham, 'the pleasures of the imagination are the pleasures which may be derived from the contemplation of any such pleasures as may happen to be suggested by the memory'. (Bentham 1907: 36) Not only was this a more prosaic representation of the pleasures of the imagination, it was also one that discounted the playful and creative aspects that Wordsworth treated as highly significant.

The stimulation of the imaginative powers was not the only uplifting effect provided by the contemplation of nature. Stimulation of the imagination gave rise to self-generated pleasure and a greater appreciation of others:

> And naked valleys, full of caverns, rocks,
> And audible seclusions, dashing lakes,
> Echoes and Waterfalls, and pointed crags
> That into music touch the passing wind
>
> Thus here imagination also found
> An element that pleased her, tried her strength,

> Among new objects simplified, arranged
> Impregnated my knowledge made it live,
> And the result was elevating thoughts
> Of human Nature....
> (Wordsworth 1959: 308)

Contemplating nature also stimulated virtue. 'And it was from Wordsworth that Mill derived his notion of the cultivation of feelings: Moral life can be affected by our enjoyment of nature.' (Britton 1953: 72)

Wordsworth differed from Bentham on this matter primarily in distinguishing pleasures in terms of their uplifting effect on character. This, and other, elements of Wordsworth's thought found a place alongside his Benthamism in Mill's political theory.[17] Mill turned to Wordsworth to augment Benthamite utilitarianism.

### Understanding Mill on Pleasure

Mill's partial defection from Benthamite utilitarianism was met with considerable hostility from those who remained wedded to its tenets. Mill 'was no longer the perfect Benthamite; his defence of Wordsworthian poetry and ideals at the London Debating Society, where hitherto he had been the shining star of Benthamism, estranged him from the ranks of the orthodox. John Morley recalled many years afterwards that Mill's "radical friends used to get angry with him for loving Wordsworth".' (Woods 1961: 49)

Wordsworth's influence encouraged Mill to temper the strict quantification of pleasure inherent in felicific calculus. He retained a commitment to the 'greatest happiness' principle. In developing the notion of qualitatively higher pleasures, however, he modified his understanding of human being and added a non-quantifiable element to felicific calculus.[18] In Wordsworth's poetry 'Mill had experienced, without fully realising it, ... the transcendent, the divine, for which Benthamite utilitarianism had no place at all. Throughout the rest of his life Mill tried to unite Wordsworth with Bentham, so to speak, "value" with "fact", "purpose" with "process", in a single unified philosophy.' (Bluhm 1965: 446-7)

Mill did not think of himself as having abandoned Benthamite utilitarianism and a general commitment to rationalism. He could not convince Roebuck of this, however:

> It was in vain I urged upon him that the imaginative emotion
> through which an idea when vividly conceived excited in us, is not

an illusion but a fact, as real as any of the other qualities of objects; and far from implying anything delusive in our mental apprehension of the object, is quite consistent with the most accurate knowledge and most perfect practical recognition of all its physical and intellectual laws and relations. The intensest feeling of the beauty of a cloud lighted by the setting sun, is no hindrance to my knowing that the cloud is vapour of water, subject to all the laws of vapours in suspension.... (A 1: 157)

Reason and beauty were both sources of satisfaction. 'Mill's "individual" possessed an inner spirit which defied rational investigation alone.' (Davis 1985: 348)

Mill's sense of the developmental nature of human character was another change in his political theory that resulted from Wordsworth's influence. By treating certain pleasures as conducive to the enhancement of character, he added a dynamic element to the static formula propounded by Bentham. According to Britton: 'Nothing more clearly marks the advance of John Stuart Mill upon the moral philosophy of James Mill and Bentham than this turning away from the purely intellectual disciplines to "the internal culture of the individual" as understood by Wordsworth.' (1953: 73) For Mill, calculations of felicity must take into account the evolutionary nature of individuals and avoid instantaneous judgements of the value of actions.

The end-result was a version of utilitarianism in which a place was found for the pursuit of the 'higher' pleasures. 'Higher' pleasures enhanced the appreciation of the pleasures derivative of the imagination and other-feeling. This enhancement reflected the development of character. Mill's calculus incorporates quality and development. This presented a logical problem for Mill. It was necessary to his philosophy, however, given the intellectual influences he sought to reconcile:

At the age of fifteen John Stuart Mill gave his enthusiastic adherence to the Benthamite system of morals.... he felt that all previous moralists had been superseded, and that here indeed was the commencement of a new era in thought. And, in fact to the end of his days he professed the fundamental logic and psychology of Utilitarianism. But at the same time his attitude towards their distinctive moral teaching changed very greatly indeed.... In later years he was inclined to judge the rightness or wrongness of an action very largely by its probable effects upon the character of the individuals immediately concerned. Mill was a Wordsworthian.

(Britton 1953: 45)

Mill's conception of pleasure represents a confluence of the influences of Bentham and Wordsworth. Bentham's influence ensured that Mill remained cognisant of the centrality for being of pleasure and pain and the need to justify public policies in terms of these basic elements. Wordsworth expanded his conception of pleasure to provide an expanded understanding of human motivation and a sense of character development. 'After long study and analysis he added intuition and poetry to his mental arsenal and revised utilitarianism. Benthamism was crude but the doctrine could be made useful if it were combined with human culture and high moral ideas.' (Staley 1986: 298)

## The Classical Economists, Comte and Understanding Mill on History and the Stationary State

Bentham and Wordsworth were not the only thinkers to influence Mill's political theory. Mill's views on historical development and the stationary state can be understood as the product of his exposure to the works and theories of the classical economists and Auguste Comte.

### The Classical Economists

James Mill's curriculum for his son involved immersing him in the works of the major classical economists (Smith, Ricardo and Malthus). Like many intellectuals of his time, Mill absorbed a great deal from them. Duncan has argued that both Mill and Marx were heavily influenced by 'the classical political economy of Smith, Malthus and Ricardo, which seemed to friends and enemies alike to be peculiarly appropriate to the society in which it emerged. Although the responses of Marx and Mill differed greatly,' Duncan continued, 'their social theories were each influenced particularly by certain key notions and concerns in the classical economics...'. (1973: 38)

Mill's absorption of the principles of the classical economists was enhanced through direct contact with Ricardo. Ricardo was an *habitué* of James Mill's study. As a result, Mill became 'acquainted with the dearest of his [father's] friends, David Ricardo, who by his benevolent countenance, and kindliness of manner, was very attractive to young persons, and who after I became a student of political economy, invited me to his house and to walk with him in order to converse on the subject.' (A 1: 55)

Ricardo was not the only classical economist whose ideas influenced Mill's political theory. Thomas Malthus was another important influence. 'Above all,' MacCunn wrote, 'he had read Malthus, and significantly he tells us that it was Malthus who first turned his thoughts to social questions. We may say he repaid the debt. For to the last, social questions always turned his thoughts to Malthus.' (1964: 45–6)

While Ricardo and Malthus shaped Mill's thinking, Adam Smith provided much of the intellectual framework for all three. Mill's theories reflected two key elements of Smith's works. The first was a positive conception of economic development (positive in the sense that productive and distributive capacities were increasing and in the sense that this increase was considered desirable). The second was an awareness of the possibility of economic stagnation.

According to O'Brien, Smith's view that societies generally demonstrated economic improvement, and did not merely change, resulted from the influence of natural law philosophy on his thought. Of the intellectual influences on classical economics, O'Brien argued, 'the most important by far, at least for Adam Smith (and through him for classical economics in general) was the influence of the natural-law philosophers'. (O'Brien 1975: 22) According to O'Brien, four propositions were basic to natural law theory: 'that there is an underlying order in material phenomena; that this underlying order is discoverable...; that discovery of the underlying order leads to the formulation of natural laws which, if followed, lead to the best possible situation; and that positive legislation should reflect these natural laws'. (O'Brien 1975: 22)

Smith foresaw a bright future due to the natural propensity of society to progress: 'He proceeded to demonstrate that society was in fact constantly improving; that it was being propelled, willy-nilly, toward a positive goal.' (Heilbroner 1972: 59) This was not a result of conscious direction on any person's part. Society 'moved because there was a concealed dynamic beneath the surface of things which powered the social whole like an enormous engine'. (Heilbroner 1972: 59) The possibility for progress was almost infinite for Smith and, so long as government did not interfere unduly, 'there is virtually endless opportunity for society to improve its lot'. (Heilbroner 1972: 65)

But 'virtually endless' is not endless. 'In the very long run, well beyond the horizon, one could just discern the final destination for society.' (Heilbroner 1972: 65) That destination was far in the distance and of little concern for Smith. 'Smith ... had a theory of eventual economic stagnation.... But for Smith the approach of a stationary state in which growth had ceased does not seem to have been an immediate problem.' (O'Brien 1975: 35) Smith was intent on fostering enthusiasm for a largely unregulated economy, not on introducing elements of gloom. This fell to Malthus and Ricardo whose theories identified many dark clouds that hung over Smith's bright future. Their sobering influence had a marked effect on classical economists and, as a result, on Mill.

Few documents could have had as much effect on his contemporaries as Malthus's *An Essay on the Principle of Population as It Affects the Future Improvement of Society*. The publication of the first version of that essay, in 1798, marked the end of unbridled optimism. In this essay Malthus argued that rather than 'ascending to an ever higher level, society was caught in a hopeless trap in which the human reproductive urge would inevitably shove humanity to the sheer brink of the precipice of existence. Instead of being headed for Utopia, the human lot was forever condemned to a losing struggle between ravenous mouths and the eternally insufficient stock of Nature's cupboard....' (Heilbroner 1972: 76)

Malthus's premise was that 'while the number of mouths grows geometrically, the amount of cultivatable land grows only arithmetically'. (Heilbroner 1972: 87) Malthus resiled from his extreme pessimism in a later version of the *Essay* and adopted a contingent pessimism. The contingency was the extent to which people could control their urge to procreate. (Heilbroner 1972: 89) Mill accepted this view.

Whereas Malthus's re-examination of Smith's doctrine was blunt and direct, Ricardo's was more subtle. Ricardo identified divisions among the members of Smith's progressive society into those who benefited from such progress and those who did not.

For what Ricardo foresaw was the end of a theory of society in which everyone moved together up the escalator of progress sketched out by Smith. On the contrary, Ricardo saw that the escalator worked with different effects on different classes, that some rode triumphantly to the top, while others were carried up a few steps and then were kicked back down to the bottom. Worse yet, those who kept the escalator moving were not those who rose with its motion, and those who got the full benefit of the ride did nothing to earn their reward.

(Heilbroner 1972: 77)

For Ricardo, and ultimately for Mill, Smith had left a crucial element out of his description of economy relations; this was class.

Ricardo was mainly concerned with the division between middle and upper classes, or industrialists and aristocrats. (Heilbroner 1972: 77)

He was not particularly concerned with the working classes, but his works stimulated suspicions that all was not well with Smith's world. 'The apparent confidence of classical political economy evaporated in Ricardo's cool and sharp analysis. He had pointed to a clear division of interests between landlords, seeking to maintain a destructive protectionism, and the other sections of society.' (Duncan 1973: 51) Mill was deeply influenced by Ricardo's analysis. Mill wrote that 'inequalities of wages are generally in an opposite direction to the equitable principles of compensation erroneously represented by Adam Smith as the general law of the remuneration of labour. The hardships and the earnings ... are generally in an inverse ratio to one another.' (PPE 3: 383)

Mill absorbed four elements from classical economics into his political theory. These were: a sense of the developmental nature of society; the idea of the stationary state; a concern with the problem of population; and, finally, a sense of the problem for his society that class presented. To these influences were added that of Auguste Comte. Together, these intellectual cross-currents allow for a proper understanding of Mill's conception of historical development and understanding of the stationary state.

### Comte

Comte's influence on Mill was twofold. First, Mill adopted his view of the centrality of intellectual development for social development. Second, he accepted Comte's idea that history proceeded in stages. Both of these ideas represented significant divergences from the general tenets of classical economics and provided Mill with the means for a reassessment and reorientation of his political theory. 'The writers by whom, more than by any others, a new mode of political thinking was brought home to me', Mill wrote, 'were those of the St Simonian school.... Among their publications ... was one which seemed to me far superior to the rest.... This was the early work of Auguste Comte....' (A 1: 171–3)

The classical economists believed in the progressive nature of development in the productive forces but did not distinguish this from social progress. Economic development was their object to the exclusion of much else and, for Mill, this left them with a limited understanding of history. According to Heilbroner, Smith's system presupposed 'that eighteenth-century England will remain unchanged forever. Only in quantity will it grow: more people, more goods, more wealth; its quality will remain unchanged. His are the dynamics of a static community; it grows but it never matures.' (Heilbroner 1972: 70)

While Ricardo and Malthus introduced important elements into classical economics, they maintained a limited conception of history, and as a result provided little that went to the creation of a science of society.

> The admission that political economy dealt only with a limited area of human activity made the elaboration of a general science of society all the more urgent, if the universality of scientific method was to be upheld. It was the promise of such a general science of society which drew Mill to Comte, whose enterprise he once called 'very nearly the grandest work of the age'. Yet his reception of Comte's philosophy only throws into relief his greater debt to Ricardo and his father.
>
> (Thomas 1992: 303)

Comte provided Mill with a sense that history was more than merely the development of productive forces. Davidson argued that 'it was peculiar to Mill, as compared with his British predecessors, that he widened the conception of Political Economy. Influenced by Comte, though not by him alone, he viewed it as inseparably associated with the philosophy of society, thereby conjoining consideration of economic theory and principles with that of their social applications.' (Davidson 1957: 130)

Comte's understanding of progress was much more sophisticated than that of the classical economists. Central to this understanding was the notion that quantitative and qualitative improvement were inextricably linked.

> Civilization develops, to an enormous degree, the action of Man upon his environment: and thus, it may seem, at first, to concentrate our attention upon the cares of material existence, the support and improvement of which appear to be the chief object of most social occupations. A closer examination will show, however, that this development gives the advantage to the highest human faculties, both by the security which sets free our attention from physical wants, and by the direct and steady excitement which it administers to the intellectual functions, and even the social feelings.
>
> (Comte 1893: 125)

Comte's conception of the nature of development was also different from that of the classical economists, especially Smith's. Smith focused on the stabilising and harmonising effects of the economy. Comte accepted that society contained such stabilising forces but argued that these were overridden at times by other disruptive forces. He communicated this sense of the dual nature of social forces to Mill. Comte's 'peculiar use of the terms "statics" and "dynamics", the former indicating the equilibriating mechanisms of non-evolutionary phenomena, and the latter the behaviour of evolutionary phenomena in society, was taken over by J.S. Mill.' (O'Brien 1975: 26)

For Comte and Mill society was characterised by moments of stability and change and evolved through a number of discernible stages. 'Mill learned to appropriate the emphasis of Comte and the St Simonians that history moved through a sequence of inevitable successive stages....' (Davis 1985: 349–50) Mill wrote that this aspect of Comte's theory gave his thinking on these matters 'a scientific shape'. (A 1: 173)

Comte's influence on Mill was primarily a result of his view that transitions between the three stages of social development were governed by natural laws. Comte wrote:

> We have indicated the general direction of the human evolution, its rate of progress, and its necessary order. We may now proceed at once to investigate the natural laws by which the advance of the human mind proceeds. The scientific principle of the theory appears to me to consist in the great philosophical law of the succession of the three states: – the primitive theological state, the transient metaphysical, and the final positive – through which the human mind has to pass, in every kind of speculation. (1893: 131)

These forms of social organisation differed with respect to their intellectual foundations. Each period represented a progression because the intellectual achievements possible within it were far greater.

Those progressions were not smooth. 'The passage from one social system to another can never be continuous and direct. There is always a transitional state of anarchy which lasts for some generations at least....' (Comte 1893: 9) For Comte and Mill, social progress was not the relatively smooth transition it was for the classical economists and was bought at the price of temporary and necessary social instability.

Comte referred to these transitional periods as times of 'intellectual anarchy'. (Comte 1893: 23) Intellectual anarchy was the result of a lack of a comprehensive intellectual system that could provide for the progressive development of society. In the transition from Metaphysical to Positive stages, 'the old philosophy is in a state of imbecility; while the development of the positive philosophy, though always proceeding, has not yet been bold, broad, and general enough to comprehend the mental government of the human race'. (Comte 1893: 3) This period of intellectual anarchy would only cease with the development of a coherent and comprehensive positive philosophy.

## Understanding Mill on History

The task of integrating Comte's philosophy with that of the classical economists was central to Mill's intellectual project. According to Platteau: 'To transform the political economy of his masters into an instrument for social and economic progress was probably the only claim to originality which J.S. Mill was ready to voice.' (Platteau 1985: 4) Mill sought to reinterpret the historical progression that the classical economists assumed but, in his view, did not fully understand. He did this to achieve a more complete, and more scientific, understanding of social progress. This understanding made prediction possible.

Mill expanded his understanding of social progress and the forces that brought it about, under Comte's influence. His conception of history changed and came to reflect parameters that were not part of classical economics.

> The Comtian position is reproduced by Mill, and much is made of Comte's distinction between 'Social Statics' and 'Social Dynamics' ... the first having for its province social order ... and the second considering social states as succeeding each other in time, and aiming at ascertaining the laws of social progress.... As to social progress, it is evident that it depends on the varying range of men's knowledge and the nature of their beliefs. Every great change of a social kind is preceded by a change in people's conceptions and convictions; so that social progress is amenable to invariable laws.
> 
> (Davidson 1957: 120–1)

Mill also came to see social progress as more than economic increase. Progress was economic, intellectual, and social. The classical economists, Mill decided, were constrained by a preoccupation with the economic relationships of the day. They could not imagine a future without those economic relationships. In Mill's view, the classical economists could not think beyond 'their eternal circle of landlords, capitalists, and labourers, until they seem to think of the distinction of society into those three classes, as if it were one of God's ordinances, not man's, and as little under human control as the division of day and night'. (MM 4: 226) As a result, none of them considered 'as a subject of inquiry, what changes the relations of those classes to one another are likely to undergo in the progress of society'. (MM 4: 226–7)

Classical economists provided no means by which social progress could be understood and facilitated. Comte's works made it clear that their theories resulted in a limited understanding of history. According to Mueller, 'in his *Spirit of the Age* articles, Mill was under the influence of Comte's *Trait de Politique Positive* which suggested the need for determining the pattern of development and for determining the kind of society that would be in harmony with the contemporary state of development'. (1968: 103) Later works by Comte, Mueller continued, caused Mill to insist 'more and more on the scientific study of history as the means of determining which institutions were outmoded and as a means of determining the direction of political reform'. (1968: 103)

Comte's view that social development was determined by the growth of social feelings was also reflected in Mill's understanding of history. Growth in cooperation was an important indicator of social progress and moral improvement was central to human history. Comte's influence, Mill believed, meant that he had avoided the error

> of regarding the intellectual as the only progressive element in man, and the moral as too much the same at all times to affect even the average of crime. M. Comte shows, on the contrary, a most acute sense of the causes which elevate or lower the general level of moral excellence; and deems intellectual progress in no other way so beneficial as by creating a standard to guide the moral sentiments of mankind, and a mode of bringing those sentiments effectively to bear on conduct. (ACP 10: 322–3)

Ricardo had identified problems in the relations between the classes but he did not provide a clear indication of the means through which such tensions might be resolved. Comte led Mill to see intellectual improvement as vital to this resolution; as were cooperation and moral improvement. A Ricardian sense of the roots of social injustice was combined with a Comtian understanding of the nature of social progress as the overcoming of this injustice. The final product was Mill's conception of the historical process.

## Understanding Mill on the Stationary State

Comte's views on the role of morals and the intellect also led to Mill's revision of the classical economists' views on the stationary state.[19] Comte's influence meant that Mill did not equate economic development with social development. A society may become static economically, but remain dynamic with respect to the intellectual and moral capacities of its members. 'Thus if any doubt had burdened

Mill's reform efforts because of his anticipation of an end to economic progress, the burden was removed by the Comtian and Saint-Simonian notion of social progress as it derived from the theory of historical progress and social consensus.' (Mueller 1968: 123)

The stationary state which for most other classical economists was 'an imminent horror ... becomes in Mill a prospect to be positively welcomed. He could see no pleasure in expansion for its own sake. Increased production might be an important aim for poor countries, but for advanced ones a better distribution of existing wealth was more important still.' (Thomas: 1992: 315) Thus, 'Mill broke with the mainstream tradition of both Ricardian and Smithian political economy in arguing that the future period in which economic growth would have virtually ceased need not be ... a nightmare to be avoided, but might rather open to the human species many prospects superior to those currently available.' (Claeys 1987: 133)

Mill's understanding of the stationary state reflected the combined influence of Comte and the classical economists. 'He accepted the Ricardian view of a falling rate of profits but coloured the final outcome with the Comptian notion of a happy stationary state.' (Davis 1985: 352) Mill's 'happy stationary state' would be marked by the absence of the social tensions to which Ricardo had made Mill more sensitive, and would be brought about through the mechanisms of social readjustment, through intellectual and moral improvement, suggested in Comte's works.

## Conclusion

The influence of Bentham, Wordsworth, the classical economists and Comte provided Mill with the stimulation and conceptual and intellectual tools that gave form and content to important elements of his understanding of pleasure, history and the stationary state. A lack of familiarity with each of these influences would lead to a failure to understand key elements of Mill's political theory.

## A SOCIAL-HISTORICIST READING

### Introduction

Situating Mill's works in terms of their psychological and intellectual determinants provide two means for understanding those works.

Situating them in terms of the social conditions within which they were produced provides another. From this perspective, Mill's political theory is a product of his times and can only be understood in this context. 'It is necessary to understand not just the doctrine, but the circumstances to which the doctrine was a response. This is a preliminary essential in dealing with all serious writers on moral, political and social questions ... with Mill it is central to the doctrine itself.' (Cowling 1963: 3) For Berlin, 'the Essay on Liberty deals with specific social issues in terms of examples drawn from genuine and disturbing issues of its day...'. (1959: 30) In the same vein, Forget argued that 'Mill's recantation [of the wage fund doctrine] was not motivated by internal inconsistencies, but was a calculated political act, undertaken by an individual aware of the role he played in shaping public opinion.' (Forget 1992: 32)

Many political theorists have considered their times to be marked by manifest and significant change and have developed their theories in order to contribute to or influence these changes. Certainly, Mill felt his times to be decisive. He wrote that his times were 'pregnant with change; and that the nineteenth century will be known to posterity as the era of one of the greatest revolutions of which history has preserved the remembrance, in the human mind, and in the whole constitution of human society.' (SOA I 22: 227–8)[20]

Mill believed that 'he was living in a critical phase in the history of the world, a transitional period in which old opinions, old institutions, and the old religion were disintegrating ... and where the task of the mature, reasonable writer and mature reasonable philosopher was the provision of a body of received doctrine to supply the want caused by this disintegration'. (Cowling 1963: 3–4) 'The Spirit of the Age' articles, for example, were written 'especially to point out in the character of the present age, the anomalies and evils characteristic of the transition from a system of opinions which had worn out, to another only in process of being formed'. (quoted in 'Introduction' to SOA 22: 227)

In Cowling's view, Mill carried 'a sense of historic mission which gives greater confidence than he might have otherwise had, and induced an earnestness of manner deriving from consciousness of obligation to propagate what he had conceived to be opinions suitable to the time and point-in-history at which he had arrived...'. (1963: 3) Mill's sense of his public role sometimes caused him difficulty, according to Alexander: 'The attempt to modify his opinions in accordance with the time and to allow his criticism to be determined by what he supposed to be the needs of the public, could land Mill in some embarrassing situations. He often was obliged to impede the too thorough acceptance of ideas he himself first proposed.' (1965: 66)

Mill's positions on the role of government, 'self-regarding' actions, education, socialism, and tradition or custom can be understood as responses to the social context in which he found himself. The most important aspect of Mill's social context was the onset of industrialisation. Two features of the newly emerging industrial society shaped Mill's political theory. The first was the appearance of major urban populations. The second was the development of an industrial working class. The growth of cities led to Mill's position on the proper role of government and his development of the category of self-regarding actions. The problems posed by the rise of the industrial working class produced Mill's views on socialism, traditions and customs, and education.

## The Growth of the City and Understanding Mill on the Proper Role of Government and Self-Regarding Actions

Two features of the growth of the city are important for an understanding of Mill's views on the role of government and his category of self-regarding actions. These are the emergence of a large concentrated population and, what may be termed, 'mass culture'. The problem of a large urban population was behind Mill's views on the role of government. The phenomenon of mass culture led Mill to develop the category of 'self-regarding' actions.

### *The Growth of the City*
One of the most significant social changes that Great Britain underwent during Mill's lifetime (1806–73) was a rapid increase in the populations of towns. 'During the first 30 years of the century Birmingham and Sheffield doubled in size, Liverpool, Leeds, Manchester and Glasgow more than doubled. London, in 1815 was above the million mark, and five years later numbered 1 274 000).' (Thomson 1951: 11–12) By 1851 'suburbanism, at least around London, had begun: and more than 3 254 000 people lived in the capital, constituting a city of unprecedented size.' (Thomson 1951:137) This resulted not just from an increase in the overall population but from a concurrent movement of that population into the existing towns.

Population increase and urban expansion at this time was marked by a lack of planning and coordination. The field was left to individual initiative, and not all individuals acted with the best of intentions. 'The new structure of society came into existence piecemeal, by the unco-ordinated efforts of individuals progressing forcefully, but ignorantly, in unknown fields, under conditions which placed the unscrupulous, unimaginative, hard-bitten type at a great material advantage.' (Evans 1965: 18)

These entrepreneurs had little interest in the welfare of those who inhabited the new areas created in the cities and towns, and no regula-tory agencies existed to force them to take such an interest. Many of these new areas 'were built with a sole eye to individual profit by men ignorantly moving into the unknown, they were in fact nothing but close-packed squalid slums, with the merest mockery of any attempt at the provision of sanitation, fresh air, garden room, or any other civi-lized amenity.' (Evans 1965: 18–19) The development of towns of this type created a social problem and an intellectual problem. As Webb observed, 'the town was the greatest challenge faced by modern Britain'. (1968: 116)

## Understanding Mill on the Proper Role of Government

The economic and social forces that produced the town resulted in social problems that could not be ignored. 'It is indisputable that the process of industrialisation put English institutions under considerable strain. Population was increasing fast; urbanisation, which was quicker than mechanisation, made misery at least more obtrusive.' (Duncan 1973: 24) Mill addressed the problems this presented in his political theory. That these problems went to the heart of liberal theories of government meant that Mill had to formulate a new understanding of the proper role of government. The sacred principle of non-interference had clearly failed and the 'invisible hand' had pushed society to the brink of degradation.

The squalor of the cities and towns had resulted 'because through ignorance, and in the sacred name of laissez-faire, there were no laws of sanitation, or of drainage, or even of building'. (Webb 1968: 94) *Laissez-faire* approaches could no longer be adopted with absolute certainty as a result of the problems. The significant role for govern-ment that Mill detailed was a direct result of the social conditions generated by the development of unregulated urbanisation. Thus 'the life and thought of John Stuart Mill exemplify the intellectual and theo-retical adjustments which had to be made in the prevailing creed of Radicalism by honest men who sought a new creed more appropriate to the changing social scene'. (Thomson 1951: 48) That social scene required significant state intervention into the economy and society, as the activity of unregulated individuals had created the problems society faced.

Benevolent societies had helped to lessen the effects of the substantial and rapid rise in urban population (Milliken 1963: 110ff), but attention shifted quickly to the responsibilities of government in this situation. 'No rapid solution of the dreadful "condition of the people" was possible. That was not a problem, but a process: the building up of the modern state.' (Evans 1965: 89) Mill's works were significant to the generation of a philosophical base, or justification, for that state.

Mill sought to revitalise liberal theory to make it capable of dealing with the changed social context. 'Liberalism, if it was not to lose its public, had to revise the letter of its law, and this in fact was what it did.... A thoroughgoing revision of liberal theory ... required a re-examination of the nature and functions of the state, the nature of liberty, and the relationship between liberty and legal coercion.' (Sabine 1973: 637) According to Sabine, this revision came in two 'waves'. The first was comprised of the theories of Herbert Spencer and John Stuart Mill whose work, Sabine argued, 'is the clearest proof of the urgency, not to say the inevitability, of the revision'. (Sabine 1973: 638)

This development in Mill's thought was not a natural outgrowth of the theories that had been his staple as a youth. It was a direct product of social changes that invalidated the theory that underpinned the classical liberal's commitment to minimal government. Mill's expanded sense of the proper role of government was a development in liberal thought that was necessitated by his social context. Mill provided intellectual support for governments engaging in many activities they had not previously undertaken and the expansion of their social role included significant interference in the lives of most people.[21]

### Understanding Mill on Self-Regarding Actions

Problems with respect to social infrastructure were not the only ones created by the growth of the city. It also presented problems with respect to the rules that governed social interaction. The development of major urban centres meant that existing lifestyles needed to be 'modernised'. Mill's category of 'self-regarding' actions was a response to this need. Two aspects of the problem of mass culture explain Mill's concept of 'self-regarding' actions. The first is that large urban masses meant more frequent contact between strangers or mere acquaintances. The second was the way in which increasing populations magnified the weight of public opinion.

The growth of the city required the development of a notion of 'acceptable' behaviour that could function effectively in the context of increased levels of anonymous, or near-anonymous, social interaction. Tolerance toward the actions of others could not be based upon familiarity. The city was not only bigger than its predecessors, it was more impersonal. This meant that general rules, or rules that could be applied without prior knowledge of the other, were necessary.

One possible solution for this problem was to allow public or majority opinion to dictate acceptable social behaviour. Mill rejected this on the basis that it would restrict the individual's scope for self-expression. The weight of opinion that a majority could exert would crush individuals. The end result of such pressure would be widespread uniformity. The threat to the individual 'as Mill conceived it ... came from the total social as well as legal and political pressure exerted by the collectivity known as "society".' (Himmelfarb 1974: 20)

Group pressure constrained individuals in smaller communities. A large community magnified this pressure and constraint increased. 'Everyone ... lived "as under the eye of a hostile and dreaded censorship"; conformity was the first thing thought of; they liked in crowds; they exercised choice only among things commonly done....' (Anschutz 1963: 24–5) For Mill, stifling conformity was the result of a mass society in which people did not govern themselves through principles that encouraged difference. Intellectual freedom was constrained, in Mill's England, as a result of 'the intolerant temper of the national mind; arising ... from the general habit, both in opinion and in conduct, of making adherence to custom the rule of life...'. (PPE 3: 935)

Intolerance was not peculiar to his era, but with the increase in population density its inhibiting effect became an irresistible force. The 'Spirit of the Age' articles 'opened with a diagnosis of the malady of the times: the increased power of the masses and the decreased power of the individual'. (Himmelfarb 1974: 43) Mill believed that such a force was growing and needed to be resisted through the acquisition of new attitudes and social conventions. 'The disposition of mankind ... to impose their own opinions and inclinations as a rule of conduct on others ... is hardly ever kept under restraint by anything but want of power; and as the power is not declining, but growing, unless a strong barrier of moral conviction can be raised against the mischief, we must expect ... to see it increase.' (OL 18: 227) Mill's goal was to generate this 'strong barrier of moral conviction' from which could develop a tolerant attitude to behaviour that disturbed moral sensibilities.

Mill's category of 'self-regarding' actions was central to his attempt to describe that attitude which was conducive to progressive social coexistence in more highly concentrated communities. Most of the actions individuals take will affect others in a densely populated society. To provide others with the latitude necessary for them to live their own lives, people needed to consider carefully whether they were merely affected by a 'self-regarding' activity, or whether the behaviour was outside that category and therefore open to intervention. Mill's category of 'self-regarding' actions was not an abstract construction for hypothetical situations. It was devised for those who found themselves in unfamiliar concentrations in his England.

The category of self-regarding actions is meaningless when treated as some abstract formula designed for all times and all places. It is both more comprehensible and more interesting, however, when understood as an attempt to provide some guidance to people who found themselves in an urban environment for which they were ill-prepared. According to Gildin, 'in the social context within which Mill wrote *On Liberty* 'there was no agreement as to where the right of an individual to do as he thinks best ends and where the right of society to compel him to do as it thinks best begins, or even as to whether there exists a well-defined province within which the individual has the right to do whatever he pleases'. (Gildin 1964: 288) The concept of self-regarding actions was an attempt to provide this 'well-defined province'.

## The Rise of the Working Class and Understanding Mill on Socialism, Traditions and Customs and Education

A much greater concentration of people was not the only feature of Mill's society important for an understanding of his political theory. Mill's society was also marked by rapid industrialisation. A crucial effect of this, for Mill's political theory, was the rise of the urban industrial working class. With the development of the industrial town came the industrial working class. This created new tensions within English society. Cities did not merely grow, they grew in particular ways and the structure of Mill's society was solidifying into the class division often associated with capitalist societies. The struggles that resulted from attempts by members of the working class to find a place in society provide a necessary context for an analysis of Mill's political theory.

Mill's positions with respect to socialism, traditions and customs, and education were direct responses to the efforts of members of the

working class to secure social position and to protect their needs and interests. These efforts were conducted on economic and political fronts. The former, which primarily involved the development of worker co-operatives, explains Mill's considerations of and responses to socialist ideas. The latter, which involved moves for Parliamentary representation, explains his views on traditions and customs and the need for general education.

### Worker Co-operatives

The disadvantages experienced by members of the working class of Mill's time created a sense of injustice on their parts with respect to the existing social order. This sense of injustice resulted in their desire for other forms of social organisation. Socialism was often presented to and by members of the working class as an answer to their problems. Like many other intellectuals of his time, Mill was forced to address the question of the desirability of socialism. His sense that the social tensions created by the conditions of working people required a consideration of other forms of social organisation led him to encourage socialist experiments. If Mill can be said to have adopted a socialist position, which is something that he claimed he did (see A 1: 199), it was only as a response to calls for justice from members of the working class.

The fact that they owned nothing of value apart from their labour meant that members of the working class were poorly placed in any struggle with their employers over wages and conditions. The position of employers was further strengthened by the use of child-labour and the lack of government regulation. Wages and prices were beyond the control of the workers and their labour was only as valuable as the employers and retailers determined.

Workers began to form co-operatives to counteract that power. Among the new developments in Mill's England 'the greatest novelty of all is the spirit of combination which has grown up among the working classes...'. (Cn 18: 125) The early attempts at co-operation proved sufficiently successful that they soon spread and were extended to a variety of economic activities, as Thomson explained:

> The Co-operative movement [was] founded in 1844 when a group of twenty-eight Lancashire working men opened a little store in Toad Lane, Rochdale.... It was the most solid and impressive piece of working-class self-help which emerged from the many experiments of the period.... By 1851 there were some 130 Co-operative stores

in the north of England and in Scotland. Within twenty years their methods spread to wholesale trading as well as retail, and to production as well as to distribution.

(Thomson 1951: 150)

Co-operatives directly challenged the dominant classes. They were also a repudiation of the attitude of superiority and paternalism through which the dominant classes viewed the working class.

The success of worker co-operatives caused a strong reaction from the ruling elites. The advent of support networks created by and for the working class was not necessarily new, but alarm was caused due to the fact that these networks were more extensive than any previously seen. Briggs has observed that associations which provided social security for their members across Britain 'were so large that they were viewed with suspicion by those who scented danger when working-men from different parts of the country were gathered together in national federal bodies'. (Briggs 1979: 303)

The co-operatives served to clearly differentiate the interests of the workers from that of employers. Many spokespeople of the employers sought to dissuade workers from their independence and self-help through reference to some shared interest. Mill admonished those who continued to suggest 'that the interest of labourers and employers ... is one and the same. It is not to be wondered at that this sort of thing should be irritating to those to whom it is intended to be a warning.' (TLC 5: 656) Mill accepted that it was in the interests 'of labourers and employers that business should prosper, and that the returns to labour and capital should be large. But to say that they have the same interest as to the division,' he continued, 'is to say that it is the same thing to a person's interest whether a sum of money belongs to him or to somebody else.' (TLC 5: 657)

## Understanding Mill on Socialism

Mill was convinced the working class would 'not much longer tolerate its subordinate position'. (Sarvasy 1985: 319) Mill advised the Committee on the Savings of the Middle and Working Classes 'that there was a growing awareness by the workers of their unjust condition'. (Hughes 1979: 538) He accepted this sense of injustice but sought to prevent it from leading to social breakdown. For this reason Sarvasy emphasised Mill's 'growing concern in the post-1840 period with the consequences of increasing polarization between capitalists and labourers. This theme provides an historical explanation of Mill's embrace of socialism and focuses interpretation on a key structural component of Mill's thought: class analysis.' (1985: 314)

Mill's intention was to moderate class antagonism. His defence of socialism was designed to reduce the militancy of the working class. He believed that what he called 'socialist experiments' provided 'a most useful education of those who took part in them, by cultivating their capacity of acting upon motives pointing directly to the general good, or making them aware of the defects which render them and others incapable of doing so'. (A 1: 241) If Mill could be understood to have embraced socialism it was to prevent rather than promote radical social change.

## Working-Class Political Power and Understanding Mill's Views on Traditions and Customs and Education

The increasing strength and militancy of the working class also explain Mill's defence of traditions and customs and belief in the need to ensure that education was widely available in the community and that all children were exposed to some measure of education. Mill believed that the working class would secure significant political power in the immediate future. His major concern was the lack of preparedness of members of that class for the acquisition of that power. He did not oppose their claims for political power but sought to temper the urgency of those claims by indicating the essential prerequisites for the proper possession and use of that power. These included an appreciation of, if not respect for, traditional or customary practices and some level of formal education.

### Working-Class Political Power

Claims for political power had been expressed in England before Mill was born; his lifetime was marked by more vehement and violent moves by its members for a share of political power more in keeping with their economic contribution. 'The organisation and mobilisation of the working class clearly took a far more serious form with the development of the Chartist movement in the violent decade following the financial crisis of 1836 and the economic crisis of 1837.' (Duncan 1973: 32) Mill considered Chartism to be 'the first open separation of interest, feeling, and opinion, between the labouring portion of the commonwealth and all above them'. (COL 4: 369)

Movements aimed directly at securing working-class representation in Parliament were a direct result of the failure on the part of the working class to secure a larger share of economic power. 'The failure

of the early trade union movement drove labour from the industrial to the political field, in which an attempt was made to remedy social and economic abuses by changing the character of Parliament....'
(Milliken 1963: 98) Chartists sought to reform Parliament to make it more representative of the population and, as a result, more reflective of the interests of the working class.

They failed to achieve their aims directly. But the Chartists' struggle had two major effects. First, it stimulated and encouraged subsequent calls for reform. Second, it made those in positions of political authority aware of the lengths to which working people would go to secure their political power. 'Chartism ... left a deep and permanent mark on English history. It was the first widespread and sustained effort of working-class self-help; it was directed to the cause of parliamentary democracy and constitutional reform; and the impetus it gave to eventual political reform on one hand and to trade unionism on the other was never wasted.' (Thomson 1951: 87) Chartism may have collapsed, but 'its cloudy goals and ephemeral organizations were ... replaced by tough-minded and practical work for the attainment of economic and political power'. (Webb 1968: 248)

The revolution in France served as a further reminder of the potential inherent in the struggle for political power by members of lower classes. Both sides of the social division in Britain couldn't fail to be impressed, whether positively or negatively, by the events in France. 'The French Revolution served as a model of violent and creative change, and an indication that men could substantially alter their institutions if they wished.' (Duncan 1973: 19)

Those in political and social control in England probably overestimated the strength and vehemence of claims for reform. Briggs suggested that 'the English working classes were not as revolutionary in the late 1830's and 1840's as many frightened contemporaries thought or as many militant Chartists hoped...'. (Briggs 1979: 302) Though this does not mean that they were happy: 'Through the first half of the century Labour was in a state of smouldering revolt....'
(Sommervell 1950: 85) The upshot of all this was that, in England, working-class movements were paid considerable attention throughout the nineteenth century and, on occasion, were violently suppressed by the government. Working-class pressure for political reform was never far from the political agenda and reforms had to be considered, even if 'only as concessions to extreme pressure, and as alternatives to riot'.
(Thomson 1951: 40)

No one who thought about politics could ignore calls for reform.

None could neglect consideration of the effects on society of granting increased political power to the working class. Mill recognised that the masses possessed 'a growing power'. (ACP 10: 325) He wrote of the working classes as 'deeply and increasingly discontented, and whose discontent now speaks out in a voice which will not be unheard'. (quoted in Duncan 1973: 227) This meant that Mill believed that 'the Claims of Labour have become the question of the day'. (COL 4: 365)

He did not pale at the prospect of a working class with considerable political representation. Rather, he supported such an extension of the franchise: 'With regard to the working classes, the chief topic of my speech on Mr. Gladstone's Reform Bill was the assertion of their claims to the suffrage.' (A 1: 277) He was not blind, however, to the problems that might result if the working class was incapable of appropriately exercising their newly gained power. Mill's 'major fear [was] ... of a legislative class tyranny, through their premature admission to the franchise.' (Duncan 1973: 228)

That the working class would succeed in achieving political representation meant the entry into parliament of a group with interests different from those previously represented.

It is known to even the most inobservant, that the working classes have, and are likely to have, political objects which concern them as working classes, and on which they believe, rightly or wrongly, that the interests and opinions of the other powerful classes are opposed to theirs. However much their pursuit of these objects may be for the present retarded ... it is as certain as anything in politics can be, that they will before long find the means of making their collective electoral power effectively instrumental to the promotion of their collective objects. (COS 5: 707)

Mill was not 'inobservant' and had to adapt his theory to meet the prospect of the working class gaining political power.

Liberalism changed in the face of the success of claims from the working class for political representation. This change was reflected in Mill's views on traditions and customs and on education. As Sabine has pointed out, working-class representation 'meant the appearance of a group of voters who were more concerned to protect wages, hours of labour, and conditions of employment than to extend business enterprise, and who were well aware that their strength lay not in freedom of contract but in collective bargaining'. (1973: 636–7) In Sabine's view this meant that 'either liberalism would meet these requirements or the working class would not be liberal'. (Sabine 1973: 637) Mill rose to the challenge and, as Duncan argued, his 'writings reveal clearly the hesitations and dilemmas of the improving liberal at a time when demands for far reaching political and social change challenged liberal values and the partially established framework of liberal institutions.' (1973: 209)

Mill didn't abandon liberal principles. He modified them to accommodate the imminent achievement of political power by the working class.

> Armed with the vote and the strike-weapon, the workers might achieve a large share of political power in a much shorter time than had seemed possible. What could be done to educate their leaders to use this power wisely and moderately? Mill had no particle of sentimentalism in his view of the working class or of any other class, and saw with great clearness the dangers which a too-rapid advance of their powers might bring.
>
> (Britton 1953: 43)

Mill's response was not to deny them this power, but to develop principles which might serve to limit the destabilising effects of their use of this power.

## Understanding Mill on Traditions and Customs

One way in which Mill sought to amend liberalism was to tone down its radical nature. Liberalism had been a radical theoretical intervention to support middle-class claims for social recognition against resistance from the aristocracy. It was oriented to undermining claims of privilege and institutional inertia. This made it susceptible to appropriation by the working class in its challenge to the existing institutions – many of them products of liberal reforms.

> Working-class aspirations and demands faced liberal philosophers with an urgent and fundamental dilemma. The liberal-democratic creed which they expounded, and which had been focused with revolutionary effect against traditional rulers, had dangerous implications when applied to mankind at large. The new danger was the mass, demanding the right to participate in political life and power, and using the radical elements in the liberal democratic ideology to support that demand.
>
> (Duncan 1973: 229)

Mill modified radical liberal rhetoric to justify more gradual social change by advocating a respect for customs and traditions. Mill was faced with a potentially powerful working class from which came claims for significant structural alterations. He did not deny the validity of such changes, but was not convinced that all of the changes mooted would be positive and sought to slow the process of change to allow for greater consideration of their implications. His support for traditions was a direct appeal to the working class to moderate their demands and an exhortation to consider the value in the institutions they wished to undermine.

In the fourth of the 'Spirit of the Age' articles Mill wrote, with apparent nostalgia, of those communities that held a great deal of respect for the force of tradition or custom. In these communities

> there is naturally a strong, and generally a very just, reverence for the memories of its founders. This would not have been thought strange three-quarters of a century ago. Robertson, the historian, speaks with the utmost simplicity, of 'that attachment to ancient forms, and aversion to innovation, which are the unfailing characteristics of popular assemblies.' Europe had not then entered into the state of transition of which the first overt manifestation was the breaking out of the French Revolution. (SOA 22: 292)

Nostalgia for communities in which traditions and customs were respected is not a common trait of liberal political theorists. It can be explained in terms of a social context involving the threat of far-reaching and disruptive changes in the social structure. 'In the words of the working-class journalist and later Chartist leader Bronterre O'Brien, "an entire change in society – a change amounting to the complete subversion of the existing 'order of the world' is contemplated by the working-classes...".' (Briggs 1979: 290) Mill counselled respect for traditions and customs in an attempt to contain the social upheaval he considered imminent.

### Understanding Mill on Education

Mill's support for general education was another element of his attempt to deal with the impending political power of the working class. If it was inevitable that the working class would gain greater political power, then to educate them may help to ensure that they use it more wisely. According to Mill, 'we must never lose sight of the truth, that the suffrage for a member of Parliament is power over others, and that to power over others no *right* can possibly exist. Whoever wishes to exercise it, is bound to acquire the necessary qualifications.' (quoted in

Burns 1968: 319) In pre-democratic periods the upper classes had no interest in the education of the working-class 'but if the democracy obtained a large, and perhaps the principal, share in the governing power, it would become the interest of the opulent classes to promote their education, in order to ward off really mischievous errors...'. (A 1: 179)

Mill's faith in the ability of education to induce a responsible attitude in the working class led him to support significant government intervention to ensure and, if necessary, provide a general education. 'The great means for preparing the workers were education (paid for, but not provided by, the State) and cooperation in local and national government, and in public enterprises of an unofficial character.' (Britton 1953: 43)

Middle- and upper-class parents were already well placed to provide education for their children. 'Until a comparatively recent period,' Mill wrote, 'none but the wealthy ... had it in their power to acquire the intelligence, the knowledge, and the habits, which are necessary to qualify a man, in any tolerable degree, for managing the affairs of his country.' (SOA 22: 278) Mill's support for general education meant an increase in the availability of education to working-class children.

State intervention to enforce and provide general education does not fit well with the general tenor of the liberal theory in which Mill was steeped. In terms of the political changes that his society was undergoing, however, this modification to the doctrine is not surprising.

> With regard to the advance of democracy, there are two different positions which it is possible for a rational person to take up, according as he thinks the masses prepared, or unprepared, to exercise the control which they are acquiring over their destiny.... If he thinks them prepared, he will aid the democratic movement.... If, on the contrary, he thinks the masses unprepared for complete control over their government – seeing at the same time that, prepared or not, they cannot long be prevented from acquiring it – he will exert his utmost efforts in contributing to prepare them; using all means ... for making the masses themselves wiser and better.... (Cn 18: 127)

Mill's adoption of the latter view resulted in his support for popular and accessible education. This was a means of ensuring that the working class could be made more able to handle the political power he thought they would acquire. It would make them more able to participate in politics and more able to see a national and not simply a class interest.

## Conclusion

Mill's views on traditions and customs and on education may be understood as responses to the major social tensions of his day. Mill was led to modify liberalism in his attempt to address the claims of workers. This modification was not designed to prevent the working class from achieving political power, but was intended to lessen its impact. On one hand, Mill sought this through instilling a respect for past practices so that new modes were not adopted before the previous ones had been fully and carefully assessed. The introduction of popular education, on the other hand, was intended to ensure that all those to whom political power would come were more deliberate in their use of that power. The effect of this education would ensure, Mill believed, that the working class used its power in the interests of all.

Mill's support for socialism can also be understood as an attempt to respond to the pressures for social change that were coming from the working class. To reject socialism outright would not have diminished the tension. To support social experiments and to encourage milder forms of socialism might serve to stem the tide of change and to preserve the institutions Mill supported.

In the same way, the purpose and meaning of Mill's positions on the role of government and his concept of 'self-regarding' actions can only be understood in light of the growth of the city. Independent of this context they lose reference and/or sense. Both reflect responses to social problems that, for a theorist who understood his role in shaping his society, were intellectual problems. These key elements of Mill's political theory are clear reflections of the effect his social location had upon his theories.

## CONCLUSION

To understand Mill's works, then, requires that those works are read in terms of a context or history. History is central whether that history is personal, intellectual or social. To read Mill's works without recognising that they were stimulated and shaped by contextual factors is to misunderstand them. Mill's positions on associationism, necessity, individuality and women so clearly express the psychological effects of his upbringing that they cannot be appreciated without reading them in terms of that upbringing. The divergent intellectual influences to which Mill was exposed make sense of his particular understanding of pleasure, history and the stationary state. The changes that British society underwent in his time provide the background necessary to understand Mill's writings on the proper role of government, self-regarding actions, socialism, traditions and customs, and education.

To fail to read Mill's works in their appropriate context is not simply to misunderstand them. It is also to treat him as an intellectual somehow disengaged from the communities to which he belonged. Mill was a person of Great Britain in the nineteenth century. To disconnect him from the period in which he found himself is to overlook his strong sense of situation and engagement. To read him without context would be to read him as though he had never lived.

# 4 Reading Mill within a Linguistic Framework

## INTRODUCING LINGUISTIC READING

Chapter 1 outlined three forms of linguistic analysis: taxonomic, reconstructive and therapeutic. A taxonomic approach involves situating a theorist's use of particular words in terms of a taxonomy of uses for those words. The reconstructive approach is oriented to refining the use of words in discussions of politics to reduce confusions that have grown up around their use in the general community. The goal is to make the meaning of words more specific and consistent within the specialist community engaged in the study of politics. A therapeutic approach involves either of two activities. The first is addressing the divergence of uses with respect to particular words in order to understand something of the divisions within a community that shares a language. The second is to identify pathologies which result from a separation between a consideration of the meaning of a word and the activity of which the use of that word is part.

While all of the forms of linguistic analysis discussed in Chapter 1 are consistent with the principles of linguistic philosophy, the taxonomic and therapeutic seem more applicable to a reading of Mill's works. The former allows for a consideration of Mill's use of a word in terms of the possible uses available for that word. The therapeutic approach is applicable due to Mill's commitment to ideas about the meaning of words that led him to separate meaning from use and commit the philosophical pathologies to which Wittgenstein referred.

The reading that follows is somewhat more idiosyncratic than the traditionalist reading and the intellectual and social historicist readings – the psychological historicist reading is more controversial. First, because it combines two variations on the linguistic approach. Second, because it is applied to a specific thinker. Most linguistic analysts study groups of word-users and their analyses deal with particular word-users as one of a number of users. Mill's works, then, would appear as one of the variety of works that are read in linguistic studies. An example of this approach is Pitkin (1967). A third reason for the idiosyncrasy of this reading of Mill is that it is more self-consciously linguistic than

113

most of the analyses that are represented as deriving from a linguistic conception of political theory. Fourth, because in order to maintain some consistency in the exemplification of the three conceptions of political theory, the same concepts are covered as those dealt with in Chapters 2 and 3. This chapter is intended to provide a sufficiently consistent and coherent reading of Mill's works to exemplify the linguistic conception as both an alternative understanding of political theory and an alternative way of reading the works of political theorists.

In Chapters 2 and 3 Mill's works could be read in terms of intellectual projects to which he appeared committed (Mill often sounded like a traditionalist or historicist). This reading is not in terms of Mill's intellectual project. This does not have the same implications as would be involved in attempting a behaviouralist reading of his works. The difference in this case is that linguistic analysis is oriented to the way that others use words without requiring that those others understand or are committed to linguistic analysis.

Linguistic analysis does not rely upon an individual word-user's commitments or intentions because an individual word-user can make a meaningful utterance only if s/he uses words in accordance with the rules or conventions that govern meaningful use. This holds even when there are a number of ways of using a word meaningfully and, therefore, a number of rules or conventions that govern meaningful use.

The only point at which a word-user's intentions may be considered significant is when they intend to do something in using a word. One form of linguistic analysis, speech act theory, relies upon the idea that word-users intend to achieve effects through their use of words. This intention to create effects can only be fulfilled when the word is used in a way that relies upon conventional use. A user can intend to create confusion and can intend to puzzle hearers. A word-user cannot intend to use a word unconventionally and intend to use it meaningfully for an audience familiar with the conventions that usually apply. As speech act theory suggests, an intention to create effects is part of the use of words; but these effects can only be achieved under limited circumstances. They cannot be achieved simply through an intention that they result. The effects themselves rely upon conventions and can only be achieved through adherence to, or careful play around, conventions.

At this stage it may be helpful if I introduce the way that I have approached a linguistic reading of Mill's work through a discussion of ordinary language analysis. Ordinary language analysis was and is an influential form of linguistic analysis. The 'ordinary' in ordinary language analysis is important and, in my view, best understood to refer to the conventional nature of word-use, rather than to the use of words in everyday interactions.[22] To be ordinary in one sense is to be consistent across a community. Ordinary use, therefore, can also be found in technical discourses.[23] While technical discourses are anything but everyday, they contain ordinary use and speech acts that are committed through ordinary use. The variety of uses that may be identified in taxonomic analysis reflects both the variety of things done when using words (with multiple meanings being produced from the different things that are being done) and the fact that words can function within everyday and technical discourse.[24] Mill's works contain both everyday and technical uses of words (sometimes the same word is used in both ways). As a result, his works can reflect more than one way of using a particular word.

The point at which meaning fails in Mill's works is the point at which he attempted something out of the ordinary. This can arise for philosophers when they cease to use words as part of the activities with which they ordinarily occur. A therapeutic approach can be applied in this case because Mill's understanding of his role in society reflected orientations common to the type of philosopher Wittgenstein rejected. Mill sought to uncover or discover the true meaning of words in order to enhance their powers of reference. He looks on language as 'one of the principal instruments or helps of thought; and any imperfection in the instrument, or in the mode of employing it, is confessedly liable ... to confuse and impede the process, and destroy all ground of confidence in the result'. (SOL 7: 19)

For Mill, words were tools for rendering the world clearer. Those who were 'not previously versed in the meaning and right use of the various kinds of words' could not attempt to philosophise, as this 'would be as if some one should attempt to become an astronomical observer, having never learned to adjust the focal distance of his optical instruments so as to see distinctly'. (SOL 7: 19) Mill might be thought of as a reconstructionist when we read that he understood 'the proper office ... of a clear thinker, would be to make other men's thoughts clear for them, if they cannot do it for themselves, and to give words to the man of genius, fitted to express his ideas with philosophical accuracy'. (UAPT 18: 6) That is, until we discover that Mill believed that 'an analysis of what propositions mean is an analysis of what kinds of knowledge there can be – what kind of thing one can know...'. (Skorupski 1989: 48)

A problem for this chapter derives from the hostility to the linguistic approach on the part of traditionalists and historicists. Most of these types of political theorists simply reject the limitations that derive from the linguistic approach. They cannot, as linguistic ontology and episte-mology require, leave everything as it is. Most, if not all, traditionalists cannot abandon questions that, from a linguistic perspective, are patho-logical. Most, if not all, historicists cannot accept the lack of a social or political objective that a linguistic conception requires.[25] The result is that they are continually disappointed by linguistic analysis or find it perverse. My hope is that readers who are committed to either of these other conceptions can set aside their prejudices – at least for the dura-tion of their reading of this chapter.

## INTRODUCTION

Two of the approaches to linguistic analysis outlined in Chapter 1 will be used in discussing Mill's use of words. The taxonomic mode is used to discuss Mill's treatment of the uses of 'education', 'history', 'indi-viduality' and 'custom'. The therapeutic approach is used in discussing Mill's attempted interventions into the use of 'women', 'pleasure', 'association' and 'stationary state'. Some of these discussions rely upon speech act theory and look to meaningful use in terms of the things that are done in using these words. For example, the different meanings available for 'individuality' revolve more around the issue of whether the word is being used to praise or condemn another for their differ-ence, than on the issue of the differences that result in individuality. An important feature of Mill's use of 'higher' and 'lower' in connec-tion with 'pleasure' was his desire to influence behaviour toward the former and away from the latter. Mill was not simply trying to name types of 'pleasure' he was attempting to persuade his readers to pursue certain pleasures rather than others.

The final section introduces other insights into Mill's use of words that derive from a linguistic perspective. Mill's category 'self-regard-ing' represented an odd intervention in language use which is interesting to the extent to which it reflects the use of the word 'private'. One of the most intriguing aspects of Mill's works, from a linguistic perspective, was his rejection of attempts to determine the 'proper' role for government. Mill rejected this on the basis that the proper role of government cannot be specified ahistorically. In doing so his discussions come closest to reflecting the ontology and episte-mology of a linguistic conception of political theory. Mill's suggestion that he came to adopt a 'qualified socialism' is interesting, from a linguistic perspective, in the way that the rejection of this suggestion introduces the question of the meaningful use of the word 'socialism'.

## TAXONOMIES OF USE IN AND FROM MILL'S WORKS

Understanding the meaning of words requires a sensitivity to the variety of uses to which words are put. In his discussions of 'education', 'history', 'individuality' and 'custom', Mill both alluded to, and adopted, some of the uses available for the words. His works indicate two uses of the word 'education' and a particular understanding of 'history' (coupled with a curious use of 'progress'). His works also reflect two forms of use for both 'individuality' and 'custom' that derive from the speech acts performed in using them.

To understand Mill's use of 'individuality' and 'custom' – and other words discussed in later sections – requires some sense of speech-act theory and, in particular, of Austin's notions of illocutionary and perlocutionary acts (see Austin 1976). According to Searle, Keifer and Bierwisch, 'the theory of speech acts starts with the assumption that the minimal unit of human communication is not a sentence or other expression, but rather the performance of certain kinds of acts, such as making statements, asking questions, giving orders, describing, explaining, apologizing, thanking, congratulating, etc.' (1980: vii) Austin referred to these speech acts as illocutionary acts.[26]

Illocutionary acts are performances intended to be taken as such.[27] They require no response from a hearer (though they may be part of a larger ritual in which a response is usually forthcoming). A promise can be made, for example, without that promise being taken seriously and somehow affecting the behaviour of others. When a speech act does affect another, this effect is, in Austin's terminology, perlocutionary. 'Perlocutionary acts have to do with those effects which our utterances have on hearers which go beyond the hearer's understanding of the utterance.' (Searle, Keifer and Bierwisch 1980: vii)[28]

Correlated with the notion of illocutionary acts is the notion of the consequences or *effects* such acts have on the actions, thoughts, or beliefs, etc. of hearers. For example, I may *persuade* or *convince* someone, by warning him I may *scare* or *alarm* him, by making a request I may *get him to do something*, by informing him I may

> convince him (*enlighten*, *edify*, *inspire him*, *get him to realize*). The italicized expressions above denote perlocutionary acts. (Searle 1980: 25)

Understanding what Mill was doing when he used words like 'individuality' and 'custom' requires understanding the speech-act Mill committed in using them, including the attempt to produce perlocutionary effects.

In his discussions of 'individuality' and 'custom' Mill sought to change the things that people did in using these words. His intention was to address these words in terms of their use in illocutionary and perlocutionary acts. Mill believed that 'individuality' had come to be used as a criticism or means of belittling and rejecting others. He rejected this use and sought to encourage the use of 'individuality' in complimenting or recommending. He is not as decisive in his reflections on the use of 'custom'. In all instances, he uses 'custom' to refer to a longstanding practice. On some occasions, though, he used 'custom' in commending practices. At other times, he used it in rejecting practices.

## 'Education'

Like most users of the word 'education' Mill uses it to refer to a formal process through which some knowledge or understanding is imparted to another. The key question, then, relates to that which is imparted in an 'education'. Mill adopted the use in which 'education' is a form of shaping of individuals but not of indoctrinating them. Mill rejected that use in which 'education' was simply imparting that which was already known. He used 'education' to refer to the shaping of an individual's character. The only remaining question is whether there is any real differences between these uses.

'Education' can be used to refer to a process in which a person is provided with a set of information which they internalise. To be properly educated is to properly absorb the information provided. 'Education' is a relationship in which an educator provides information held to be true in a field of human inquiry to those being educated in that field. 'Education', in this use, refers to the transmission of material – such as classifications of animals and plants, or the parts of the human body.

'Education' is also used to describe one process through which an individual acquires certain character traits or undergoes a particular attitudinal shift. 'Education', in this use, is present when people are exposed to influences designed to change them in some way. Mill's use of 'education' was generally consistent with this use. Mill rejected those uses in which 'education' was the transmission of some content. His use of 'education' necessarily involves the development of the mental capacities of the person educated. This development is primarily an increase in that individual's ability to acquire information for themselves and to think for themselves.

Mill believed that 'education' had come to mean the imparting of information. 'Modern education is all *cram* – Latin cram, mathematical cram, literary cram, political cram, theological cram, moral cram. The world already knows everything, and has only to tell it to its children, who, on their part, have only to hear, and lay it to rote (not to *heart*).' (OG 1: 337) Mill believed that one of the main obstacles to reform in 'education' was the dominance of this understanding of 'education'. The result was that 'the object of education is, not to qualify the pupil for judging what is true or what is right, but to provide that he shall think true what we think true, and right what we think right – that to teach, means to inculcate our own opinions, and that our business is not to make thinkers or inquirers, but disciples.' (Cn 18: 140)

In a paper on reform in education Mill quoted with approval the following passage from a speech by Sir William Molesworth:

> The so-called education, provided for the working classes of England, deficient as it is admitted to be in quantity, is immeasurably more deficient in quality; as *instruction*, it is lamentably meagre, incomplete and inappropriate; as *education*, as nearly as possible, absolutely null. All instruction consists in the mere repetition of by rote of certain words, to which the children affix either no idea at all, or ideas too indistinct to have any hold on their minds, or influence on their conduct. (RIE 21: 66)

According to Mill, 'knowledge comes only from within; all that comes from without is but *questioning*, or else it is mere *authority*'. (OG 1: 332) 'There is a language very generally current in the world,' he wrote, 'which implies that knowledge can be *vicarious*; that when a truth has become known to *any one*, all who follow have nothing to do but passively to receive it....' (OG 1: 331) In Mill's view, however, simply being told something did not lead to truly knowing it. Instead, he argued 'if I would *know* it, I must place my mind in the same state in which he has placed his; I must make the thought my own thought;

I must verify the fact by my own observation, or by interrogating my own consciousness'. (OG 1: 331)

'Education', for Mill, provided people with the ability to make choices that better reflected their interests. In his view, 'the end of education is not to teach, but to fit the mind for learning from its own consciousness and observation...'. (OG 1: 338) As a result, he demanded

> schools in which the children of the poor should learn to use not only their hands, but their minds, for the guidance of their hands; in which they should be trained to the actual adaptation of means to ends; should become familiar with the accomplishment of the same object by various processes, and be made to apprehend with their intellects in what consists the difference between the right way of performing industrial actions and the wrong. (COL 4: 378)

Mill believed that by this means these children would acquire 'habits of order and regularity, of the utmost use in after-life, and which have more to do with the formation of character than many persons are aware of.' (COL 4: 378)

A proper university curriculum, Mill argued, 'would have the classics and logic taught far more really and deeply than at present, and ... add to them other studies more alien than any which yet exist to the "business of the world", but more germane to the great business of every rational being – the strengthening and enlarging of his own intellect and character'. (Cn 18: 139) Mill did not dismiss what he referred to as 'empirical knowledge', but was 'content with infusing into the youth of our country a spirit, and training them to habits, which would ensure their acquiring such knowledge easily, and using it well'. (Cn 18: 139)

Mill was not always consistent, however, in his use of 'education' and sometimes used 'education' to refer to a more deliberate shaping. 'Admitting the omnipotence of education,' he wrote, 'is not the very pivot and turning point of that education a *moral sense* – a feeling of duty, or conscience, or principle, or whatever name one gives it – a feeling that one *ought* to do, and to wish for, what is for the greatest good of all concerned.' (JSM–HTMC 3: 1031). This is also reflected in Mill's comment that he and his father sought to 'alter people's opinions ... to know what was their real interest'. (A 1: 113) This understanding of 'education' is also reflected in Mill's comment that 'education works by conviction and persuasion as well as by compulsion'. (OL 18: 277)

These passages reflect a tendency to use 'education' to refer to one form of social engineering in which people were shaped in specific and deliberate ways. This comes close to the use of 'education' to refer to a process through which educators reproduce themselves in the educated. Individuals are not simply given the wherewithal to make up their own minds, but are directed to hold certain things to be true. For the most part, Mill used 'education' to refer to a process through which individuals were made more able to think for themselves. At times, however, his use was more in line with that in which 'education' is the acquisition of attitudes considered desirable by the educators.

Despite, or indeed because of, these inconsistencies, Mill's works offer an opportunity to examine different uses of the word 'education'. The inconsistencies in Mill's use also introduce the question whether education is ever taken to be as open as Mill's sometimes suggested it was. Given that 'education' has no true referent, this discussion cannot conclude with a definition of 'education'. Both of the uses identified through a reading of Mill's use are available. Each has a specific effect on the nature of the 'education' provided by those who adopt it.

### 'History'

Mill followed conventional use in using 'history' to refer to past events and to a record of past events. He followed a variant of conventional use in referring to 'history' as a pattern and even a pattern of progress. Mill's use of 'progress' was somewhat unusual, however, in that it was not intended to imply improvement. In this context, Mill used 'progress' to refer to continuation within a pattern.

For Mill, 'history' was a resource to be combed for indications of the future. In a discussion 'Of the Inverse Deductive, or Historical Method' (SOL 8: 911–930) Mill referred to 'the general facts of history' (SOL 8: 917); 'the facts of history' (SOL 8: 917); 'the evidence of history' (SOL 8: 926); 'the indications of history' (SOL 8: 928), 'the facts of universal history' (SOL 8: 930); and 'the main facts of history' (SOL 8: 930). Mill's use goes beyond a simple reference to 'history' as record and reflects the intellectual project that Mill outlined in the *System of Logic*. This project was to detect a pattern in history. In short, Mill was concerned with charting 'the whole course of history'. (SOL 8: 928)

That, for Mill, 'history' had a course meant that it occurred in stages in which the succession from one stage to another was governed by discernible laws of causation. (SOL 8: 912) A scientific interest in 'history' was an interest in the derivation of these laws. 'History accordingly does, when judiciously examined, afford Empirical Laws of Society.' (SOL 8: 916)

Mill thought that those who used 'history' to refer to a pattern referred to either of two patterns. The first was a cycle or orbit; the second a progress or trajectory. (SOL 8: 913) Mill noted that 'one of the thinkers who earliest conceived the succession of historical events as subject to fixed laws, and endeavoured to discover these laws by an analytical survey of history, Vico, ... adopted the former view'. (SOL 8: 913) Mill, on the other hand, used 'history' to refer to 'a trajectory or progress, in lieu of an orbit or cycle'. (SOL 8: 913) For Mill, then, 'Philosophy of History ... [was] at once the verification, and the initial form, of the Philosophy of the Progress of Society.' (SOL 8: 930)

Mill's use of 'progress' was somewhat unusual in that he used it without intending to connote improvement. While he wrote that 'progressiveness ... [was] an idea involved in every just conception of social phenomena as the subject of a science' (SOL 8: 912), he also wrote that 'the words Progress and Progressiveness are not here to be understood as synonymous with improvement and tendency to improvement'. (SOL 8: 913) The most sense that can be made of this is that, in Mill's use, 'progress' is a synonym for the continuation of a pattern. The pattern itself need not lead to a better or higher state. Yet Mill also wrote that 'the general tendency is, and will continue to be, saving occasional and temporary exceptions, one of improvement; a tendency toward a better and happier state.' (SOL 8: 914)

This creates problems for understanding Mill's use of 'history'. 'History' refers to a predictable pattern of events which follows a trajectory. While this trajectory is generally toward a more desirable state, the pattern is not necessarily one of improvement. Mill seems to be toying with conventional uses of 'progress' in 'history' and threatens to lapse into language idling.

## 'Individuality'

In discussing 'individuality' Mill took the position that the word was being used to discipline or constrain those at whom it was directed. In opposition to this, Mill used 'individuality' as a recommendation or means for praising and not for criticising or rejecting. He believed that 'individuality' had come to be used in the same way as 'perversity' or 'abnormality' and, as a result, that people were not being encouraged to demonstrate 'individuality'. In responding to this, Mill was led into

a defence of 'eccentricity' – which might be understood to be an intermediate term with hazier illocutionary or perlocutionary aspects.

Mill's object is evident in oppositions he constructed between
'conformity' and 'individuality'. He even went so far as to develop an
historical account of that putative opposition:

> There has been a time when the element of spontaneity and individ-
> uality was in excess, and the social principle had a hard struggle with
> it.... But society has now fairly got the better of individuality; and
> the danger which threatens human nature is not the excess, but the
> deficiency, of personal impulses and preferences. Things are vastly
> changed, since the passions of those who were strong by station or
> by personal endowment were in a state of habitual rebellion against
> laws and ordinances, and required to be rigorously chained up to
> enable the persons within their reach to enjoy any particle of secu-
> rity. In our times, from the highest class of society down to the
> lowest, every one lives as under the eye of a hostile and dreaded
> censorship. (OL 18: 264)

In Mill's account, those with the courage or strength of mind to resist
this censorship were marked with labels that indicated that they were
dangerous and to be avoided. Words that indicated divergences from
the norm, such as 'individuality', were used to mark those to be
shunned or treated with caution. People, Mill wrote, who 'are of a
strong character, and break their fetters, ... become a mark for the
society which has not succeeded in reducing them to commonplace, to
point at with solemn warning as "wild," "erratic," and the like...'.
(OL 18: 267–8) In Mill's view, people who displayed 'any marked
demonstration of individuality' were classed by those who conformed
as 'wild and intemperate whom they are accustomed to look down
upon'. (OL 18: 271)

He believed that his society was characterised by 'a mass of influences hostile to Individuality'. (OL 18: 275) These influences could
only be resisted if 'the intelligent part of the public can be made to feel
its value – to see that it is good there should be differences, even
though not for the better, even though, as it may appear to them, some
should be for the worse'. (OL 18: 275)

Mill even came to the view that eccentricity, a word not usually used
to compliment, had to be used positively. He suggested that 'no society
in which eccentricity is a matter of reproach, can be in a wholesome
state'. (PPE 3: 209) 'Precisely because the tyranny of opinion is such

as to make eccentricity a reproach,' he wrote, 'it is desirable, in order to break through that tyranny, that people should be eccentric. Eccentricity has always abounded when and where strength of character has abounded; and the amount of eccentricity in a society has generally been proportional to the amount of genius, mental vigour, and moral courage which it contained.' (OL 18: 269)

Like everyone else, Mill used 'individuality' to refer to behaviour that differed from the norm. Unlike most other users, however, Mill used 'individuality' positively, as a commendation or recommendation. His challenge was with the illocutionary and perlocutionary acts in which 'individuality' was used in criticising and in inducing conformity. If nothing else, his discussions of 'individuality' highlight the ways in which the use of words have pronounced political effects.

## 'Custom'

Like all users, Mill used 'custom' to refer to practices that have been observed within a community consistently and over a significant period of time. His works highlight the fact that either of two illocutionary or perlocutionary acts can be committed in using 'custom'. One of these is to criticise longstanding practices and induce others to change those practices. The other is to praise those practices and to encourage others to follow them. Mill used 'custom' in both of these ways.

Using 'custom' to commend a practice and persuade others to follow it can take a variety of forms. Take the statement: 'It is customary for men of our culture to shake hands upon being introduced.' This is more than a report that these men tend to shake hands when they are introduced. When uttered to a person not of that culture, or one who wants to be treated as a man, it is to suggest to that person that he should shake hands upon being introduced to another man if he wishes to avoid confusion or ill-will.

Some users go further than recommending that a particular behaviour be adopted, and use 'custom' to induce, or enforce, conformity. Take the utterance: 'The custom in our family is that women learn to play the piano.' This is more than mere observation or recommendation and constitutes a ground for enforcing the learning of the piano for a daughter who may be expressing reluctance. In this case the use of 'custom' is part of attempting to ensure conformity to longstanding practice.

Recommending that someone follow a practice or persuading them to follow it is only one set of illocutionary and perlocutionary acts performed in using 'custom'. 'Custom' can also be used to diminish a practice and to bring another to depart from longstanding practice. Take the statement: 'These days, people get married because it is a custom to get married; they have no real reason to do so.' This use of 'custom' communicates a lack of necessity with respect to marriage and suggests that there are no reasons, apart from 'custom', for getting married. People who follow 'custom' are marked as unthinking and incapable of choosing for themselves. That people would rather be thought of as thinking and capable of choosing for themselves means they will be induced to think of the act of getting married differently and may even be induced to desist from getting married.

This latter use characterises a number of Mill's uses of 'custom'. In *On Liberty*, Mill referred to a 'despotism of custom', which, he argued, 'is everywhere the standing hindrance to human advancement, being in unceasing antagonism to that disposition to aim at something better than customary, which is called, according to circumstances, the spirit of liberty, or that of progress or improvement'. (OL 18: 272) Later, he added, that 'the progressive principle ... whether as the love of liberty or of improvement, is antagonistic to the sway of Custom, involving at least emancipation from that yoke; and the contest between the two constitutes the chief interest of the history of mankind.' (OL 18: 272) One of the most extreme forms of this use of 'custom' was Mill's statement that 'the greater part of the world has, properly speaking, no history, because the despotism of Custom is complete'. (OL 18: 272–3)

On other occasions, however, Mill used 'custom' in recommending and defending certain longstanding practices. He wrote of 'the limits which custom and prescription had set to the indulgence of each man's fancies or inclinations, or of attachment to anything which belonged to them as a nation, and which made them feel their unity as such.' (C 10: 137) Even *On Liberty* contains the following: 'I have said that it is important to give the freest scope possible to uncustomary things ... but independence of action, and disregard of custom are not solely deserving of encouragement ... and customs more worthy of general adoption, may be struck out....' (OL 18: 269–70)

The co-existence of two uses of the word 'custom' is no evidence of a lack of meaning on Mill's part. 'Custom' can be used to recommend and to criticise, to encourage and to discourage conformity. Mill might be said to have engaged in or promoted confusion with respect to his attitude to 'custom'. This view, however, presumes that 'custom' has only one proper use.

## PATHOLOGIES OF USE IN MILL'S WORKS

Mill's use of 'education', 'history', 'individuality' and 'custom' did not go beyond ordinary use and can be understood in terms of the conventions that govern the use of these words and the activities in which they are used meaningfully. He did not always use words in ways that followed ordinary use, however, and sometimes explicitly rejected conventional use. His view that meaning was a function of reference, rather than use, meant that he sometimes refused to be bound by the conventions that allowed for the meaningful use of words. He rejected common use of the word 'women' on the grounds that it is used in the maintenance of patriarchy. He appended words such as 'higher' and 'lower' to 'pleasure' to reflect what he took to be a real distinction between types of 'pleasure'. He used 'stationary state' unconventionally because he could not use it pessimistically, as it was used in the discourse of classical economics. He used 'necessity' in a way that reflected what he took to be its true meaning and suggested that other users were misguided in their use. He used 'association' in the same context as 'natural tie' without acknowledging that they belong to incompatible ways of talking about the mind.

### 'Women'

Mill believed that the way in which the word 'women' was used had contributed to undesirable social outcomes. This resulted from the way that its use went beyond the naming of physiological types and was bound up with maintaining male dominance in society. Mill believed that he understood something about 'women' that was not generally recognised and knew more than others of the truth about men and women. Viewed as an intervention around use, rather than meaning, Mill's project can be understood as attempting to discourage the use of 'women' as part of the recreation of patriarchy.

Mill believed that 'women' was used to designate a category of beings fitted for a particular and limited set of social functions. In short, Mill rejected what might be called, the grammar of the word 'women' which involved an unconscious shift from the designation of a category of people with particular physiological characteristics or reproductive roles to the designation of a category of people with specific social functions.

Mill objected to 'ideas and institutions by which the accident of sex is made the groundwork of ... a forced dissimilarity of social functions'.

(PPE 3: 765) He denied that the word 'women' could be used to identify consistent patterns of difference 'in bodily strength'. (OM 21: 42) On the other hand, Mill accepted that 'it would ... be extreme folly to suppose that ... differences of feeling and inclination only exist because women are brought up differently from men...'. (SOW 21: 334) He also suggested that 'women' might be subject to 'greater nervous susceptibility' than 'men', which made 'women' more suitable for certain functions and less so for others. (SOW 21: 307)

These differences, however, did indicate 'that the *nature* of the two sexes adapts them to their present function and position, and renders these appropriate to them.' (SOW 21: 276) Nor were these differences reflected in superior members of both sexes. Mill doubted whether there was 'any distinction between the highest masculine and the highest feminine character'. (LTC 12: 184) He suggested that 'the women, of all I have known who possessed the highest measure of what are considered feminine qualities, have combined with them more of the highest *masculine* qualities than I have ever seen in any but one or two men, and those one or two men were also in many respects almost women'. (LTC 12: 184)

Urbinati has suggested that in Mill's writings the words 'masculine' and 'feminine' took on different meanings. For him 'what is called "feminine" and "masculine" involves the existence of qualities that would be good for everyone to possess in order to develop their character in the best way.' (Urbinati 1991: 629) The result was that, for Mill, 'what people commonly call feminine and masculine are not incompatible properties at all. Rather, they are *human* attributes that for social and historical reasons are distributed separately among men and women and misleadingly called "feminine" and "masculine".' (Urbinati 1991: 629)

According to Urbinati, 'Mill introduced the distinction between what we call today sex and gender, that is, between biological (female and male) and social (feminine and masculine) spheres.' (1991: 628) From this she inferred that, for Mill, 'psychological qualities are not linked to sexual determinations and that, properly speaking, "masculine" and "feminine" do not exist, or, if they do, only as cultural and social products'. (Urbinati 1991: 628-9)

Urbinati's reading of Mill's works provides one way in which he can be understood to have done something in and to language. This should not be taken too far. Mill could not introduce a distinction into a language, as Urbinati suggested. At most, he could discuss ways in which words are used in order to point out the variety of activities, including undesirable ones, that were being performed in using words. Mill was mistaken when he believed that he could do anything more than note the consequences of the use of the word 'women'. That he could not merely describe word-use led him to attempt some sort of intervention into word-use. This attempt to do more than was available through the use of a word is a manifestation of the pathology Wittgenstein believed was common among philosophers.

## 'Pleasure'

Mill's attempt to make sense of a notion of 'higher' and 'lower' pleasures also reflected his view that meaning was reference. He assumed that he was referring to some demonstrated difference that required the use of qualifiers for the word 'pleasure'. The test which he applied to determine the quality of a pleasure ended up circular, however, and a clear indication that Mill could not do what he was trying to do. In short, Mill was not referring to some real difference. His reflections on this subject, however, do go some way toward indicating the extent to which 'higher' and 'lower' function to legitimise activities valued by cultural elites. Mill's works allow for an appreciation of the illocutionary and perlocutionary effects of appending 'higher' and 'lower' to 'pleasure'. These words function as ways of recommending some activities over others and inducing people to engage in one form of pleasure rather than another.

The word 'pleasure' is used as part of an individual's reporting about the state of mental states. To say 'I experience pleasure from listening to music' (or, more likely, 'I enjoy listening to music') is to tell others about oneself. To say that another experiences pleasure ('She takes pleasure in listening to music') is only meaningful in the presence of behavioural indicators conventionally taken to indicate the presence of pleasure. Reporting on another's 'pleasure' introduces the issue of the meaningful use of 'pleasure' when it is intended to refer to what another is experiencing.

Certainly, 'pleasure' is used as in talking about others. To refer to a person as a 'pleasure seeker' is to register disapproval. Judging the 'pleasures' of others is a common activity; though, usually it is represented to be simply describing or observing. Pairs of words such as 'higher' and 'lower' are often used in judging. That these words are not always recognised as judgements, or recommendations, creates problems for those who want to use them in this way. If a person cannot understand why one 'pleasure' is better than another they cannot be influenced in the desired manner.

To overcome this problem, and to correct misguided or recalcitrant people, Mill introduced an external measure through which pleasures were demonstrated to be 'higher' or 'lower'. The following passage is typical of Mill's attempt to demonstrate qualitative differences among 'pleasures':

> If I am asked, what I mean by difference of quality in pleasures, or what makes one pleasure more valuable than another, merely as a pleasure, except in being greater in amount, there is but one possible answer. Of two pleasures, if there be one to which all or almost all who have experience of both give a decided preference, irrespective of any feeling of moral obligation to prefer it, that is the most desirable pleasure. If one of the two is, by those who are competently acquainted with both, placed so far above the other that they prefer it, even though knowing it to be attended with a greater amount of discontent, and would not resign it for any quantity of the other pleasure which their nature is capable of, we are justified in ascribing to the preferred enjoyment a superiority in quality, so far outweighing quantity as to render it, in comparison, of small account. Now it is an unquestionable fact that those who are equally acquainted with, and equally capable of appreciating and enjoying both, do give a most marked preference to the manner of existence which employs their higher faculties. Few human creatures would consent to be changed into any of the lower animals, for a promise of the fullest allowance of a beast's pleasures.... (U 10: 211)

Mill's test for determining 'higher' and 'lower' pleasures appears to be public, in that it seems to rely on behavioural indicators and can be checked with respect to meaningful use through reference to those indicators. But the test refers only to the behaviour of a limited portion of the population (i.e. those who agree with Mill).

The test is perverse in that it relies on the behaviour of particular people. It becomes farcical when even the behaviour of those Mill considers 'qualified' to judge is unreliable. Mill is honest enough to accept that everyone, including those who can discriminate between 'pleasures', is drawn to pursue the 'lower' form.

> It may be objected, that many who are capable of the higher pleasures, occasionally, under the influence of temptation, postpone them to the lower. But this is quite compatible with a full appreciation of

the intrinsic superiority of the higher.... It may be further objected, that many who begin with youthful enthusiasm for everything noble, as they advance in years sink into indolence and selfishness. But I do not believe that those who undergo this very common change, voluntarily choose the lower description of pleasures in preference to the higher. I believe that before they devote themselves exclusively to the one, they have already become incapable of the other. Capacity for the nobler feelings is in most natures a very tender plant, easily killed, not only by hostile influences, but by mere want of sustenance.... (U 10: 212–13)

Mill's honesty undermines his test and reveals it to be what can often be found in discussions of 'pleasure': an attempt to influence the behaviour of others.

Mill was not doing something altogether unusual in introducing a distinction between 'higher' and 'lower' 'pleasures'. This practice will persist as long as there are people who wish to commit illocutionary and perlocutionary acts in which certain 'pleasures' are discounted and through which others are induced to pursue particular 'pleasures'. Like many others, Mill wanted people to recognise greater value in some activities. He attempted to do this by identifying real differences between 'pleasures'. In recognising that those he relied on to demonstrate differences in quality were not reliable guides he rendered his test meaningless – in that it lacked any consistent behavioural indicators which regularly registered a difference in quality. That Mill could not even rely on the behaviour of those who shared his prejudices highlights the illocutionary and perlocutionary acts committed by those who, like Mill, appended words that indicated difference in quality when using 'pleasure'.

### 'Stationary State'

That Mill used the phrase 'stationary state' reflected his exposure to the developing technical discourse of economics. His use was not consistent with the conventions that governed its use in economics, however. Mill may have been correct in responding to a tendency on the part of classical economists to think that the terms of economic discourse referred to more than just economic conditions. He was not correct to think that he could employ the phrase without the negative or pessimistic connotations it had for economists. The question is not whether a 'stationary state' is more than simply an economic state. It was used by classical economists to refer to a society that was stagnant in all respects. Mill could not meaningfully use the phrase in any other way. All that was open to him was to point out that economists exceeded the limits of technical discourse in using 'stationary state' in the way that they did.

That set of practices referred to by 'economics' is a technical activity governed by particular rules or conventions that result in meaningful communication. While it was less developed in Mill's day, it still makes sense to think of the rules or conventions for the meaningful use of terms by economists as belonging to a language available only to a limited set of technical users. This is not to say that the language of economics does not overlap with non-technical or ordinary language. It simply means that the rules or conventions that govern the meaningful use of terms in economics are sufficiently particular to require an understanding of those rules or conventions.

Part of understanding rules or conventions for meaningful use is an appreciation of the relationship between the various terms that are part of that technical language. Knowing how to use a term is knowing how it fits into what may be called a conceptual web. Knowing how to play chess, for example, is more than knowing the ways that chess pieces can be moved according to the rules of chess. It is also to understand the relative worth of the pieces. It is knowing what winning is and understanding the usefulness of different pieces to different strategies for winning. Not to understand that the king is the central chess-piece for both white and black is not to understand chess.[29]

The technical discourse of economics is a conceptual web in which certain terms are primary and others secondary. Terms such as 'capital', 'population', 'wages', 'profits', 'labour' are primary. The phrase 'stationary state' is secondary. Whether a state is 'stationary' is determined by the core terms that represent key economic indicators.

Something of the conceptual web of classical economics is present in the following passage written by Thomas Malthus.

The command of a certain quantity of food is absolutely necessary to the labourer in order to support himself, and such a family as will maintain a merely stationary population. Consequently, if poorer lands which required more labour were successively taken into cultivation, it would not be possible for the corn wages of each individual labourer to be diminished in proportion to the diminished produce; a greater proportion of the whole would necessarily go to labour; and the rate of profits would continue regularly falling till the accumulation of capital would cease. Such would be the necessary course of profits and wages in the progressive accumulation of capital, as applied to the progressive cultivation of new and less fertile land, or the further improvement of what had been before cultivated; and on the supposition here made, the rates both of profits and of real wages would be highest at first, and would regularly diminish together, till they both came to a stand at the same period, and the demand for an increase in produce ceased to be effective.

(Malthus 1989: 299)

The terms in this passage to which attention may usefully be directed are: population, labour, wages, profits, demand, accumulation, and capital. Population depends upon the ability of labourers to support their families. Wages are determined by the labour required in production. The more wages provided to the labourer the less profits are derived. This, in turn, leads to a decline in the rate of the accumulation of capital. This decline ultimately leads to decline in the rates of profits and wages. This leads to a decline in demand for produce.

The core term here is 'capital' and the crucial process is the accumulation of capital. The rate of this accumulation is a result of the derivation of profits which is affected by the level of wages. The level of wages is a function of the amount of labour required in production. Wages are, however, independent of the productivity of labour. The more production is shifted to areas that require greater amounts of labour, the less profits result and the accumulation of capital reduces.

The amount of labour available is independent of the amount of capital available. The effects of an increase in population will vary according to whether the amount of capital also increases. If it does not, then the wages that are paid to labourers allow only for the maintenance of the existing population.

But, independently of any particular efforts of prudence on the part of the poor, it is certain that the supplies of labour and the supplies of capital do not always keep pace with each other. They are often separated at some distance, and for a considerable period; and sometimes population increases faster than capital, and at other times capital increases faster than population. It is obvious, for instance, that from the very nature of population, and the time required to bring full-grown labourers into the market, a sudden increase of capital cannot effect a proportionate supply of labour in less than sixteen or eighteen years; and, on the other hand, when capital is stationary from want of will to accumulate, it is well known that population in general continues to increase faster than capital, till the wages of labour are reduced to that standard which, with the actual habits of the country, are no more than sufficient to maintain a stationary population.

(Malthus 1989: 306–7)

These core and peripheral terms work according to conventions that govern the presentation of economic phenomena. Either through carelessness or the early stages in the development of economic discourse, technical terms that were part of the language of economics were mixed with those which belonged to popular, non-technical, discourse.

In the early stages of the development of economics as a technical discourse, economists may well have found it impossible to distinguish their activity as economists from their activity as social and political commentators. The following quotation from Adam Smith is an example of this combination of the technical and the non-technical.

It deserves to be remarked, perhaps, that it is in the progressive state when the society is advancing to the further acquisition, rather than when it has acquired its full complement of riches that the condition of the labouring poor, of the great body of people, seems to be the happiest and the most comfortable. It is hard in the stationary, and miserable in the declining state. The progressive state is in reality the cheerful and the hearty state to all the different orders of the society. The stationary is dull, the declining melancholy.

(Smith 1976: 99)

Smith's use of 'progressive' in connection with the acquisition of riches is a conventional technical use. His linking of 'progressive' with 'cheerful' and 'hearty', of 'stationary' with 'dull', 'declining' and 'melancholy' may have been common among writers of his time but is not a technical use.

'Stationary state' is used to refer to social conditions, not economic conditions. The sense in which 'stationary' is being used here is one in which a society is understood to be standing still. No problem is occasioned by the use of 'stationary state' to refer to an economy. An economy can be meaningfully described as stationary when the rates of accumulation of capital or riches do not change. The centrality of these to an economy makes meaningful their use as part of the definition of a 'stationary state'.

The problem lies in the presumption that a society can be described as static if standard measures of economic activity show no increase.

To use 'stationary state' to indicate a standing-still in all aspects of a society goes beyond technical use. Mill recognised this. Instead of simply noting this impropriety on the part of classical economists, however, he sought to use the phrase without the negative connotations it had within classical economists. He might be understood to have corrected the failure of economists to use economic discourse to refer to economics by drawing attention to the way in which a stationary economic state could be understood as a positive social state. This would be to presume, however, that the phrase could be meaningfully used in an unconventional manner – remembering that at all times the issue is not the true nature of a 'stationary state'.

Mill recognised that the 'impossibility of ultimately avoiding the stationary state ... must have been, to the political economists of the last two generations, an unpleasing and discouraging prospect; for the tone and tendency of their speculations goes completely to identify all that is economically desirable with the progressive state, and with that alone'. (PPE 3: 752) Unlike the classical economists he did not 'regard the stationary state of capital and wealth with the unaffected aversion so generally manifested towards it by political economists of the old school'. (PPE: 753–4)

The reason for this was that Mill was 'comparatively indifferent to the kind of economical progress which excites the congratulations of ordinary politicians; the mere increase of production and accumulation'. (PPE 3: 754) Mill's departure from the conceptual web of economics is even clearer when he argued that 'a stationary condition of capital and population implies no stationary state of human improvement. There would be as much scope as ever for all kinds of mental culture, and moral and social progress ... when minds ceased to be engrossed by the art of getting on.' (PPE 3: 756)

To use 'stationary state' to imply more than a static economic condition may be taken to exceed the possibilities made available within economic discourse. Classical economists were not economists when they claimed that 'stationary state' referred to more than an economic state. Mill did not correct their use, however; he simply rejected it. His use was unconventional and, as a result, meaningless.

Before leaving this discussion of Mill's use of 'stationary state' I think it worth noting that the colonisation, as Habermas might put it, of political discourse by economic discourse appears to have increased. That most discussions of politics seem to be governed by economic terms makes economics the dominant discourse. Mill's strategy of reconstructing the terms of economics is not an effective strategy, as it creates

creates meaningless uses while it perpetuates the colonisation. Putting economics back in its place by reminding economists that their discourse does not include all possible social and political objects may be a better strategy; though the genie is probably well and truly out of the bottle.

## 'Association'

In its technical use within psychological discourse, 'association' is used to refer to an artificial link within the mind. The use of 'artificial' in this instance is intended to indicate that the link is not necessary, in the sense of being a link to which the mind is not predisposed. The character that results from the development of a plethora of associations can also be understood to be artificial. Mill clearly departed from this way of talking about the mind and character when he used 'natural tie' in the same context. By using 'association' and 'natural tie' Mill combined two ways of talking about the mind. He was not wrong to do so, in the sense that he somehow got the mind wrong. He was simply inconsistent in the way that he wrote about the mind.

'Association' figures in a number of different technical and non-technical discourses. 'Voluntary associations' is part of legal discourse. 'Political associations' is part of the discourse of politics.[30] In the technical discourse of psychology, 'association' is used to refer to a process in which certain experiences are recorded and connected in the mind. Experiences are said to be 'associated' when they have been linked such that the re-experience or recall of one leads to the recalling of the other.

In 'associationist' discourse the mind was a *tabula rasa* or blank slate. '*Rasa*' or 'blank' indicates both emptiness and without predisposition. '*Tabula*' or 'slate' connotes a capacity to be inscribed. 'Association' refers to the processes of inscription and connection which, in turn, may be characterised by two further images: absorption and moulding. The primary unit is an experience. When an experience or sensory event (a sensation or set of related sensations) occurs in the mind it is inscribed upon or absorbed by the mind. When an experience occurs at the same time as another experience these experiences become part of the same record. When two experiences are recorded together, whenever one is called up the other is also brought to mind. These experiences are said to be 'associated'. Associations are reinforced through repetition – the inscription becomes more permanent. They are weakened when one of the two associated experiences does not occur with the other.

Minds contain stronger or weaker 'associations'. They are constellations of associated experiences in which each set of associations has significance for the behaviour or attitudes to be expected of an individual. 'A desire, an emotion, an idea of the higher order of abstraction, even our judgments and volitions when they have become habitual, are called up by association, according to precisely the same laws as our simple ideas.' (SOL 8: 856) In this way of speaking, the mind is a complex and evolving set of 'associations' that result in particular responses to externally and internally generated stimuli.

'Natural ties' play no role in associationist discourse (unless the process of inscribing and connecting is taken to be 'natural'). An associationist represents the mind as formed through experiences and not through associations that are not the result of experiences. To introduce 'natural ties' as something different from 'associations' makes for confusion in the representation of the mind.

Because of his belief that he could represent the mind in some true or complete fashion Mill ended up saying nothing meaningful about the mind. Consider the following passage:

> I had always heard it maintained by my father, and was myself convinced, that the object of education should be to form the strongest possible associations of the salutary class; associations of pleasure with all things beneficial to the great whole, and of pain with all the things hurtful to it. This doctrine appeared inexpugnable; but it now seemed to me on retrospect, that my teachers had occupied themselves but superficially with the means of forming and keeping up these salutary associations. They seemed to have trusted altogether to the old familiar instruments, praise and blame, reward and punishment. Now I did not doubt that by these means, begun early and applied unremittingly, intense associations of pain and pleasure, especially of pain, might be created, and might produce desires and aversions capable of lasting undiminished to the end. But there must always be something artificial and casual in associations thus produced. The pains and pleasures thus forcibly associated with things, are not connected with them by any natural tie ... (A 1: 141)

In this passage Mill suggests not only that 'associations' are superficial, artificial and unnatural, but that this is somehow not enough.

He even introduced an anti-associative capacity of the mind and wrote: 'the habit of analysis has a tendency to wear away the feelings ... and no associations whatever could ultimately resist this dissolving force'. (A 1: 141) Analysis was not simply a cause of the dissolving of connection, for Mill; it was also an alternative source of connection. Thus, 'we owe to analysis our clearest knowledge of the permanent sequences in nature; the real connexions [*sic*] between Things, not dependent on our will and feelings'. (A 1: 141)

The consequence of all this is that Mill was not, as he thinks, closer to a true representation of the mind; instead, he was further from sense in describing the mind. In retaining both 'associations' and 'natural ties' Mill ends up outside both ways of talking about the mind.

For conventional users, 'associations' are inscriptions and connections introduced by external factors. For them, there is no distinction between 'natural' and 'artificial' connections. Minds are blank. 'Associations' are simply connections. What they are and how they are achieved is clear. For Mill, on the other hand, connections can be either 'artificial' or 'natural'. 'Artificial' and 'natural' are not part of the same way of talking about the mind. The issue, from a linguistic perspective, is not adequacy, it is consistency. That Mill did not commit himself fully to the language of 'associationism' but did not deny it meant that he ended up with nonsense.

## 'Necessity'

Mill's discussion of the idea of 'necessity' may be understood as linguistic. He argued that the word had been tainted by ordinary use and could not be properly used in philosophical discussions in which the freedom, or lack thereof, of the will was discussed.[31] In his view in its popular use 'necessity' implied inevitability, but that it needn't do so when used by philosophers. The key question, in this context, was whether these connotations can be understood to be simply a product of a mixing of ordinary and technical use.

In its technical use 'necessity' operates with 'free will' to constitute different terms used in philosophical discussions of the extent to which individuals are able to control their actions. To suggest that actions are 'necessary' or are a result of 'necessity' is to represent actions as determined by factors other than an individual's volition. 'Free will' on the other hand is used to deny this and to affirm the power of an individual's volition.

Mill didn't reject the position he called 'Philosophical Necessity'. He merely questioned the use of the term 'necessity'. In his view, those who had used the term in philosophical discussions had represented 'human volitions and actions to be necessary and inevitable'. (SOL 8: 836) Actions that were of 'necessity' could not be otherwise. Mill attributed this connotation to the mixing of ordinary and technical uses of 'necessary' and 'necessity'. The error of treating 'necessity' or 'of necessity' as 'irresistible' was a function of popular use of 'necessity'.

> This error is almost wholly an effect of the associations with a word; and ... would be prevented, by forbearing to employ, for the expression of a simple fact of causation, so extremely inappropriate a term as Necessity. That word, in its other acceptations, involves much more than mere uniformity of sequence: it implies irresistibleness. Applied to the will, it only means that the given cause will be followed by the effect, subject to all possibilities of counteraction by other causes: but in common use it stands for the operation of those causes exclusively, which are supposed too powerful to be counteracted at all.... The application of the same term to the agencies on which human actions depend, as is used to express those agencies of nature which are really uncontrollable, cannot fail, when habitual, to create a feeling of uncontrollableness in the former also. (SOL 8: 839)

Such an habitual connection meant, for Mill, that those who used the word 'necessity' were misled by its usual associations.

> That whatever happens, could not have happened otherwise unless something had taken place which was capable of preventing it, no one surely needs hesitate to admit. But to call this by the name 'necessity' is to use the term in a sense so different from its primitive and familiar meaning, from that which it bears in the common associations of life, as to amount almost to a play upon words. The associations derived from the ordinary sense of the term will adhere to it in spite of all we can do: and though the doctrine of Necessity, as stated by most who hold it, is very remote from fatalism, it is probable that most necessitarians are fatalists. (SOL 8: 839)

His view that 'necessity' did not connote fated, led Mill to question the use of the term in philosophical discussions.

In the end, Mill decided that no resolution of the philosophical issues involved would be possible if 'necessity' continued to be used. He considered the use of 'necessity' to be 'one of the most signal instances in philosophy of the abuse of terms, and its practical consequences one of the most striking examples of the power of language over our associations'. (SOL 8: 841) As a result, he argued, the issue could not be resolved 'until the objectionable term is dropped'. (SOL 8: 841)

That Mill believed that he could get closer to understanding the issue properly meant that his was not a linguistic intervention. His argument, that technical discourse had lost coherence as a result of the effect that the use of words in popular use had on the use of the same word in technical discourse, relies on the view that the connotations of 'necessity' are a result of popular use and not technical use. Mill's assumption that the connotations of popular use need not be mirrored in technical use is questionable. If, as Mill seems to suggest, there are two different ways of representing human volition (as free and unfree), then Mill's use of 'necessity' without a connotation of unfree seems odd. This is a result of his view that the issue can be resolved, which led him to resolve it by disturbing one of the ways of representing human volition.

## OTHER INSIGHTS DERIVED FROM A LINGUISTIC FRAME-WORK

That Mill was prone to philosophical pathologies does not mean that he was always oblivious to problems that derived from them. His rejection of attempts to specify a 'proper' role for 'government' might be understood in this light. A linguistic framework also offers some insights into Mill's category of 'self-regarding' actions. A consideration of 'self-regarding' within the linguistic framework also sheds light on the use of the word 'private'. Commentators who rejected Mill's statement that he had adopted a 'qualified Socialism' also provide grist to a linguistic mill in that they open up questions about the meaningful use of the word 'socialism'.

### The 'Proper' Role of 'Government'

While there remain interesting things to be said about 'government' (Sparkes 1994: 17) and 'governance' (Kooiman 1993), Mill's work is not particularly interesting on this ground. Mill's discussion of the use of 'proper' in the context delimiting a proper role for government, however, is interesting from a linguistic perspective. Mill rejected the project of specifying a 'proper' role for 'government' on the ground that it was a misguided enterprise. Mill's objection was not precisely a linguistic one, but it does point to an important philosophical pathology in this instance.[32] In his view, no role could be predetermined for government because what was required of government changed over time. For Mill, the question of the proper role of government was a contextually situated question that had no general, timeless, or absolute answer.

Mill believed that his times were particularly characterised by a turning to this question of the 'proper' role of government. He claimed that 'one of the most disputed questions both in political science and in practical statesmanship at this particular period, relates to the proper limits of the functions and agency of governments'. (PPE 3: 799) The problem with this question, he argued, was the presumption that the 'proper' functions of government could be delimited. Against this presumption Mill argued that 'the necessary functions of government ... [are] not capable of being circumscribed by those very clear lines of demarcation, which, in the inconsiderateness of popular discussion, it is often attempted to draw round them'. (PPE 3: 800)

In some ways Mill's argument parallels Wittgenstein's approach to attempts to determine meaning by separating words from the context in which they are used. Pitkin summarised the position in the following way:

> In our craving for generality, we try to abstract from all the partic-
> ular, concrete cases in which an expression might actually be used,
> to contemplate it in isolation, at rest. We try to consider it apart from
> any context; or, one might say, we create a new and special context
> of abstract contemplation. But this special context is not a context for
> speech; in it, language is not being used by one person to tell another
> something, but as an object for study. When we speculate this way
> about concepts, Wittgenstein says, 'the language-game in which they
> are to be applied is missing.' Consequently, conceptual problems
> 'arise when language *goes on holiday*'; they involve 'confusions
> which occupy us ... when language is like an engine idling, not
> when it is doing work.' (1972: 93)

Mill resisted definition of the 'proper' functions of government because he considers that such a definition must be generated in a specific social context. For him, 'the proper functions of government are not a fixed thing, but are different in different states of society'. (CRG 19: 383)

Instead Mill linked 'proper' with 'expedience' and 'convenience'. He argued that government could legitimately 'assume powers and execute functions for which no other reason can be assigned except the simple one, that they conduce to general convenience'. (PPE 3: 803) At this point his discussions clearly diverged from those generated within a linguistic approach. Mill argued that 'the admitted functions of govern-ment embrace a much wider field than can easily be included within the ring-fence of any restrictive definition'. (PPE 3: 803) In his view, these functions were justified on the ground of 'general expediency'. No function could be rejected on the basis of 'any general rule, save the simple and vague one, that it should never be admitted but when the case of expediency is strong'. (PPE 3: 803–4)

Mill's rejection of attempts to define a 'proper' role for government is interesting to the extent to which he rejected this whole activity. This view has some resonance for those who adopt a linguistic approach to reading works of political theory. Unfortunately, Mill threatened to return to philosophical pathology when he argued that a 'proper' role for government could be defined within a specific context through applying tests of 'expedience' or 'convenience' – though 'expedience' and 'convenience' may be understood to be contextually determined and the threat of philosophical pathology recedes.

## 'Self-regarding'

Interesting observations also emerge from a linguistic perspective with respect to Mill's use of 'self-regarding'. This use returns a linguistic reader to the illocutionary and perlocutionary acts committed in and through word-use. In this context, his use of 'self-regarding' can be understood in terms of speech acts performed through the use of the word 'private'. Mill used 'self-regarding' in the way that 'private' is used: to mark a phenomenon, to challenge those who wished to invade it and to ward them off. That 'self-regarding' was not ordinarily used in this way meant, of course, that Mill could not do what he attempted to do.

The word 'private' is used to mark certain objects or interactions. To call a letter 'private' is to signify that it is a letter that is not open to all. To refer to property as 'private' is to mark that property as one to which access is limited. To describe a meeting as 'private' is to announce that only certain people are allowed to attend. To announce that a letter, property or meeting is 'private' is also to induce others to treat that letter, property or meeting in particular ways. Others are called to 'respect' the privacy asserted.

Benn and Gaus emphasised the way in which the use of 'private' was about control and argued that 'a concern for one's privacy is typically a concern to be able to control the dissemination of information about oneself: to insist that a certain piece of information is private is not necessarily to assert that no one but oneself should have access to it, but rather that the access should be under one's control.' (1983: 8) To emerge from a room and direct at someone the statement 'This is a private meeting!' may well lead them to desist from entering that room or to engage in some other form of respecting the privateness[33] of the meeting. The statement is a means to maintain control over access to the meeting.

Mill used 'self-regarding' in his discussion of interference in an individual's acts and omissions. He distinguished a category of actions that were not open to legitimate interference by others. Mill wrote that 'with the personal tastes and self-regarding concerns of individuals the public has no business to interfere'. (OL 18: 285) No matter how tempting interference might be in such a case, 'purely self-regarding misconduct cannot properly be meddled with in the way of prevention or punishment'. (OL 18: 295) On the other hand, if 'a person is led to violate a distinct and assignable obligation to any other person or persons, the case is taken out of the self-regarding class, and becomes amenable to moral disapprobation in the proper sense...'. (OL 18: 281) Mill considered the protection of the self-regarding sphere to be of paramount importance. He argued that 'engines of moral repression have been wielded more strenuously against divergences from the reigning opinion in self-regarding than even in social matters'. (OL 18: 226)

From the above, Mill's category of 'self-regarding' actions can be understood as used to: identify a behaviour as belonging to a particular type or category of behaviour; to protect certain behaviour from interference from others; and to constitute a call on others to justify interference with a certain act.

The term 'self-regarding' could readily be considered perverse and, for the most part, meaningless. When viewed as a speech-act, it becomes more meaningful (though, given the limited number of English speakers who would know what was meant, it would rarely function as an effective speech-act). Once the notions that words like 'private' can be defined and understood in use, we can understand something of what Mill was trying to do in using 'self-regarding'. Mill believed that he was identifying something real about actions when he identified some as 'self-regarding'. While he was misguided in this respect, speech act theory makes some sense of what he was trying to do in using 'self-regarding'.

## 'Socialism'

One of the more interesting instances of Mill's use of words was his description of himself as having adopted a 'qualified socialism'. This comment is interesting because of commentators' responses to this self-designation. These responses highlight problems associated with using the word 'socialism' (a problem compounded by the addition of 'qualified'). The issue that arises concerns the possibility of using the word 'socialism' meaningfully.

In his *Autobiography* Mill wrote that his thinking had undergone two major shifts. The first was 'a shifting of my political ideal from pure democracy, as commonly understood by its partisans, to the modified form of it, which is set forth in my *Considerations on Representative Government*.' (A 1: 199) The second was 'a greater approximation, so far as regards the ultimate prospects of humanity, to a qualified Socialism'. (A 1: 199)

Responses from commentators to this passage provide a starting-point for any consideration of the meaning of Mill's use of 'qualified Socialism'. For some writers, Mill's use of this phrase was empty, if not wrong. In their view, he was never a 'socialist'. Anschutz described Mill's self-description as 'plainly an incredible statement'. (1963: 31) McCloskey concluded that 'Mill was never a socialist although in the *Autobiography* he claimed to have been one'. (1969: 191). A variant of this response is the argument that Mill's version of socialism was not 'really' socialism. 'Mill has been called a socialist', Bluhm wrote (neglecting the fact that Mill called himself one), 'but the kind of collectivism he envisages is a far cry from the system of government ownership which most people identify with the word "socialism" today.' (1965: 463) Duncan suggested that Mill 'did not become in any serious sense a socialist'. (1973: 244). Kurer concluded that of those who consider Mill's 'socialism' 'the majority view holds that Mill was not a socialist, let alone a committed one'. (1992: 222)

Bluhm's point about differences in the meaning of socialism in different time periods is important. It may lead to the view that contemporary readers cannot understand Mill's use because the rules or conventions that govern the meaningful use of 'socialism' have changed. This position, however, presupposes the existence of rules or conventions that govern the meaningful use of 'socialism'. For if 'socialism' was not, and is not, governed by identifiable rules or conventions then neither Mill nor the commentators identified above are saying anything meaningful.

The word 'socialism' is used in a variety of speech situations. The most important for present purposes is its use in the designation or categorisation either of a particular political order or of a particular approach to political organisation. This is reflected in descriptions such

as 'the socialism practised in China' or references such as 'the socialism of Charles Fourier'. A distinction can be made, however, between
the use of 'socialism' in popular political discussions and its use as part
of the technical discussions of political theorists or those who study,
and sometimes compare, political orders.

The meaning of popular uses of 'socialism' has been affected by the
way in which it has been used as part of illocutionary and perlocutionary acts. To refer to someone as a 'socialist' is, in many Anglophone
countries, a strategy through which others, and especially opponents in
electoral contests, can be marked as extremists, utopians, incompetent,
or, more generally, not to be trusted. The intended effect is to induce
some resistance in the audience to that person or candidate. This effect
relies on conventions associated with persuasion and not taxonomy. In
short, it does not rely on the description being in any way accurate and
actually describing the persuasion of the person who is so labelled.

Those engaged in more technical practices require other rules or
conventions that make for meaningful categories. The question of
whether Mill was a 'socialist', in this case, relies on rules or conventions that allow an individual's views on political organisation to be
designated 'socialist'. This test can only be applied if it is still meaningful to use the word 'socialism' to describe a commitment to
particular principles of social and political organisation.

In his *A Dictionary of Modern Politics*, Robertson argued that confusion over the meaning of 'socialism' was

> not because of ambiguity or vagueness, but because it is a concept
> that operates in several different ideological vocabularies. Within
> Marxism, socialism has a very technical meaning, referring to a
> phase before the establishment of true communism. Outside that
> debate, socialism does become extremely vague, and is best differ-
> entiated into a number of versions, such as Christian socialism,
> social democracy and so on.
>
> (Robertson 1993: 438)

Fetscher observed that 'Hans Muller ... has traced the history of the
term "socialism" back to Benedictine Anselm Desing (1699–1772), who
in 1753 made a distinction for polemical purposes between Christian
scholars and modern exponents of natural law who postulated a natural
sociality of man.' (Fetscher 1973: 422) Fetscher continued that

> the earliest use of the word had reference to those who took it for
> granted that man was by nature social. This would then provide a

certain connection with the later Marxian use of the word, inasmuch as Karl Marx regarded the 'unsociable sociability' of men not as a constant of nature but as a historically surmountable feature of individuals in the competitive society of capitalism. In the socialistically structured society a sort of 'natural' human sociality would evolve, and political repression of any kind could therefore become superfluous. The connection between the sense of the word employed by the enlightened bourgeois and that of the proletarian revolutionary would thus give expression to a continuity of interest in the cause of emancipation.... In their modern, anti-bourgeois sense, 'socialism' and 'socialist' first came into use only at the beginning of the 19th century. Carl Grundberg first finds the term 'socialism' in France in 1831–32, and from 1837 onwards in England; but he is unable to establish for certain whether it was derivative or an independent formation of the term. The word 'socialist' was first used in its modern sense in 1827 to describe the followers of Robert Owen.

(Fetscher 1973: 422)

Multiplicity of use did not stop Fetscher from offering his own definition:

'Socialism' can be defined here as designating a theory and a movement arising out of bourgeois society, which has set itself the aim of re-ordering man's communal life on the basis of common ownership. This theory and the movements named after it must be distinguished from the designation given to social relations in the period after the revolution. As applied to them, 'socialism' is taken in general to mean an order of society in which the means of production are communally owned and in which everyone works according to his capacities but is also differentially rewarded according to the varying quantity and quality of the work he performs. Under socialism, therefore, the privileges of differing ownership are abolished, but not the advantages of differing talents or other external contingencies.

(Fetscher 1973: 422–3)

Three different, though not unconnected, ways of using the word 'socialism' are evident in these passages. The first use is to refer to the ideas of a person who takes human beings to be naturally social. The second is to designate a set of ideas in which collective ownership is understood to be the means for achieving social harmony. The third, more technical use within Marxist discourse, is to refer to a social formation that is a precursor to communism.

The different uses currently available do not appear to differ markedly from those available to Mill. According to Mill:

> The word Socialism, which originated among the English Communists, and was assumed by them as a name to designate their own doctrine, is now, on the Continent, employed in a larger sense; not necessarily implying Communism or the entire abolition of private property, but applied to any system which requires that the land and the instruments of production should be the property, not of individuals, but of communities or associations, or of the government. (PPE 2: 203)

Mill further elaborated upon the divergent uses of the word 'socialism':

> Among those who call themselves Socialists, two kinds of persons may be distinguished. There are, in the first place, those whose plans for a new order of society, in which private property and individual competition are to be superseded and other motives to action substituted, are on the scale of a village community or township, and would be applied to an entire country by the multiplication of such self-acting units; of this character are the systems of Owen, of Fourier, and the more thoughtful and philosophic Socialists generally. The other class, who are more a product of the Continent than of Great Britain and may be called the revolutionary Socialists, propose to themselves a much bolder stroke. Their scheme is the management of the whole productive resources of the country by one central authority, the general government. And with this view some of them avow as their purpose that the working classes, or somebody in their behalf, should take possession of all of the property of the country, and administer it for the general benefit. (COS 5: 737)

In Mill's view, the term 'socialist' was 'a designation under which schemes of very diverse character are comprehended and confounded, but which implies at least a remodelling generally approaching to abolition of the institution of private property'. (COS 5: 709) For Mill 'the distinctive feature of Socialism is not that all things are held in common, but that production is carried on upon the common account, and that the instruments of production are held as common property'. (COS 5: 738)

A number of possibilities may be presented that provide different understandings of Mill's use of the phrase 'qualified Socialism'. The use of this phrase may be to indicate that the 'socialism' that Mill meant was not that proposed by 'revolutionary Socialists' or by 'English

Communists' or in 'simple Communism'. 'Qualified socialism' may have been used to distinguish the more limited, and in Mill's view more practical, forms of 'socialism'. On the other hand, Mill may have used the word 'qualified' to indicate that he had some hesitation or reservation about even the more limited forms of organisation of productive forces that could be referred to as 'socialism'.

If the first view is the better interpretation, then many of those who dismissed Mill's 'socialism' may be understood to be doing so on the basis that Mill did not support the forms of organisation of productive forces that they take to reflect 'socialism'. In this use, Mill did not advocate 'socialism' because he did not mean by it what they mean by it. This view would be persuasive if some clear rules or conventions that govern the use of the word 'socialism' could be identified. These rules would then allow the conclusion that Mill's use of 'socialism' does not reflect current rules or conventions. In this case what these commentators are actually saying is that Mill was not a 'socialist' because we could not meaningfully call him a 'socialist' since the form of organisation of productive forces that he supported as 'qualified Socialism' does not represent what could be called socialism today.

If the second view is adopted, commentators' responses to Mill's self-designation can be understood as suggestions that Mill was never wholeheartedly committed to the reorganisation of the productive forces in society along any of the lines proposed by those who, in his day, were referred to as 'socialists'. Mill was not a 'socialist', in this use, because he was never so without hesitation or reservation.

The first of these interpretations of the commentators' reactions to Mill's self-description relies upon the existence of rules or conventions. In this case, commentators deny the existence of rules or conventions which allow Mill to meaningfully describe himself as adopting a 'socialism' of any kind. The second relies upon the view that 'socialists' must be socialists without reservation or hesitation. In the end, either of these positions may be taken with respect to Mill's use of 'qualified Socialism' to describe his position on political organisation.

A variety of responses to Mill's use of 'qualified socialism' to describe the political position he came to adopt are available. One is that it was meaningless because, due to persistent confusions in use, no clear conventions exist to govern its meanings and no one could or can use the word meaningfully. Another is that Mill's use of 'qualified' renders the self-description meaningless. A third is that it is meaningful because it can be understood to mean that Mill, given his understanding that there were multiple uses of the word, supported a less radical form.

The question of whether or not Mill was a socialist gives rise to a number of considerations that go to the issue of whether the word can be used meaningfully. Popular use in Anglophone countries is generally as part of illocutionary and perlocutionary acts which, to a significant extent, are effective due to confusion over the meaning of 'socialism'. When considered in terms of technical uses among those who study politics, the use of 'socialism' cannot be understood to be governed by clear rules or conventions. This is no recent phenomenon, as Mill himself noted. Mill's use of 'socialism' provides an opportunity for a linguistic reader to note problems in the meaningful use of the word in technical discourse. Apart from attempts at stipulation, which seem to have little effect, nothing more can be said.

## CONCLUSION

Adopting a linguistic conception provides a different way of reading Mill's works and leads to very different discussions of his works. Mill's use of words can be understood in terms of the way that they partake of or reflect varieties of the use of words. This is the case with respect to his use of 'education', 'history', 'individuality' and 'custom'. His presumption that all words have referents and are meaningful in terms of the extent to which they reflect those referents resulted in pathological attempts on his part to alter the use of words to make them more appropriate for their referents. This is evident when reading his discussions of 'women', 'pleasures', 'stationary state', 'necessity' and 'association'. A linguistic approach also offers different, and sometimes more productive, ways of understanding other aspects of Mill's works. It seems to offer something for an understanding of his reflections on the 'proper' role of government, his category of 'self-regarding' actions; and his 'qualified socialism'.

Some readers may be disappointed with the preceding discussions. These readers may be dissatisfied on the basis that a linguistic approach does not allow for claims of some true meaning for any of the words Mill used or some attempt to declare upon the real nature of the world to which he attempted to refer. These limitations, however, are essential to a linguistic approach. Something positive is still achieved, in my view, through leaving readers with a sense of multiple uses of words, an appreciation of the notion of philosophical pathologies, and a sense of other insights offered within a linguistic perspective.

# 5 The Four Conceptions Reconsidered

This chapter is devoted to further reflection on the four conceptions of political theory. It is designed to address some of the issues that arise for political theorists from the preceding discussion. The question to which it is implicitly addressed concerns what political theorists might do in response to this book. The shortest, simplest and most realistic answer to this question is: nothing much different from what they have been doing. Most political theorists have already been trained in and are already committed to the basic principles of one of the conceptions outlined. Some of us will argue that one or other of the conceptions is better or is better for the times in which we find ourselves. We will never know whether this is simply self-serving. I know that I will continue to teach political theory from within a traditionalist conception. This is a result of my training, my personal inclinations at this point in time and my ability to persuade myself that there is something valuable for my students in my doing so.

Of course, some political theorists consider themselves sufficiently imaginative and creative to straddle a number of conceptions (perhaps even all of them) and write and read political theory in a number of ways at the same time. Some have told me so. I think this view is both misguided and unnecessary. Misguided because it simply perpetuates the ontological and epistemological confusion addressed in this book. Unnecessary, because in this age of the so-called decentred subject, we have the capacity to be a variety of political theorists. The only limit on this, in my view, is that we cannot be a variety of them in each moment of being. To say that we are a variety of people, or have a variety of modes of being, in our lives is not to say that we are a variety of people, or adopt a variety of modes of being, at the same time. A desire to see ourselves as having an integrated and stable identity will drive us to think of ourselves in this way though we will be wrong.

Independent of these micro-level issues, nothing is going to happen to academic practices of political theory that is likely to result in a successful disciplining of political theorists and the production of a single way of writing, teaching or reading political theory. Political theorists will continue to demonstrate little in the way of disciplinarity. This does not preclude the hope that they might demonstrate greater awareness of their commitments or predispositions and, as a result, will be more self-reflexive – this may be a forlorn hope.

Before leaving a discussion of the alternative conceptions of political theory, however, two tasks still need to be carried out. The first is to deal with readers whose predispositions have already led them to deny legitimacy or validity to one or more of the conceptions discussed in this book. Two ways of achieving this will be presented. The first is to demonstrate that all can be said to have positive features or strengths. The second is to demonstrate that all can be said to have negative features or weaknesses. Of course, strengths and weaknesses are largely in the eyes of the beholder. Some of those who behold these conceptions of political theory are predisposed to understand them in particular ways, but something more might be done to make this predisposition evident. The second general task is to outline in more detail the sensitivity to difference that this book is designed to encourage.

## POSITIVES AND NEGATIVES

### Positives

Each of the conceptions of political theory can be understood to have positive features. Proponents of a particular conception may claim that theirs is superior because of the soundness of the epistemological assumptions from which it derives. As indicated in the Introduction to this book and, as in that case, following Rorty, epistemology is not a means for determining the superiority of one of the conceptions of political theory available to political theorists.

### *Traditionalist*

One of the more important effects of adopting a traditionalist conception of political theory is that it results in a certain grandeur. To believe that you are part of a timeless tradition of great thinkers who investigate fundamental truths about politics cannot help but provide a sense of personal efficacy. To use a contemporary jargon, the traditionalist conception results in a form of empowerment for those who adopt it. This may be especially important for those who find themselves at odds with those around them and marginalised in their own time and place. The timeless quest for eternal truths provides a residual sense of purpose when no headway seems otherwise to be made. Reading Mill may be ennobling in itself, but it may also give us a sense that important things can still be said.

To over-emphasise what might be understood to the audacity, perhaps even arrogance, of the traditionalist may be to elide the sense of responsibility that also derives from this conception. This sense of responsibility may be simply in terms of keeping the tradition alive by reading and encouraging others to read the great works in a traditionalist manner. Or it may be in terms of a contribution to solving problems that are understood to have plagued humanity for much of its history. Both lead to a sense of responsibility and service. Reading Mill and encouraging others to read Mill is maintaining a tradition that links us to antiquity and beyond. It is also to open up questions that may remain a puzzle but the resolution of which could well be a boon to civilisation.

That traditionalists maintain a sense of the reality and possibility of truth also represents a strength of this conception of political theory. That conversations can be oriented to and governed by a shared sense of the possibility of truth provides, if nothing else, a motivation to speak about truth and a motivation to listen to others, like Mill, who claim to speak or write about the truth. Some traditionalists, like Strauss, may be considered better speakers than others. Other traditionalists, like Plamenatz, may be considered better listeners than others. Speaking and listening with respect to the truth are both important and flow from a traditionalist conception. Habermas's notion of an ideal speech situation in which great care is taken in speaking and listening in order that these are done without distortion is only meaningful in the context of a traditionalist conception of political theory. His reliance on speech-act theory can be understood as an acceptance that we are always doing more than we may realise in speaking and must be careful not to have effects that are undesirable for the creation of a healthy community. A category of speaking well requires that speaking is more than simply persuading. It relies on a notion of coming closer together and coming closer to something that looks very much like the truth.

The other side of speaking around the truth is that it allows for, and may well require, criticism. This criticism goes beyond allusion to internal contradiction, though it may also involve this. If truth is possible and if people disagree about it, then something in what either or both say must be wrong. This can result in speaking poorly. It can also allow for the avoidance of the paralysis brought on by many forms of relativism. Criticism may not be pleasant or always desired, though it may be necessary. Mill's works allow us to consider the possibility that some people have gotten things wrong and that some views are basically untenable.

## Historicist

One of the principal strengths of the historicist conception of political theory is that it provides a strong sense of engagement with being (in whichever form it is understood). Whether their focus is upon political theorising as the resolution of personal, intellectual or social problems, the focus is problem-oriented and the solutions produced for the problems will have practical implications. If we are all subject to personal, intellectual or social tension which requires release if it is not to become overwhelming means that the historicist offers something important to all human beings. We read Mill for his humanity and understand our own a little better.

The connection with an audience is immediate and the implications for the audience are also relatively immediate within this conception. None of us may have been subject to quite the same level of parental intervention as John Stuart Mill, but the struggle for identity in the face of parenting is familiar to those of us raised in nuclear families. We may not be caught within the same intellectual cross-currents, but many of us are still trying to weave together divergent influences in order to come to some clear intellectual position. Mill's times are not our times, but his commitment to doing something about his times can be our commitment.

We can also use reading Mill as an opportunity to reflect upon and develop techniques through which we might persuade others to adopt perspectives we take to be more valuable than those they already have. Mill may not have been the most influential writer of his times, but he was not without influence and was able to persuade others to adopt his points of view. Reading Mill and using extracts from his works may also improve our capacity to persuade to our point of view or to dissuade others from theirs. The authority of quotation may have receded somewhat, but it still operates and reading Mill may be one way in which we can give our positions greater authority.

## Linguistic

Whereas the traditionalist and historicist conceptions of political theory partake of a certain seriousness of purpose, the linguistic conception provides something of an antidote to seriousness. This isn't to say that linguistic analysis is not serious, but that it requires far greater in the way of humility. That, for the most part, linguistic political theorists will leave everything as it is, means that they do not pretend to some greater insight into the true nature of things or some deeper understanding of personal, intellectual or social tensions and necessary responses.

Another positive attribute of a linguistic conception is that it directs attention to the ways in which people communicate with each other. Even when attention is addressed to the works of those in the traditional canon, the central concern of the linguistic approach is with the possibilities available for making sense and the limits that flow from this set of possibilities. Abandoning a concern with what is going on behind a text as referent results in greater attention to the forms of language present in that text. These forms of language reflect, in turn, forms of life or grammars of living associated with being a language-user. While some language-users have a larger vocabulary or greater rhetorical skill, none is so different from all the others that their ways of using words are more important or more interesting than the ways that popular users employ words. The approach is not elitist. It does not rely on the view that some individuals are greater or more concerned or sensitive to their times. It does not require that those who adopt it treat political theorists as though they are an object of interest in their own right on the ground that they make a greater contribution to society than others.

The sorts of limitations that taxonomers of word-use place upon themselves are one manifestation of this positive attribute. The contribution of a taxonomically oriented linguistic political theorist is simply toward the clarification of word-use. This clarification might result in some positive outcome, but it might not. Some social purpose that serves as the province of the linguistic political theorist may flow from an appreciation of multiple uses for particular words. If this appreciation results in tolerance among word-users or an appreciation on their part of failures of communication, then this may be for the good. The taxonomer, however, cannot produce tolerance or prevent communication failure.

That a stipulative approach is designed to facilitate communication in the technical use of language on the part of students of politics or political scientists provides it with some greater capacity for intervention. If those interested in politics accept that problems of communication arise between them as a result of problems that result from the multiple meanings for words or unclear conventions that govern their use, then they may well welcome the assistance provided by linguistic political theorists who offer stipulation or reconstruction. The actual practice of politics may not have changed and the service will have been done for only a small section of the population, but those in that small section who are open to the gains available for stipulation or reconstruction may appreciate the efforts of linguistic political theorists.

Therapeutic interventions are probably the most ambitious of those proposed and practised by linguistic political theorists. To be part of a process of allowing others to perceive the source of their problems and to change their practices to reduce the extent to which they are led into a variety of pathological or deluded activities is no small contribution (even if the recipients of therapy are a minority of the population). That the therapeutic approach requires greater attention to attempts at communication, without a corresponding desire to interfere with these attempts in some forceful manner, is a positive feature of this approach.

That political theorists are required by the linguistic conception to descend from the intellectual heights of traditionalism or from the interpretive heights of historicism makes this an attractive conception of political theory. Mill can be read as a user of words who sometimes was unclear in his use and was sometimes prone to the sort of philosophical pathology to which a linguistic approach draws attention. He is no different from all language-users and especially from those who take themselves to be philosophers.

### Behaviouralist

Much of the value of the behaviouralist conception of political theory derives from the power that behaviouralist techniques have acquired over both politics and the social sciences. Surveys or polls have become an accepted part of studying certain aspects of politics. These forms of information-gathering are taken (by many specialists and non-specialists) to generate meaningful information about politics. They dominate much of the discussions of political issues, especially around election times. To understand the issues of methodology and method is to understand much about the limitations, and in some cases biases, of these methods which are rarely acknowledged. Behaviouralism can be a powerful tool; it can also be misused, misunderstood, or misrepresented by those who understand the legitimacy that appearing to use these methods can lend any study.

Behaviouralist political theorists are some of the few who understand and can interpret the information generated by survey methods. Their sympathy for the behaviouralist approach means that they can do much more to control the effects of behaviouralist research outcomes than simply to direct ineffectual slogans such as 'empiricist' or 'positivist' at the results generated by behaviouralist studies. Even if 'empiricist' and 'positivist' can be understood as pejoratives, they are ineffective ones. That they are not criticisms and that they are not understood by most people means that they will have no effect on the reception of results of behaviouralist studies. Only those who understand the methodological underpinnings and methods of particular studies can do anything to respond to potential and politically powerful misinterpretations of their results.

The value of behaviouralist political theory to the practice of political science may be understood in terms of the distinction that Kuhn drew between those who practise normal science and those who promote paradigm shifts. (Kuhn 1970) The behaviouralist can contribute both to the formation of hypotheses and the interpretation of results of research carried out within normal political science. Indeed, they may be understood to play a crucial role in directing and using normal political science research. They also have an important role to play in terms of the debates and controversies that are part of paradigm shifts. Obviously these paradigm shifts are not of the order of those required by critics of the behaviouralist approach to studying politics. They want the approach abandoned. These paradigm shifts occur within the general principles that gave rise to and govern behaviouralism. Political theorists could be expected to play an important role in paradigm shifts, but only if they understand the basics of behaviouralism.

A narrower positive feature of a behaviouralist approach to political theory is that it requires that political theorists not only contribute to research projects, but that part of their contribution is through providing testable hypotheses. This may prove to make behaviouralist research projects more interesting. It may also result in making claims by political theorists less interesting in that they may actually be open to resolution. Debates in politics may actually be closed through the generating of information that bears upon them. Of course, this is only on the basis that political theorists are prepared to have issues resolved through the generation of evidence. Mill may not have been without sympathy for such an approach to social and political issues, but he could not provide testable propositions for a research programme which was not to appear for almost one hundred years. Those political theorists who understand the currently available methods through which propositions are tested can have a significant role in shaping and directing the research agenda of the social and political sciences.

**Negatives**

Many of the positives asserted in the preceding section may well be questioned, not so much on the basis of whether they are in fact consequences that flow from the conception under discussion, but on the basis of whether they are positives at all. Some of the negatives attributed to the conceptions are simply different ways of understanding the consequences that were asserted to be positive. Value may well be in the eyes of the beholder. Further, whether a conception of political theory results in positive or negative attributes on the part of its adherents may reflect more about the adherent than it does about the conception.

*Traditionalist*[34]

If traditionalists can be understood to be ennobled and empowered by their conception of political theory, they can also be understood to be rendered arrogant and paternalistic. The conception may, and sometimes does, produce an elitism that means that those who are not able to engage with the tradition may be treated as objects for analysis, not as people to be heard. If only the great works and the great thinkers are worthy of attention, then little may be paid to those who have not been certified for inclusion in the great tradition. This feature of a traditionalist conception of political theory may also make its adherents aloof and unresponsive to those in their immediate vicinity. The level of disengagement that is required for the contemplation of the essential issues of human existence may not be conducive to an active and empathic concern for the plight of those who are in immediate need of political support.

One of the more serious charges against this conception of political theory is that it is systematically exclusive – certainly, its adherents would accept that not everyone is cut out to contemplate the perennial questions. From this perspective not only is the canon of traditional political theory skewed, the attitudes that are taken to be essential to it are also understood to be skewed. For example, Shanley and Pateman have argued that 'among the greatest wrongs done to women has been their exclusion from taking part as full members and citizens of the polity in political debate, deliberation and contest. The classic theorists, and the construction of the academic canon of political theory, have been instrumental in achieving and maintaining this exclusion.' (1991: 9–10)

Another negative feature that can be attributed to the traditionalist conception is that the tradition can be taken too seriously. John Gunnell devoted a significant amount of attention and words to elaborating upon the proposition that the tradition was a mythical invention that, when taken too seriously, actually impaired an interpreter's capacity to understand a text (See Gunnell 1978, 1979).

## Historicist

A reverse form of this problem may well derive from an historicist conception. If the traditionalist might be accused of taking the texts too seriously, the historicist may be accused of not taking them seriously enough. The historicist approach could easily render political theory into another form of history and make any attempt at political theorising no more than an interesting curio. Unless some commonalities can be asserted of different historical periods, a claim that may be hard to make within an historicist conception, little can be learnt from works produced in other periods or within other cultures. The question of whether a work from any other period, or at least another period removed by more than a couple of decades from that of an interpreter is worth reading, remains open.

Another negative effect that may result from adopting this conception is that it can cause a preoccupation with the motivations or reasons that theorists wrote what they did, rather than a concern with what they tried to say. In the end we may discover a great deal about the situation that provoked theorists to write and the various factors that led them to respond in the way they did, but discover very little about the works that they produced. A corollary of this tendency is to dismiss what theorists had to say on the basis of the factors that led them to write in the way they did about the matters about which they wrote. On this basis, Mill might be dismissed as someone who was 'just' responding to aspects of his psychological, intellectual or social situation.

Another negative effect of this conception is that it introduces difficult problems that go to 'closing the context' of the works in question. This can manifest itself in an endless quest to fully understand an historical situation by accumulating all of the information available about that situation. It can also lead into problems with deciding what pieces of information actually go to closing the context. The historicist could find himself locked into an extended debate as to what actually counts as a fact that goes to designating an historical context and how it should be counted as such a fact. The apparent divergences of opinion between Ellen Meiksins Wood and Neal Wood and

Richard Ashcraft, James Tully and Quentin Skinner (see Wood 1994) about how to characterise an historical context is an example of the sort of problem that may arise and the difficulty that could emerge in resolving it.

### Linguistic

One of the most often articulated objections to the linguistic conception of political theory is that it results in a conservatism on the part of political theorists (see Wertheimer 1976). Other political theorists cannot accept the sense of limitation that the linguistic conception requires. That the linguistic political theorist is committed to 'leaving everything as it is' may result in a lack of concern for, or irresponsibility toward, dealing with important political issues. Taxonomic and stipulative or reconstructive approaches may result in a passivity that is objectionable to those who seek activity. Therapy may offer some hope of achieving change, but therapy can only be successful when the patient has already shown some predisposition to identify a problem and seek a solution. The linguistic political theorist may help to achieve improvement by aiding conversation, but s/he can only do so under conditions in which that help is understood and appreciated.

Another difficulty associated with adopting the linguistic conception of political theory is that it brings to light problems with defining use that may prove to be impossible to resolve. To study use, not meaning, is a simple and evocative slogan, but when the problem of determining what use it is arises, linguistic philosophy is not quick to resolve it. Austin's adoption of locutionary, illocutionary and perlocutionary acts as means of understanding use provides some assistance in determining the variety of ways in which words are used (Austin 1976). These categories break down into a number of sub-categories, however, which makes it difficult to specify the variety of conventions that govern meaningful use. If these conventions cannot be specified, studying use might lead a political theorist in a variety of activities which may not reflect the activities of other linguistic researchers.

As it is another contextual approach, there is the problem that the context will become the dominant concern, with any particular text merely a vehicle for playing out some larger story. Indeed, the texts normally studied by political theorists may well not fit into the research agenda of the linguistic political theorist. This may lead into the problem of deciding what to study in studying political theory and, indeed, if there is anything to study which can be called political theory as opposed to simply studying any form of word use.

*Behaviouralist*

Like the linguistic conception, the behaviouralist conception may also result in a conservatism on the parts of those who adopt it. A certain amount of the hostility that has been directed to behaviouralists was driven by the fact that they were not considered sufficiently critical of the social order within which they did research. This might result from a commitment to values identical to those of the current order. Alternatively, it may result from a desire to generate the funds necessary for this form of research from institutions which, in some way or another, belong to that dominant order. The refusal to engage with normative issues and the desire to separate fact and value may be taken to be a refusal to adopt a critical position that relies upon values and which asserts that a certain order is more desirable than another.

One result of adopting a behaviouralist conception of political theory is that it can lead to an apolitical attitude. Such an attitude may be understood to be apolitical only to the extent that it results in a refusal to take positions on political issues of the day. This view may derive from the perpetuation of an understanding of science as objective. This may well be to perpetuate a largely out-of-date conception of the scientific method. It may also be to occlude the disciplinary processes that produced behaviouralism and continue to maintain it as a powerful, and in some instances, dominant research agenda.

That hypotheses or assertions must be testable may also result in a limiting of the questions that can be asked. This may be objectionable to those who see political theory as posing larger questions and adopting critical positions in the face of what are taken to be the facts within a dominant order. That hypotheses must be shaped according to the research techniques available may result in limited hypotheses of interest only to a few.

## SENSITIVITY TO DIFFERENCE

If all conceptions of political theory have positive and negative consequences for their adherents, then it might be possible to combine elements of all or some of them to achieve a superior conception of political theory. Creating a single practice as political theory could be achieved through selecting one of the conceptions as superior to the others and excluding those others as illegitimate ways of practising political theory. The second option is objectionable on the grounds that it requires either an arbitrary choice of conception or the production of a single stable set of criteria through which a choice can be made. The former option, i.e. the combinatory approach, is also objectionable as it relies on a refusal to accept that the ontologies and epistemologies of the four conceptions are tenable. In the end, the best response, in my view, is to develop what may be referred to as 'sensitivity to difference'.

Great caution must be exercised in making recommendations as to possible courses of development for political theory. That it lacks strong disciplinary processes is evident from the fact that divergent conceptions and practices are available to political theorists. Even if other disciplines or sub-disciplines could be reconstituted in close to one stroke, this is unlikely to happen to the sub-discipline of political theory. The most that can be hoped for is an increasing sensitivity to difference based upon greater self-reflexivity. In short, there is simply no way of constituting a unified discipline of political theory and, even if there was, this wouldn't be desirable.

If each of the conceptions of political theory is underpinned by respectable and persuasive ontologies and epistemologies, then to lose any of them would be to the detriment of political theory. The more important problem relates to what is to be done given a greater recognition on the part of political theorists of the commitments that lead them to practise political theory in the way that they do. First, it requires a sense of the ways in which these conceptions lead to the development of what might be called micro-disciplines within the sub-discipline of political theory. Second, it requires a tolerance toward divergent conceptions and approaches to reading and writing political theory. Third, it may open up the possibility of understanding a training in political theory to be the acquisition of a variety of skills each of which is meaningful in the context of a particular ontology and epistemology.

That political theory as a whole has no disciplinary architectonic that leads to a single conception and practice does not mean that political theory is an unregulated intellectual terrain. The usual disciplinary processes still operate within the academic world. These are marked in specific ways by patterns of promotion, publication (especially in journals), success in research grant applications and structures of patronage into which postgraduate and postdoctoral researchers are inserted. They are marked in more general ways by specific academic and intellectual networks. The only difference between the sub-discipline of political theory and other disciplines and sub-disciplines is that these processes have resulted in four practices rather than one. Each of these practices is fairly clearly marked and regulated. That they are not always acknowledged is part of the way in which they maintain themselves.

Too great a degree of self-reflexivity is actually destructive to the maintenance of disciplinarity. If an understanding of proper practice had to be justified continually and processes of disciplining made overt rather than natural or automatic, the coherence and continuation of the discipline is in doubt.

I have no doubt that the micro-disciplines of political theory will not be greatly damaged or undermined by this book. Indeed, I hope that this is not the case. The more modest aim is for some level of reconciliation to, if not extreme enthusiasm for, multiplicity and difference in the practices of political theory. In its most limited form, all that is required is an appreciation of the fact that ontological and epistemological questions, and particularly the latter, remain open. This may lead to a recognition that those who practise political theory differently do so in ways that are not necessarily misguided or false (though some of them may be inconsistent in their practices and in need of some level of disciplining by those who adhere to the conception that makes their work most meaningful). This is the beginning of sensitivity to difference. All it requires is that we can find it within ourselves to pass over other conceptions and practices of political theory in silence. (In Millian terminology, political theorists might accept difference as indication of a variety of experiments of living on the parts of political theorists.)

Political theorists do not need and could not achieve conformity in their practices. But they can develop the capacity to resist deriding or otherwise attempting to diminish the practices of those who adhere to alternative conceptions. This may result in an inability to use the works produced by those who work within other conceptions of political theory and who read the works of political theorists differently. Political theorists do not have to agree with each other about the nature of political theory. All they need for community and a collective defence of political theory is an appreciation of the value of what they are doing in reading and writing political theory. This book was designed to demonstrate how at least three of the conceptions lead to some interesting observations in reading Mill's works.

That behaviouralists will largely turn their backs on works like those produced by Mill may lead to some suspicion if not hostility on the part of adherents of other conceptions. This does create a potential for disunity, antagonism and vulnerability on the part of political theorists. In some ways the later development of the behaviouralist conception required that it push other conceptions aside in becoming a viable conception. Its development may have necessitated the sorts of shifts that displaced other conceptions and, in some instances, led to a degree of atrophy on the part of other conceptions (see Gunnell 1981). Hopefully the enthusiasm and excesses of adherents to this conception may be forgiven in light of an understanding of the relative youth of their movement and a recognition that political theorists would do well to develop their capacity to recognise difference without hostility. In the same way, adherents of the behaviouralist conception may do well to recall that the hostility they experienced is to be expected, given the excesses of early proponents and the way that they disrupted a semi-ordered intellectual terrain.

Political theorists cannot be expected to hold metaphorical hands in some act of understanding and togetherness. This is impossible because of the effects of different conceptions in legitimising and sustaining certain practices. It is also undesirable in that it may be disruptive to the processes of disciplining that are necessary to maintain the alternative conceptions and the practices that go with them.

The furthest that sensitivity to difference may be pushed is into the provision of multiple forms of training to those who study political theory in universities and other academic institutions. The basic ontologies and epistemologies of the four conceptions of political theory can be taught to those students who are able to tolerate the cognitive dissonance to which it may lead. This cannot be done in such a way as to imply either the possibility of unity in terms of the sub-discipline of political theory or that political theorists are wrong in maintaining their commitment to particular conceptions and in criticising practitioners of other conceptions. It is simply to say that students of political theory can be brought to understand that they too must make choices and evidence commitments to a particular conception without having to engage in the gainsaying of other conceptions. This may be too difficult to achieve, for it requires a sense of multiplicity which is not actually a sense of complete openness.

Universities and other academic institutions are not open fields in which every and any flower can bloom. They are fields fertilised, ploughed and oriented in such a way that some flowers will be more likely to grow and some of those more likely to blossom. Power still operates in universities and similar institutions. It has effects on all of those who form part of the university community. Some institutions will be more likely to foster particular conceptions of political theory, but this is a result of the processes of disciplinarity that operate and not of the nature of the conception that dominates. At base, sensitivity to difference requires an awareness of this.

# Conclusion

That the question 'what is political theory?' has no single answer may be taken as either a lack of consistency and coherence on the part of the group of scholars who take themselves and ask to be taken as political theorists or as a sign of multiplicity and openness on the part of that group of scholars. Perhaps it is both. Then again, it may well be neither. The latter is probably the better view. It is probably the better view because the sub-discipline of political theory, like all forms of institutionalised academic behaviour, is regulated through the use of appointment and promotion (themselves, more often than not, based upon publications – which are themselves overseen by editors and referees who bring their own understanding of the sub-discipline to bear in the determination of worth).

This book is not an implicit rejection of such processes of regulation. At most it is a call for some sensitivity to difference on the part of those who regulate. Not an unlimited and indiscriminate sensitivity, however. The four conceptions of political theory discussed in this book are coherent alternatives only because they have specific ontologies, epistemologies and methods. That they are intellectually defensible at each of these points makes them open to both understanding and use. That they can be understood and used was important to the discussions in each of the chapters (with the acknowledged limitation that the behaviouralist conception could not be demonstrated in practice in the context of a reading of Mill's works).

This book is simply an attempt to demonstrate that the differences among political theorists in their self-conceptions and practices are significant in that they identify a limited variety of self-conceptions and practices. That they are limited in number is important because it indicates that political theory can be understood as a set of sub-disciplines and not an amorphous mass of practices that have little in common.

This book hasn't been designed or written in order to promote any sweeping changes in the practices of political theorists. Even if this were possible, it is not intended. If anything, this book is a simple call for greater self-reflexivity on the part of political theorists. It may also be taken to be a call for greater humility on some of their parts. Greater self-reflexivity may result from an increased sensitivity to the specific ontologies and epistemologies that underlie the practices of political theorists. Greater humility may result from an acceptance that any particular practice of political theory cannot be a foundation for all the projects a political theorist may wish to pursue.

Whatever else happens, political theorists will continue to constitute different objects as their intellectual focus. Traditionalists will continue to understand political theory as an inquiry into the essential questions of human being and an attempt to find answers for the basic problems of human social organisation. Historicists will continue to treat a political theory as a response to 'historically' defined problems. Linguistic political theorists will understand political theory to open up possibilities for reflecting upon the use of words, and sometimes assisting in the promotion of clarity with respect to those words, via taxonomy, stipulation, or therapy. Behaviouralist political theorists will continue to generate hypotheses that can be used as part of behaviouralist research and to interpret the results of particular studies.

Even when they read the same texts each type of political theorist will adopt a different interpretive method. Traditionalists will read their books as attempts to provide answers to the essential questions. Their interpretations will be attempts to present the answers to these questions developed by the theorist whose works are being studied. Their responses to these works, if they provide any, will go to the adequacy of those answers. Historicists will interpret the books they read within more or less carefully constructed contextual frameworks from which their meaning is derived. They will characterise the works of theorists with whom they deal as responses to those contextual factors. If they respond to these works it will be in terms of the relationship between the conditions under which the theorists wrote and the conditions that currently exist. Linguistic political theorists will understand texts as particular manifestations of word-use. Their reading will attempt to characterise the particular uses to which words are put. These uses may then be utilised to provide taxonomies of use, stipulations for use, or in order to identify the pathologies that result from attempts to correct use. The behaviouralists will focus their attention either on books that present and discuss techniques for the accumulation and processing of information or on books that may facilitate the generation of hypotheses that can be tested through techniques currently available.

Observers may question the extent to which political theorists can be understood to be members of the same community given that they adopt different practices as political theory. The ability to practise a particular form of political theory depends upon receiving the appropriate training. Political theory may be understood to be a set of communities united only by the sharing of a label that indicates nothing more than institutional location. The boundaries between the communities are porous, however, and nothing prevents political theorists from being trained, or training themselves, to practise each of the conceptions. Nothing, apart from disciplinary processes, prevents a political theorist from being a member of each of the sub-communities of political theory. Disciplinary processes are powerful, but they are most effective when they are not recognised or acknowledged. This book may go some way to reducing the efficacy of the disciplinary processes which produce the four conceptions and define the practices that pertain to them, though this was not its intended effect.

The argument that the different conceptions of political theory derive from different ontological and epistemological positions is insufficient to overcome a resistance on the part of many political theorists to the idea that political theory is characterised by a set of different practices or ways of being a political theorist. They still want an answer to the question 'what is political theory?' In many instances they see their own practice as partaking of some, if not all, of the conceptions discussed in this book. This is an understandable reaction. The only problem is that it is untenable. More often than not this position derives from an insensitivity to the differences between the conceptions. If their different ontologies are not recognised and their practices are taken to be identical, then the move to a practice that is 'political theory' *simpliciter* is almost automatic. Nothing in this book will change that opinion. This is merely a recognition of the fact that no amount of writing or talking will persuade some that they are not able to act and speak for all.

A search for a single conception of political theory is not, in itself, a bad thing. It only becomes a problem if it generates an insensitivity to or a belittling of some of the conceptions of political theory which many political theorists use or support. This may be overcome if the following principles are recognised. First, each of the conceptions of political theory discussed in this book derive from coherent and defensible ontologies and epistemologies. Second, each provides the basis for a coherent self-conception as political theorist. Third, each supplies a guide for practice that allows for the achievement of ends that may themselves be defended as worthwhile (and, in some cases, will be defended as all that can be done or all that can be usefully done). Fourth, each supports a training that makes possible the constitution and regulation of an intellectual discipline. Fifth, each has positive and negative attributes both at the ontological and epistemological levels and in practice. None deserves to be dismissed or belittled. This does not mean that they will not be dealt with in these ways.

A move to a single conception of political theory may be defended on a number of grounds. A single conception would allow for some uniformity in self-presentation on the part of political theorists. A single conception would also allow all political theorists to understand and be understood by all other political theorists. A single form of training would be provided to the variety of students who undertake courses in political theory and, in some cases, train as political theorists.

Moving to a single conception would create a number of problems. It may require the collapse or unification of the ontologies and epistemologies that underpin the different conceptions of political theory currently practised. Alternatively, it would require the selection of one as the preferred conception of political theory to the exclusion of alternative conceptions. The first move would be difficult to make. It would rely upon an ability to find some ground for collapsing the ontologies and epistemologies. The second would also be difficult. It would rely upon the ability to refer to criteria that were independent of any ontology or epistemology to support the process of selecting the preferable ontology for political theory.

By far the greatest problem that stands in the way of the unification of political theory around a particular conception of political theory is the very existence of different conceptions. These different conceptions have supported the self-conceptions and practices of existing political theorists. To provide unification would require the ability of political theorists to identify with one self-conception. Any familiarity with political theorists would lead to the view that this is unlikely.

This leads to the question of whether there does or could exist a disciplining agent that could provide for this amalgamation. If political theory was open to strict regulation this may well have been done by now. That it isn't reflects the extent to which it is an academic discipline that is not directly subjected to an agency that could demand and enforce uniformity. At best this would have to happen as a result of pressures that were more covert than direct intervention. Not only do these pressures have to exist – and it can be argued that they have existed and do exist – they must persist for a sufficient duration to so isolate those who hold to a divergent conception to allow them to be forgotten or their practice rendered, at best, anachronistic.

Three reasons explain the support for unification. The first is a desire for widespread conformity. The second is a desire for the exclusion of the alternative or divergent. The final reason derives from a desire to avoid the limitation that results from the adoption of a particular conception. If political theory can be everything then so can a political theorist.

Conformity is important to the extent that it allows for understanding. The position presented in this book is that there are a number of different ways that political theorists regulate their behaviour and, as a consequence, the behaviour of those for whom they are responsible. There is uniformity in political theory, but it is to be found around particular conceptions of political theory. To be consistent is to conform to the requirements of a particular conception. To make a defence of this into a defence of conformity for all political theorists is to ignore the bases upon which the differences between political theorists can be identified.

The other possibility is to adopt one conception to the exclusion of all others. Exclusion is more difficult to defend. It may result in simplification and the reduction of confusion and misunderstanding. But the price is high. A certain amount of exclusion results from the fact that many political theorists organise themselves around particular conceptions. That some exclusion exists and may be necessary for the organisation of sub-disciplines does not mean, however, that further exclusion can be defended.

The desire for the reading-down of anything that might require limitation is readily evident on the part of many political theorists. The desire to be free from restriction in one's practice leads to a desire to be free from the restrictions suggested in this book. To be restricted is to be prevented from doing whatever one wants to do whenever one wants to do it. If political theory is not understood to require a single set of practices then to do political theory at any particular time is to adopt the practices that are available within the different conceptions of political theory.

All of these reasons for supporting unification are unsustainable. None registers the depth of the differences between the conceptions of political theory discussed in this book. To appreciate that traditionalist, historicist, linguistic and behaviouralist political theorists do different things for very different reasons is to appreciate that unification is not a solution but the maintenance of the lack of self-reflexivity evident in many of the works on and practices of political theory.

Even if this were not the case, however, to move forward together as political theorists requires that political theorists recognise their differences and avoid believing that these differences can somehow be resolved. To do this requires thinking through the depth of the ontological and epistemological differences between the four conceptions discussed in this book. Progress may be made once this has been done and some appreciation has been gained as to the significance of the different practices brought to bear in the reading of works of political theory. My own view is that progress can be understood to mean sensitivity to difference. I hope that this book has facilitated the development of a sensitivity to difference on the part of its readers. This modest goal provided the principal motivation for writing it.

# Notes

1   There has been a recent interest in something called 'postmodern politi-
    cal theory' but the characteristics of this conception and practice remain
    unclear. See White (1991) and Rengger (1992).
2   The use of 'traditionalist' in this work is not identical with its use in
    Schneewind (1991).
3   The signifiers used to mark the different conceptions of political theory
    are not intended to do more than provide a shorthand method for refer-
    ring to the different conceptions. The four signifiers selected to indicate
    different conceptions of political theory (traditionalist, historicist,
    linguistic and behaviouralist) are neither accepted by individual political
    theorists as applying to them, nor have meanings independent of the defi-
    nitions stipulated below. A typology close to the one in this book is
    contained in the following quotation from Miller: 'Political theory has
    flourished over the last 20 years but it has also become more fragmented.
    The critical study of classic texts has been replaced by a more narrowly
    historical approach, which seeks to locate texts in their political contexts.
    A very recent development, conceptual history, promises a closer rela-
    tionship between historical and contemporary theory. Conceptual
    analysis has given way to normative political theory, concerned to find
    principled justifications for political arrangements. The major cleavage
    has been between individualists, who look for universal foundations in
    postulates such as human nature, and communitarians, who begin with
    persons embedded in contingent social relationships and practices. In
    applied political theory, the major shift has been from institutional ques-
    tions to the analysis of issues in public policy, such as welfare provision
    and sexual and racial discrimination.' (1990: 421)
4   Flynn has argued that only certain types of society allow for political
    theory: 'it is only within a certain historically specific socio-political
    configuration that political reflection as such becomes possible. The
    place of the "observer" is not a place marked out from eternity simply
    waiting for someone to occupy it, nor is it my contention that it is prefig-
    ured in the transcendental structure of consciousness or communication.
    Rather ... the *place* of political reflection is generated within the history
    of the very structures on which it reflects. To claim that someone reflect-
    ing on the articulation of his own socio-political configuration is
    analogous to a disincarnated, unsituated observer attempting to discover
    the objective laws of nature ... is to actively occult the fact that only
    particular socio-political configurations engender, or permit, reflection
    on their foundations, namely, those societies that believe themselves to
    be structured by *nomos* and not by *physis*.' (1985: 247)
5   In his review of *The Cambridge History of Political Thought:
    1450–1700* Pocock wrote: 'What indeed do we mean by "political
    thought"? This volume's answer is clear, predictable and thoroughly

169

defensible: a collocation of intellectual traditions peculiar to Latin Europe, in which Greek and Latin city-state culture and philosophy, Roman jurisprudence, Jewish and Christian theology, are mediated by the disputes of Papacy, empire and kingdoms to the later disputes between Protestant and Catholic monarchies and (in the last chapters of this volume) the beginnings of Enlightenment. The dispute is conducted in the languages of theology, jurisprudence, humanism and philosophy, and may be said to have been held together by a concept of "the political" sufficiently coherent and idiosyncratically Latin and Western to raise the question whether "political thought" can be held to exist in the culture of other civilisations without radical (and externally imposed) redefinitions of its meaning.' (Pocock 1993: 11)

6   While Spragens generally appears to have adopted a traditionalist conception of political theory, the following quotation has strong historicist overtones. This combination of conceptions makes his conception of political theory unclear: 'Since the specific crises of the theorist's own society are the raw materials from which he fashions his view of political order, a knowledge of what these crises were all about and the historical setting in which they took place can add considerably to a full comprehension and appreciation of the theorist in question. Understanding the political turmoil in Athenian politics around 400 B.C. provides insight into Plato's Republic. Understanding the peculiarities of politics in Renaissance Florence helps to explain why Machiavelli wrote about the need for a strong Prince. Understanding the upheavals of the Industrial Revolution are quite vital to understanding the force and meaning of Marx's Communist Manifesto. And so on.' (Spragens 1976: 98–9)

7   For a recent discussion of this problem see Wood (1994).

8   One manifestation of the traditionalist conception of political theory as an ongoing 'conversation' is that commentators often refer to the theorist they study in the present tense. Thus, for example, Mill 'writes', 'believes' and 'argues' even though he is dead. This tendency has been followed in this chapter. For an interesting perspective on this tendency among philosophers, see Maker 1992.

9   Stove argues that Mill's argument that insufficient information meant that no final views on the nature of the two sexes is absurd. 'By 1869 a great deal was known, at least to some people, about the differences between the sexes even among barnacles, insects, and flowers. The difference in the nature of the two human sexes form a subject far more interesting than any of those, and the materials for the study of it are more easily available. That this subject matter remained a closed book to John Mill, we can easily believe. But it is utterly impossible to believe that, by 1869, no one whatever had picked up even the least little bit about it. Yet this is what Mill says, over and over again...'. (1993: 5) Hekman, on the other hand, suggests that Mill's argument that insufficient information was available was a function of the absence of a science of ethology, or 'the scientific study of the laws of character formation'. (Hekman 1992: 683) According to Hekman, Mill 'presupposes that women have a "nature" different from that of men and sets out to answer

the question of how the environmental influences that form woman's character relate to that basic nature. His answer to this question is that we cannot tell. In the present state of society, he states, it is impossible to ascertain the natural differences between the sexes because of the deplorable state of the study of ethology.' (1992: 683)

10    Annas (1977: 184), Garforth (1979: 111–12) and Hughes (1979: 530–1) misrepresent Mill's positions with respect to women's natures by failing to note that Mill was referring to women as they were presently found and not as they might be. Thus, the natural tendencies of women they assert Mill proposes are not natural tendencies but those inculcated into them as Mill finds them.

11    Whether Mill's view that it was the responsibility of government to foster the development of individuals meant that he supported laws against pornography is taken up in Dyzenhaus (1992) and Skipper (1993).

12    'Whoever succeeds in an overcrowded profession, or in a competitive examination; whoever is preferred to another in any contest for an object which both desire, reaps benefit from the loss of others, from their wasted exertion and their disappointment. But it is by common admission, better for the general interest of mankind, that persons should pursue their objects undeterred by this sort of consequence.' (OL 18: 292)

13    'Gradually it has become clear to me what every great philosophy so far has been: namely, the personal confession of its author and a kind of involuntary and unconscious memoir...'. (Nietzsche 1968: 203)

14    Mazlish argued that Carlyle's limited knowledge of Mill meant that he did not fully appreciate Mill's 'Spirit of the Age' articles: 'He wished independence from his father, only in order that he might feel he had incorporated "freely" in himself that which he judged good in his father's beliefs. At no point did he wish to reject root and branch what his father, and his father's generation, stood for. Reading the "Spirit of the Age" without knowing John Stuart Mill or his personal development, Carlyle could be forgiven for not seeing this.' (1975: 241–2)

15    Feuer has provided an interesting interpretation of James's behaviour and theories: 'James Mill could never forget that his wife was not the one he loved. His utilitarianism was as much the outcome of a personal quarrel with society as his son's *On Liberty*.' (Feuer 1976: 103)

16    In an article on Mill's and Constant's ideas on liberty, Laschs comes very close to asserting that Mill failed to acknowledge an intellectual debt to Constant. 'With characteristic fairness, Mill lays no claim to wholesale originality. He praises Wilhelm von Humboldt for his advocacy of the principle of liberty, Goethe for his view of self-development, and Joseph Warren for stressing the sovereignty of the individual. These are proper acknowledgments of thinkers who preceded Mill in holding one or another of his views. Astoundingly, however, he never tips his hat to the thinker who embraced virtually all the significant theories of *On Liberty* in a series of publications that appeared more than forty years before Mill's book.' (1992: 87)

17    Donner attributed Mill's changed conception of pleasure to his mental breakdown: 'One of the features of Mill's well-known mental crisis in

his youth was a concept of utility substantially different from the ortho-dox Benthamite conception, which Mill came to regard as deficient. Mill saw that Bentham's concept was excessively narrow, and he sought to overcome its limitations by enlarging his own concept. The result is a complex mental-state account of utility which includes the quality of pleasurable experiences along with the quantity in the estimation of their worth.' (1991: 8–9)

18  'The pleasures associated with the exercise of the intellect, feelings, imagination, and moral sentiments Mill claimed were "refined" pleasures and superior to the crude, original, and mainly physical pleasures. Moreover, the superior pleasure, Mill wrote, could be identified only by "the feelings and judgement of the experienced". An individual having no experience of the higher kind of pleasure, possessed no capability to make proper judgement about qualitative difference in pleasures. Mill's claim that happiness must include higher quality pleasures was thus in conflict with the classical utilitarian principle that each was the best judge of his own interest and his "mental and bodily health". The conflict between the two claims forced Mill to adopt a dualistic position regarding the individual's pursuit of pleasure.' (Kim 1988: 106)

19  Thomas suggested a different intellectual confluence to explain Mill's views on the stationary state. Thomas explains Mill's position in terms of a combination of Wordsworth with the classical economists. 'The stationary state in Mill's work becomes a way of fusing the inexorable laws of political economists with the cult of nature in romantic poetry, making the former seem less callous and the latter more useful.' (1992: 316)

20  'Thus, if J.S. Mill's broad goals and accomplishments are to be compre-hended, we must look less to his father's beliefs than to those historical influences which both of them identified, felt and shared. In the most general terms, these influences were of the same sort that had driven Socrates and his circle to examine the idea of government and to do so within the context of a broad theory of human nature and human knowl-edge. The decisive historical event for the Socratics was the Spartan defeat of Athens; for James Mill and his fellow radicals, the French and American revolutions. This, of course, is a common theme in the history of ideas and is illustrated, to choose only a few examples, by Hobbes's *Leviathan*, by Rousseau's *Social Contract*, and by Locke's *Second Treatise of Civil Government*. In each of these – and illustrations can be multiplied into the dozens – we find the philosopher discovering in the social turmoil the need to reassess any number of traditional convictions and maxims adopted uncritically by the masses and now found to be the source of the trouble.' (Robinson 1982: 33–4)

21  'Mill sanctioned, at one time or another, the following governmental acts of intervention in the economy: the state ownership of land in the case of Ireland; the aiding of workers thrown out of work by the introduction of machinery; the curtailment of inheritance; the granting of a right to relief; the enforcement of a legal restraint against those who brought children into the world who were a burden on society; the regulation of marriage; the introduction of an income tax; the regulation of joint-stock

companies; the regulation or nationalization of monopolistic industries; the provision of compulsory education; the regulation of colonies; the provision of funds for scientific discoveries, universities and scholars; and the regulation of the hours of work for children.' (Paul 1960: 148) Kurer has argued that this does not mean that Mill supported anything more than a minimal welfare state (see Kurer (1991)).

22  Ryle identified two uses of ordinary. In one use, '"ordinary" means "common", "current", "colloquial", "vernacular", "natural", "prosaic", "non-notational", "on the tongue of Everyman", and is usually in contrast with dictions which only a few people know how to use, such as the technical terms or artificial symbolisms of lawyers, theologians, economists, philosophers, cartographers, mathematicians, symbolic logicians and players of Royal Tennis.' (Ryle 1970: 108) In the other use "ordinary" 'is in contrast with "non-stock" or non-standard".' (Ryle 1970: 109)

23  'A philosopher who maintained that certain philosophical questions are questions about the ordinary or stock uses of certain expressions would not therefore be committing himself to the view that they are questions about the uses of ordinary or colloquial expressions. He could admit that the noun "infinitesimals" is not on the lips of Everyman and still maintain that Berkeley was examining the ordinary or stock use of "infinitesimals", namely the standard way, if not the only way, in which this word was employed by mathematical specialists. Berkeley was not examining the use of a colloquial word; he was examining the regular or standard use of a relatively esoteric word. We are not contradicting ourselves if we say that he was examining the ordinary use of an unordinary expression.' (Ryle 1970: 111)

24  'There is no sharp boundary between "common" and "uncommon", "technical" and "untechnical".... The edges of "ordinary" are blurred but usually we are in no doubt whether a diction does or does not belong to ordinary parlance.' (Ryle 1970: 108–9)

25  Wertheimer took up, and in some senses reproduced, many of these objections to the linguistic approach in his article 'Is Ordinary Language Analysis Conservative?' (1976: 405–22)

26  'Some of the English verbs denoting illocutionary acts are "state", "describe", "assert", "warn", "remark", "comment", "command", "order", "request", "criticize", "apologize", "censure", "approve", "welcome", "promise", "object", "demand", and "argue". Austin claimed there were over a thousand such expressions in English.' (Searle 1980: 23)

27  Pocock has suggested that 'all speech ... is performative in the sense that it does things to people. It redefines them in their own perceptions, in those of others and by restructuring the conceptual universe in which they are perceived.' (1984: 39)

28  'In the sequence of utterances, "Please leave the room", "You will leave the room" and "Will you leave the room?" the same proposition, that you will leave the room, is expressed in the performance of three different illocutionary acts. One a request, one a prediction, and one a question.' (Searle, Keifer and Bierwisch 1980: viii)

29    In a discussion of Brutus's soliloquy in Shakespeare's *Julius Caesar*, in which Brutus articulates his intention to kill Caesar because he is a tyrant, Pocock wrote: 'In using so potent a word as "tyrant", Brutus invokes a whole world of reference structures, into which his other words, his intended act, and his verbalized state of consciousness now enter in such a way that it qualifies them all; so that "Caesar", "kill", "intend", and even "I" take on new meanings retrodictively as they enter the world that "tyrant" invokes.' (Pocock 1984: 27)

30    Kurer refers to Mill as adopting an 'associationist' position, but in this case is using 'associationist' to refer to those who support or encourage the creation of workers' associations. (Kurer 1992: 223)

31    Mill made a similar argument about the use of 'interests'. According to Mill, Bentham 'distinguished two kinds of interests, the self-regarding and the social: in vulgar discourse, the name is restricted to the former kind alone. But there cannot be a greater mistake than to suppose that, because we may ourselves be perfectly *conscious* of an ambiguity in our language, that ambiguity therefore has no effect in perverting our modes of thought. I am persuaded, from experience, that this habit of speaking of all the feelings which govern mankind under the name of *interests*, is almost always in point of fact connected with a tendency to consider *interest* in the vulgar sense, that is, purely self-regarding interest, as exercising, by the very constitution of human nature, a far more exclusive and paramount control over human nature than it really does exercise.' (ROB 10: 14)

32    Mill's objection is also interesting in the light of resistance to governments undertaking certain tasks or functions on the basis that they are not what government is really about. Privatising, 'contracting out' and other means of reducing the role of government are often justified in terms of the idea that 'government' has some true and proper meaning that makes it improper for a government to undertake many activities.

33    I follow Benn and Gaus in using 'privateness' as a better, if more awkward, word than 'privacy'. See Benn and Gaus (1983: 3).

34    **Normative Analytical Political Philosophy**
      The traditionalist conception of political theory came under sustained attack from a variety of sources. One of the forms in which it was revived, in my view, was as normative political analysis or normative analytical political philosophy. Criticisms of the ontology and epistemology fundamental to the traditionalist conception, particularly from within a linguistic framework, resulted in a silencing of traditionalist political theorists. Normative analytical political theorists were one group who broke this silence and returned to issues central to a traditionalist conception. The following is a discussion of the way in which traditionalist political theory was silenced and regained something of its voice as normative analytical political philosophy.

      In 1956, Laslett wrote that 'the tradition has been broken.' (1956: vii). In the English speaking world, he concluded, 'political philosophy is dead'. (1956: vii) Laslett identified sociologists as among those who had killed traditionalist political theory. Included in their ranks were 'Marxists, who have erected a system in which statements of sociological description and determinism tend to fill the function of philosophic analysis.' (1956: vii) Others, according to Laslett, adopted a sociology of knowledge approach, derived from Mannheim's' work. From this perspective, not only were 'political activity and political thinking ... shown to be sociologically determined, but all thinking and all knowing as well.' (1956: viii) Another aspect of the sociological attack, in Laslett's account, was in terms of a shift to social science modelled on the natural sciences. In the face of this shift, Laslett wrote, 'it is only natural that the social and political philosopher should feel inhibited'. (1956: viii)

For this discussion, however, the most important point from which a traditionalist conception of political theory came under attack was a particular group of philosophers (which included the sources from which linguistic political theorists drew). 'It was Russell and Wittgenstein, Ayer and Ryle who convinced the philosophers that they must withdraw unto themselves for a time, and re-examine their logical and linguistic apparatus.' (1956: ix) In Laslett's view, this re-examination did not require silence on the part of traditionalists, but he did acknowledge that 'in the earlier phase of the movement, the linguistic philosophers talked as if the only function of philosophy in the future was to be the exposure of linguistic confusions', (1956: x)

Laslett was convinced that the silence was not final and that even in 1956 there were 'small signs' upon which might be based 'an expectation of a rebirth of traditional political philosophy'. (1956: x) Pettit argued that the 'long silence' was broken – and, in this account, a traditionalist conception reborn – in the early 1960s. Hart and Barry published works that, according to Pettit, 'used techniques associated with current analytical philosophy to resume the sort of discussion of grand themes which had been the hallmark of the nineteenth century'. (Pettit 1993: 9) This was possible, despite the impact of analytic philosophy, because 'consistently with thinking that the main job of philosophy is to carry forward the sort of programme described by Wittgenstein or Ryle or Austin, one may believe that a subsidiary job is to sort out the commitments that can rationally be sustained.' (Pettit 1993: 10)

According to Pettit, 'there are two distinct areas where normative questions arise, according to the lore of analytical philosophers: in the theory of the good ... and in the theory of the right. The theory of the good is the theory in which we are instructed on what properties, in particular what universal properties, make one state of the world better than another; we are instructed on what properties constitute values, specifically impersonal values that do not need to refer to any particular individuals or indeed any particular entities.... The theory of the right ... is the theory in which we are told what makes one option right and another wrong, among the options in any choice; the choice may be a personal decision among different acts, or a social decision among different basic structures'. (Pettit 1993: 22)

The search for 'universal properties' and 'impersonal values' clearly recalls a traditionalist conception and is evidence that normative analytical political philosophy can be understood to be a contemporary form of the traditionalist conception of political theory.

Further evidence to this effect emerges from Pettit's discussion of Rawls's *A Theory of Justice*. In Pettit's account, Rawls 'is interested not in the different views we actually hold as to what is politically right, but in what beliefs we ought to hold about what is politically right.' (Pettit 1993: 12) Further, the device of the 'original position' illustrated something that, according to Pettit, was 'very important' in Rawls's approach to political philosophy. This was: 'that the principles to be chosen should play a public role in the life of society, being treated like a device or covenant.... The principles are to be general in form, not mentioning particular persons; they are to be universal in application, applying potentially to everyone; and, most important, they are to be publicly recognized as the final court of appeal for resolving people's conflicting claims'. (Pettit 1993: 13–4)

The approach was to 'take a certain specification of the original position and consider what principles it would lead us to endorse as principles of justice. If we find a match or equilibrium between those principles and our considered judgements, then that is fine. If we do not, then we must think again.' (Pettit 1993: 14)

In 1989, Hamlin and Pettit produced a co-edited work entitled *The Good Polity: Normative Analysis of the State* (1989). This work derived from, and contributed to, a literature which was 'analytic in character and is devoted to the variety of issues involved in the assessment of social and political institutions.... It is characterized by an emphasis on rationality, bargaining and contract, combined with the more traditional concerns with liberty, equality, rights and the like. It is informed by the concepts of decision theory, game theory, public-choice and social-choice analysis, while staying in touch with standard questions of political evaluation. We think of it as the literature of normative political analysis.' (Hamlin and Pettit 1989: 1)

Some of the techniques employed in examining fundamental issues in politics might have changed, but the tenor was clearly that typical of a traditionalist conception of political theory.

The main difference that might be asserted between normative analytical and traditionalist political theory is that the former results in a greater degree of circumspection. The normative analytical political philosopher checks conclusions against a background of 'considered judgements'; the traditionalist against a background of truth. The question that arises concerns the extent to which these are different. This may be considered in the context of another writer who has adopted this approach, Will Kymlicka.

According to Kymlicka, 'political philosophy is ... a matter of moral argument, and moral argument is a matter of appeal to our considered convictions.' (Kymlicka 1990: 7) For him, 'the fact is that we have an intuitive sense of right and wrong, and it is natural, indeed unavoidable, that we try to work out its implications...'. (Kymlicka 1990: 7) Kymlicka further develops the logic of this approach in the following passage: 'we all have moral beliefs, these beliefs can be right or wrong, we have reasons for thinking they are either right or wrong, and these reasons and beliefs can be organized into systematic moral principles and theories of justice. A central aim of political philosophy, therefore, is to evaluate competing theories of justice to assess the strengths and coherence of their arguments for the rightness of their views.' (Kymlicka 1990: 7–8)

When it came to judging success 'in the enterprise of political philosophy,' Kymlicka wrote, 'I believe that the ultimate test of a theory of justice is that it cohere with, and help illuminate our considered convictions about justice.' (1990: 7) This meant that 'if a theory of justice matches our considered intuitions, and structures them so as to bring out their internal logic, then we have a powerful argument in favour of that theory'. (Kymlicka 1990: 7)

Theories of justice may not be the only point of agreement that result from considered intuitions, however. 'On Dworkin's view, every plausible political theory has the same ultimate value, which is equality. They are all "egalitarian" theories.... That suggestion is clearly false if by "egalitarian theory" we mean a theory which supports an equal distribution of income. But there is another, more abstract and more fundamental, idea of equality in political theory – namely, the idea of treating people "as equals". (Kymlicka 1990: 4)

Kymlicka accepted Dworkin's position and asserted, as a result, that the difference between what he called a traditional approach and the one he adopted and advocated is that 'whereas the traditional view tells us that the fundamental argument in political theory is whether to accept equality as a value, this revised view tells us that the fundamental argument is not whether to accept equality, but how best to interpret it.' (Kymlicka 1990: 5)

Kymlicka's argument here may be used to defend the view that normative analytical political philosophy is different from the traditionalist conception in that it relies upon a particular set of shared intuitions or convictions that may be taken to derive from membership of a particular community. To accept this, however, would be to elide the commitment to universality that Pettit asserted and the 'more abstract and more fundamental' ideas upon which Kymlicka relied.

Normative analytical political philosophy is better understood as a return to a traditionalist conception, following the assault upon this form that resulted from the linguistic turn in philosophy. That traditionalists had been silenced by those who rejected their project meant that they had to regain their voice. A slightly more tentative or weaker voice, perhaps, but the sort of voice that represents a return to the convictions that motivate traditionalists.

Fundamental to this book is the view that no advocate of any of the conceptions of political theory discussed ought to be silenced or allow themselves to be silenced. This is not to say that advocates of one conception cannot learn to be more careful in the presentation of their views as a result of an interaction with advocates of another. That some of those who adopted a traditionalist conception of political theory regained their voice in normative analytical political philosophy is some evidence of the necessity of maintaining a traditionalist conception as one of those available to those who wish to be a political theorist. That other conceptions are equally valid and available means that traditionalists must accept, as all advocates of a conception must, that they will be subject to criticism. Hopefully, though, they will not be subject to rejection and silencing in the way that they were. Whether it is by way of an appeal to some belief in universality of background assumptions or intuitions or by way of an appeal to the truth, the traditionalist conception in which universal principles are pursued by those who look to essential features of politics or an understanding of politics remains an important and valuable enterprise.

# References

Abercrombie, N, S. Hill and B. Turner. 1988. *The Penguin Dictionary of Sociology*. 2nd edn. London: Penguin.

Alexander, E. 1965. *Matthew Arnold and John Stuart Mill*. London: Routledge and Kegan Paul.

Annas, J. 1977. 'Mill and the Subjection of Women'. *Philosophy* 52(200): 179–94.

Anschutz, R. P. 1963. *The Philosophy of John Stuart Mill*. Oxford: Oxford University Press.

Apter, D. E. 1957. 'Theory and the Study of Politics'. *The American Political Science Review* 51(3): 747–62.

Arneson, R. J. 1981. 'Prospects for Community in a Market Economy'. *Political Theory* 9(2): 207–27.

Austin, J. L. A. 1976. *How to Do Things with Words*. 2nd edn. Oxford: Oxford University Press.

Barry, N. P. 1982. *An Introduction to Modern Political Theory*. London: Macmillan.

Beer, J. 1978. *Wordsworth and the Human Heart*. London: Macmillan.

Benn, S.I. and G. Gaus. 1983. 'The Public and the Private: Concepts and Action'. in *Public and Private in Social Life*, eds Benn and Gaus. Canberra: Croom Helm.

Bentham, J. 1907. *An Introduction to the Principles of Morals and Legislation*. Oxford: Clarendon.

Bentley, A. 1956. 'The Process of Government'. in H. Eulau, S. J. Eldersveld and M. Janowitz, *Political Behavior: A Reader in Theory and Research*. Glencoe (Ill.): The Free Press.

Berger, F. R. 1978. 'Mill's Concept of Happiness'. *Interpretation* 7(3): 95–117.

Berki, R. N. 1977. *The History of Political Thought: A Short Introduction*. London: Dent.

Berlin, I. 1959. *John Stuart Mill and the Ends of Life*. London: Edgar G. Dunstan and Co.

Berlin, I. 1969. *Four Essays on Liberty*. Oxford: Oxford University Press.

Bloom, A. 1980. 'The Study of Texts' in *Political Theory and Political Education*, ed. M. Richter. Princeton (NJ): Princeton University Press.

Bloom, H. 1972. 'The Myth of Memory and the Natural Man' in *Wordsworth: A Collection of Critical Essays*, ed. M. H. Abrahms. Englewood Cliffs (NJ): Prentice Hall.

Bluhm, W. T. 1965. *Theories of the Political System: Classics of Political Thought and Modern Political Analysis*. Englewood Cliffs (NJ): Prentice Hall.

Boucher, D. 1985. *Texts in Context: Revisionist Methods for Studying the History of Ideas*. Dodrecht: Martinus Nijhoff.

Briggs, A. 1979. *The Age of Improvement 1784–1867*. London: Longman.

Britton, K. 1953. *John Stuart Mill*. Harmondsworth (Eng.): Penguin.

Burns, J. H. 1968. 'J.S. Mill and Democracy, 1829–61', in *Mill: A Collection of Critical Essays*, ed. J. B. Schneewind. London: Macmillan.

Catlin, G. 1950. *A History of the Political Philosophers*. London: George Allen and Unwin.

Claeys, G. 1987. 'Justice, Independence, and Industrial Democracy: The Development of John Stuart Mill's Socialism'. *Journal of Politics*. Vol 49(1): 122–47.

Collini, S. 1977. 'Liberalism and the Legacy of Mill'. *The Historical Journal* 20(1): 237–52.

Comte, A. 1893. *The Positive Philosophy of Auguste Comte*. Vols I & II, freely translated and condensed by H. Martineau. London: Kegan Paul, Trench, Trubner.

Condren, C. 1979. *Three Aspects of Political Theory*. Melbourne: Macmillan.

Cowling, M. 1963. *Mill and Liberalism*. Cambridge University Press.

Cranston, M. 1958. *John Stuart Mill*. London: Longmans, Green and Co.

Crespigny, A. de and K. Minogue. 1975. 'Introduction' in *Contemporary Political Philosophers*, eds A. de Crespigny and K. Minogue. London: Methuen.

Danford, J. W. 1978. *Wittgenstein and Political Philosophy: A Reexamination of the Foundations of Social Science*. Chicago: University of Chicago Press.

Davidson, W. L. 1957. *Political Thought in England: The Utilitarians from Bentham to Mill*. Oxford: Oxford University Press.

Davis, E. G. 1985. 'Mill, Socialism and the English Romantics: An Interpretation'. *Economica* 52(2): 345–58.

Derrida, J. 1973. *Speech and Phenomena and Other Essays on Husserl's Theory of Signs*. Evanston: Northwestern University Press.

Deutsch, K. W. 1971. 'On Political Theory and Political Action'. *The American Political Science Review* 65(1): 11–27.

Deutsch, K. W. and L. N. Rieselbach. 1965. 'Recent Trends in Political Theory and Political Philosophy'. *The Annals of the American Academy of Political and Social Science* (360): 139–62.

Donner, W. 1991. *The Liberal Self: John Stuart Mill's Moral and Political Philosophy*. Ithaca: Cornell University Press.

Donner, W. 1993. 'John Stuart Mill's Liberal Feminism'. *Philosophical Studies* 69(23): 155–66.

Duncan, G. 1973. *Marx and Mill: Two Views of Social Conflict and Social Harmony*. Cambridge: Cambridge University Press.

Duncan, G. 1983. 'Political Theory and Human Nature', in *Politics and Human Nature*, eds I. Forbes and S. Smith. London: Frances Pinter.

Dunn, J. 1968. 'The Identity of the History of Ideas'. *Philosophy* 43(164): 85–104.

Dunn, J. 1985. *Rethinking Modern Political Theory*. Cambridge: Cambridge University Press.

Dyzenhaus, D. 1992. 'John Stuart Mill and the Harm of Pornography'. *Ethics* 102(3): 534–51.

Easton, D. 1973. *The Political System: An Enquiry into the State of Political Science*. 2nd edn. New York: Alfred Knopf.

Eckstein, H. 1969. 'The Condition and Prospect of Political Thought', in

*Contemporary Political Thought: Issues in Scope, Value and Direction*, eds J. A. Gould and V. V. Thursby. New York: Holt. Rinehart and Winston.

Euben, J. P. 1986. 'The Battle of Salamis and the Origins of Political Theory'. *Political Theory* 14(3): 359–90.

Eulau, H. 1969. 'Tradition and Innovation: On the Tension between Ancient and Modern Ways in the Study of Politics', in *Behaviouralism in Political Science*, ed. H. Eulau. New York: Atherton Press.

Eulau, H. and J. G. March 1969. *Political Science*. Englewood Cliffs (NJ): Prentice Hall.

Evans, R. J. 1965. *The Victorian Age: 1815–1914*. London: Edward Arnold.

Fann, K. T. 1969. *Wittgenstein's Conception of Philosophy*. Oxford: Basil Blackwell.

Fetscher, I. 1973. 'Socialism', in *Marxism, Communism and Western Society: a Comparative Encyclopedia*, Vol. VII. ed. C. D. Kernig. New York: Herder and Herder.

Feuer, 1976. 'John Stuart Mill as a Sociologist: The Unwritten Ethology', in *James and John Stuart Mill: Papers of the Centenary Conference*, eds J. M. Robson and M. Laine, Toronto: University of Toronto Press.

Flathman, R. E. 1973. *Concepts in Social and Political Philosophy*. New York: Macmillan.

Flathman, R. E. 1987. *The Philosophy and Politics of Freedom*. Chicago: University of Chicago Press.

Flynn, B. C. 1985. 'Political Theory and the Metaphysics of Presence.' *Philosophy and Social Criticism* 11(3): 245–58.

Forget, E. L. 1992. 'J.S. Mill and the Tory School: The Rhetorical Value of Recantation'. *History of Political Economy* 24(1): 31–58.

Froman, L. J. 1962. *People and Politics: An Analysis of the American Political System*. Englewood Cliffs (NJ): Prentice Hall.

Garforth, F. W. 1979. *John Stuart Mill's Theory of Education*. New York: Barnes and Noble.

Gaus, G. F. 1983. *The Modern Liberal Theory of Man*. London: Croom Helm.

Germino, D. 1967. *Beyond Ideology: The Revival of Political Theory*. New York: Harper and Row.

Germino, D. 1972. 'Some Observations on Recent Political Philosophy and Theory'. *The Annals of the American Academy of Political and Social Science* (400): 140–8.

Germino, D. 1975. 'The Contemporary Relevance of Classics of Political Theory', in *Handbook of Political Science*: Vol. 1, eds F. I. Greenstein, and N. W. Polsby. Reading (Mass.): Addison-Wesley.

Gildin, H. 1964. 'Mill's *On Liberty*', in *Ancients and Moderns: Essays on the Tradition of Political Philosophy in Honour of Leo Strauss*, ed. J. Cropsey. New York: Basic Books.

Glaser, W. 1969. 'The Types and Uses of Political Theory', in *Contemporary Political Thought: Issues in Scope, Value and Direction*, eds J. A. Gould and V. V. Thursby. New York: Holt, Rinehart and Winston.

Glassman, P. 1985. *J.S. Mill: The Evolution of a Genius*. Gainesville: University of Florida Press.

Goodin, R. E. and P. Pettit. eds 1993. *A Companion to Contemporary Political Philosophy*. Oxford: Basil Blackwell.

Gould, J. A. and V. V. Thursby. 1969. *Contemporary Political Thought: Issues in Scope, Value and Directions*. New York: Holt, Rinehart and Winston.

Greaves, H. R. G. 1966. *The Foundations of Political Theory*. 2nd edn. London: G. Bell.

Greenleaf, W. H. 1972. 'Theory and the Study of Politics'. *British Journal of Political Science* 2. (Part 4): 467–78.

Gunnell, J. G. 1978. 'The Myth of the Tradition'. *The American Political Science Review* 72(1): 122–35.

Gunnell, J. G. 1979. *Political Theory: Tradition and Interpretation*. Cambridge (Mass.): Winthrop.

Gunnell, J. G. 1981. 'Encounters of a Third Kind: The Alienation of Theory in American Political Science'. *American Journal of Political Science* 25(3): 440–61.

Hacker, A. 1961. *Political Theory: Philosophy, Ideology, Science*. New York: Macmillan.

Hacker, A. 1969. '"Capital" and Carbuncles', in *Contemporary Political Thought: Issues in Scope, Value and Direction*, eds J. A. Gould and V. V. Thursby. New York: Holt, Rinehart and Winston.

Hamlin, A. and P. Pettit. 1989. 'Introduction' in *The Good Polity: Normative Analysis of the State*. eds A. Hamlin and P. Pettit. Oxford: Basil Blackwell.

Harding, A. 1994. 'The Origins of the Concept of the State'. *History of Political Thought* 15(1): 57–72.

Hayek, F. A. 1951. *John Stuart Mill and Harriet Taylor: Their Friendship and Subsequent Marriage*. London: Routledge and Kegan Paul.

Heap, J. L. 1977. 'Verstehen, Language and Warrants'. *The Sociological Quarterly* 18: 177–84.

Heilbroner, R. L. 1972. *The Worldly Philosophers: The Lives, Times and Ideas of the Great Economic Thinkers*. 4th edn. New York: Simon and Schuster.

Heilbroner, R. L. 1975. 'The Paradox of Progress: Decline and Decay in *The Wealth of Nations*', in *Essays on Adam Smith*. eds A. S. Skinner and T. Wilson. Oxford: Clarendon.

Hekman, S. 1992. 'John Stuart Mill's *The Subjection of Women*: The Foundations of Liberal Feminism'. *History of European Ideas* 15 (4–6): 681–6.

Held, D. 1991. 'Editor's Introduction', in *Political Theory Today*, ed. D. Held. Cambridge: Polity.

Himmelfarb, G. 1974. *On Liberty and Liberalism: The Case of John Stuart Mill*. New York: Alfred A. Knopf.

Hirschmann, N. J. 1989. 'Freedom, Recognition and Obligation: A Feminist Approach to Political Theory'. *American Political Science Review* 83(4): 1227–44.

Hughes, P. 1979. 'The Reality versus the Ideal: J.S. Mill's Treatment of Women, Workers and Private Property.' *Canadian Journal of Political Science* 12(3): 523–42.

Hund, J. 1991. 'Wittgenstein versus Hart: Two Models of Rules for Social and Legal Theory'. *Philosophy of the Social Sciences* 21(1): 72–85.

Jacobson, N. 1978. *Pride and Solace: The Function and Limits of Political Theory*. Berkeley: University of California Press.

Kamm, J. 1977. *John Stuart Mill in Love*. London: Gordon and Cremonesi.

Kim, K. S. 1988. 'Moral Rules and J.S. Mill's Educational Mandate'. *Journal of Moral Education* 17(2): 105–13.

Knights, M. 1993. 'Petitioning and the Political Theorists: John Locke, Algernon Sidney and London's "Monster" Petition of 1680'. *Past and Present* 138: 94–111.

Kuhn, T. 1970. *The Structure of Scientific Revolutions*. 2nd edn. Chicago: University of Chicago Press.

Kooiman, J. 1993. *Modern Governance*. London: Sage.

Kurer, O. 1991. 'John Stuart Mill and the Welfare State'. *History of Political Economy* 23(4): 713–30.

Kurer, O. 1992. 'J.S. Mill and Utopian Socialism'. *The Economic Record* 68(202): 222–32.

Kymlicka, W. 1990. *Contemporary Political Philosophy: An Introduction*. Oxford: Clarendon.

Laschs, J. 1992. 'Mill and Constant: a Neglected Connection in the History of the Idea of Liberty'. *History of Philosophy Quarterly* 9(1): 87–97.

Laslett, P. 1956. 'Introduction', in *Philosophy, Politics and Society*, ed. P. Laslett. Oxford: Basil Blackwell.

Lockyer, A. 1979. '"Traditions" as Context in the History of Political Theory'. *Political Studies* 27(2): 201–17.

MacCunn, J. 1964. *Six Radical Thinkers: Bentham, J.S. Mill, Cobden, Carlyle, Mazzini, T.H. Green*. New York. Russell and Russell.

Macpherson, C. B. 1973. *Democratic Theory: Essays in Retrieval*. Oxford: Clarendon.

Magid, H. 1963. 'John Stuart Mill', in *History of Political Philosophy*, eds L. Strauss and J. Cropsey. Chicago: Rand McNally.

Maker, W. 1992. '(Postmodern) Tales from the Crypt: The Night of the Zombie Philosopher'. *Metaphilosophy* 23(4): 311–28.

Malthus, T. R. 1989. *Principles of Political Economy*. ed. J. Pullen. Cambridge: Cambridge University Press.

Masters, R. D. 1990. 'Evolutionary Biology and Political Theory'. *American Political Science Review* 84(1) 195–210.

Mazlish, B. 1975. *James and John Stuart Mill: Father and Son in the Nineteenth Century*. New York: Basic Books.

McCloskey, H. J. 1964. 'The Nature of Political Philosophy'. *Ratio* 6(1): 50–62.

McCloskey, H. J. 1969. 'Mill's Liberalism', in *Mill: A Collection of Critical Essays*, ed. J. B. Schneewind. London: Macmillan.

McDonald, L. C. 1968. *Western Political Theory*. Part 1. New York: Harcourt, Brace, Jovanovich.

McPherson, M. S. 1982. 'Mill's Moral Theory and the Problem of Preference Change'. *Ethics* 92(2): 252–73.

Merriam, C. E. 1970. *New Aspects of Politics*. 3rd edn. Chicago: University of Chicago Press.

Miller, D. 1990. 'The Resurgence of Political Theory'. *Political Studies* 38: 421–37.

Miller, D. 1983. 'Linguistic Philosophy and Political Theory', in *The Nature of Political Theory*, eds Miller, D. and L. Siedentop. Oxford: Clarendon.

Miller, D. 1976. *Social Justice*. Oxford: Clarendon.

Milliken, E. K. 1963. *The Victorian Era, 1820–1901*. London: George G. Harrap and Co.

Mueller, I. W. 1968. *John Stuart Mill and French Thought*. Freeport (NY): Books for Libraries Press.

Nagel, T. 1989. 'What Makes a Political Theory Utopian?' *Social Research* 56(4): 903–20.

Nietzsche, F. 1968. *Basic Writings of Nietzsche*, trans. and ed. W. Kaufman. New York: The Modern Library.

O'Brien, D. P. 1975. *The Classical Economists*. Oxford: Oxford University Press.

Oppenheim, F. E. 1981. *Political Concepts: A Reconstruction*. Oxford: Basil Blackwell.

Oswald, D. J. 1990. 'J.S. Mill's *a priori* Deductive Methodology: A Case Study in Post-Modern Philosophy of Science'. *Review of Social Economy* 48(2): 172–97.

Packe, M. St. J. 1954. *The Life of John Stuart Mill*. London: Secker and Warburg.

Panichas, G. E. 1983. 'Mill's Flirtation with Socialism and Communism.' *The Southern Journal of Philosophy* 21(2): 253–69.

Pappe, H. O. 1960. *John Stuart Mill and the Harriet Taylor Myth*. Melbourne: Melbourne University Press.

Parekh, B. C. 1968. 'The Nature of Political Philosophy', in *Politics and Experience*, eds P. King and B. C. Parekh. Cambridge: Cambridge University Press.

Paul, E. F. 1978. 'J.S. Mill: The Utilitarian Influence in the Demise of "Laissez-Faire"'. *Journal of Libertarian Studies* 2(2): 135–49.

Pettit, P. 1993. 'Analytical Philosophy', in *A Companion to Contemporary Political Philosophy*, eds R. E. Goodin and P. Pettit. Oxford: Backwell.

Pitkin, H. F. 1967. *The Concept of Representation*. Berkeley: University of California Press.

Pitkin, H. F. 1972. *Wittgenstein and Justice: On the Significance of Ludwig Wittgenstein for Social and Political Thought*. Berkeley: University of California Press.

Plamenatz, J. P. 1963. *Man and Society: A Critical Examination of Some Important Social and Political Theories from Machiavelli to Marx*. Vols 1 & 2. London: Longman.

Plamenatz, J. P. 1968. *Consent, Freedom and Political Obligation*. 2nd edn. Oxford: Oxford University Press.

Platteau, J. P. 1985. 'The Political Economy of John Stuart Mill, or The Co-existence of Orthodoxy, Heresy and Prophecy'. *International Journal of Social Economics* 12(1): 3–26.

Pocock, J. G. A. 1971. *Politics, Language and Time*. London: Methuen.

Pocock, J. G. A. 1984. 'Verbalizing a Speech Act', in *Language and Politics*, ed. M. J. Shapiro. Oxford: Basil Blackwell.

Pocock, J. G. A. 1993. 'Review of *The Cambridge History of Political Thought 1450–1700*'. *London Review of Books* 15(7 Jan.): 11.

Rees, J. C. 1969. 'A Re-Reading of Mill on Liberty', in *Essays in the History of Political Thought*, ed. I. Kramnick. Englewood Cliffs (NJ): Prentice-Hall.

Rengger, N. J. 1992. 'No Time Like the Present? Postmodernism and Political Theory'. *Political Studies* 40: 561–70.

Ricoeur, P. 1971. 'The Model of the Text: Meaningful Action Considered as a Text'. *Social Research* 38(3): 529–62.

Robertson, D. 1993. *A Dictionary of Modern Politics*. London: Europa.

Robinson, D. N. 1982. *Toward a Science of Human Nature*. New York: Columbia University Press.

Robson, J. M. (ed.) 1963–1991. *The Collected Works of John Stuart Mill*. Toronto: University of Toronto Press.

Rorty, R. 1980. *Philosophy and the Mirror of Nature*. Oxford: Basil Blackwell.

Rorty, R. 1984. 'The Historiography of Philosophy: Four Genres', in *Philosophy in History*, eds R. Rorty, J. B. Schneewind and Q. Skinner. Cambridge: Cambridge University Press.

Rorty, R. 1985. 'Pragmatism and Literary Theory II: Philosophy without Principles'. *Critical Inquiry* 11: 459–65.

Ryan, A. 1970. *The Philosophy of John Stuart Mill*. London: Macmillan.

Ryan, A. 1974. *J.S. Mill*. London: Routledge and Kegan Paul.

Ryle, G. 1970. 'Ordinary Language', in *Philosophy and Ordinary Language*, ed. C. E. Caton. Urbana: University of Illinois Press.

Sabine, G. 1973. *A History of Political Theory*. 4th edn, revised by Thorson, T. L. New York: Dryden.

Sabine, G. H. 1939. 'What is a Political Theory?' *The Journal of Politics* 1(1): 1–16.

Sandoz, E. 1972. 'The Philosophical Science of Politics beyond Behavioralism', in *The Post-Behavioral Era: Perspectives on Political Science*, eds G. J. Graham and G. W. Carey. New York: David McKay.

Sarvasy, W. 1985. 'A Reconsideration of the Development and Structure of John Stuart Mill's Socialism.' *The Western Political Quarterly* 38(2): 312–33.

Sawyier, F. H. 1985. 'Philosophy as Autobiography: John Stuart Mill's Case'. *Philosophy Research Archives* 11: 169–80.

Schneewind, J. B. 1968. 'Introduction' in *Mill: A Collection of Critical Essays*. ed. J. B. Schneewind. London: Macmillan.

Schneewind, J. B. 1991. 'MacIntyre and the Indispensability of Tradition'. *Philosophy and Phenomenological Research* 51(1): 165–8.

Schwartz, P. 1972. *The New Political Economy of J.S. Mill*. London: Weidenfeld and Nicolson.

Searle, J. R. 1980. *Speech Acts: An Essay in the Philosophy of Language*. Cambridge: Cambridge University Press.

Searle, J. R., F. Kiefer, and M. Bierwisch. 1980. 'Introduction.' in *Speech Act Theory and Pragmatics*, eds Searle, Kiefer and Bierwisch. Dodrecht: D. Reidel.

Shanley, M. L., and C. Pateman. 1991. 'Introduction' in *Feminist Interpretations and Political Theory*, eds M. L. Shanley and C. Pateman. Cambridge: Polity.

Skinner, Q. 1988a. 'Meaning and Understanding in the History of Ideas', in *Meaning and Context: Skinner and His Critics*, ed. J. Tully. Cambridge: Polity.

Skinner, Q. 1988b. 'Motives, Intentions and Interpretation', in *Meaning and*

*Context: Skinner and His Critics*, ed. J. Tully. Cambridge: Polity.

Skinner, Q. 1988a. 'Some Problems in the Analysis of Political Thought and Action', in *Meaning and Context: Skinner and His Critics*, ed. J. Tully. Cambridge: Polity.

Skipper, R. 1993. 'Mill and Pornography'. *Ethics* 103(4): 726–30.

Skorupski, J. 1989. *John Stuart Mill*. London: Routledge.

Smith, A. 1976. *An Inquiry into the Nature and Causes of the Wealth of Nations*. Vol. 1. ed. R. H. Campbell and A. S. Skinner. Oxford: Clarendon.

Smith, G. W. 1980. 'The Logic of J.S. Mill on Freedom'. *Political Studies* 28(2): 238–52.

Sommervell, D. C. 1950. *English Thought in the Nineteenth Century*. London: Methuen.

Sparkes, A. W. 1994. *Talking Politics: A Wordbook*. London: Routledge.

Specht, E. K. 1986. 'The Language-Game as Model-Concept in Wittgenstein's Theory of Language', in *The Philosophy of Wittgenstein*. Vol. 6: *Meaning*, ed. J. V. Canfield. New York: Garland.

Spragens, T. A. 1976. *Understanding Political Theory*. New York: St. Martin's Press.

Staley, C. E. 1986. 'Hollander on Mill's Economics and Thomas on Mill's Bibliography'. *Scottish Journal of Political Economy* 33(3): 298–322.

Stove, D. 1993. 'The Subjection of John Stuart Mill'. *Philosophy* 68(263): 5–13.

Strauss, L. 1957. 'What is Political Philosophy?' *The Journal of Politics* 19(3): 343–68.

Strauss, L. 1959. *What is Political Philosophy? and Other Studies*. Illinois: Free Press.

Struhl, P. R. 1976. 'Mill's Notion of Social Responsibility'. *Journal of the History of Ideas* 37(1): 155–62.

Sturm, D. 1979. 'Process Thought and Political Theory: Implications of a Principle of Internal Relations'. *The Review of Politics* 41(3): 375–401.

Ten, C. L. 1980. *Mill on Liberty*. Oxford: Clarendon.

Thomas, W. 1992. 'Mill', in *Great Political Thinkers*, Oxford: Oxford University Press.

Thompson, D. F. 1976. *John Stuart Mill and Representative Government*. Princeton (NJ): Princeton University Press.

Thomson, D. 1951. *England in the Nineteenth Century (1815–1914)*. Harmondsworth: Penguin.

Tinder, G. 1974. *Political Thinking: The Perennial Questions*. Boston: Little, Brown.

Tushnet, M. 1989. 'Rights: An Essay in Informal Political Theory'. *Politics and Society* 17(3): 403–45.

Urbinati, N. 1991. 'John Stuart Mill on Androgyny and Ideal Marriage'. *Political Theory* 19(4): 626–48.

Voeglin, E. 1952. *The New Science of Politics: An Introduction*. Chicago: University of Chicago Press.

Warren, M. 1989. 'What is Political Theory/Philosophy?' *PS* 22(3): 606–12.

Webb, R. K. 1968. *Modern England: From the Eighteenth Century to the Present*. New York: Dodd, Mead and Co.

Weldon, T. D. 1953. *The Vocabulary of Politics*. Harmondsworth: Penguin.

Wertheimer, A. 1976. 'Is Ordinary Language Analysis Conservative?' *Political Theory* 4(4): 403–22.

White, S. K. 1991. *Political Theory and Postmodernism*. Cambridge: Cambridge University Press.

Wittgenstein, L. 1963. *Philosophical Investigations*, translated by G. E. M. Anscombe. Oxford: Basil Blackwell.

Wolin, S. 1968. 'Paradigms and Political Theories', in *Politics and Experience*, eds P. King and B. C. Parekh. Cambridge: Cambridge University Press.

Wolin, S. 1960. *Politics and Vision*. Boston: Little, Brown.

Wood, E. M. 1994. 'Radicalism, Capitalism and Historical Contexts: Not Only a Reply to Richard Ashcraft on John Locke'. *History of Political Thought* 15(3): 323–72.

Wood, E. M. and N. Wood. 1978. *Class Ideology and Ancient Political Theory: Socrates, Plato and Aristotle in Social Context*. Oxford: Basil Blackwell.

Wood, N. 1978. 'The Social History of Political Theory.' *Political Theory* 6(3): 334–67.

Woods, T. 1961. *Poetry and Philosophy: A Study in the Thought of John Stuart Mill*. London: Hutchinson.

Wordsworth, W. 1938. *Poetry and Prose: With Essays by Coleridge*. Hazlitt and De Quincey. Oxford: Oxford University Press.

Wordsworth, W. 1959. *The Prelude or Growth of a Poet's Mind*. 2nd edn ed. E. de Selincourt. Oxford: Oxford University Press.

Zabeeh, F. 1971. 'On Language Games and Forms of Life', in *Essays on Wittgenstein*, ed. E. D. Klemke. University of Illinois Press.

Zerilli, L. M. 1991. 'Machiavelli's Sisters: Women and "the Conversation" of Political Theory'. *Political Theory* 19(2): 252–76.

Zweig, K. 1979. 'Smith, Malthus, Ricardo and Mill: The Forerunner of Limits to Growth'. *Futures* 2(6): 510–23.

# Subject Index

# Author Index